AMINTAPHIL: The Philosophical Foundations of Law and Justice

Volume 13

Series Editors

Mortimer Sellers, University of Baltimore, Baltimore, USA

Ann E. Cudd, Boston University, Boston, USA

The *AMINTAPHIL book series* considers the philosophical foundations of law and justice from the perspectives of academic philosophy, practical political science and applied legal studies. The American Section of the International Association for the Philosophy of Law and Social Philosophy ("AMINTAPHIL") supervises the series, which dedicates each volume to the most pressing contemporary problems in legal theory and social justice. AMINTAPHIL holds biennial meetings of leading scholars in philosophy, law, and politics to discuss the philosophical basis of vital questions. The AMINTAPHIL volumes present the ultimate results of these discussions.

Gordon Albert Babst • Win-chiat Lee
Editors

Contemporary Facets of Injustice

Springer

Editors
Gordon Albert Babst
Chapman University
Orange, CA, USA

Win-chiat Lee
Department of Philosophy
Wake Forest University
Winston-Salem, NC, USA

ISSN 1873-877X ISSN 2351-9851 (electronic)
AMINTAPHIL: The Philosophical Foundations of Law and Justice
ISBN 978-3-031-93782-8 ISBN 978-3-031-93783-5 (eBook)
https://doi.org/10.1007/978-3-031-93783-5

This Springer imprint is published by the registered company Springer Nature Switzerland AG
The registered company address is: Gewerbestrasse 11, 6330 Cham, Switzerland

Contents

Introduction

Gordon A. Babst

Abstract Injustice itself is too infrequently the subject of direct rumination, with one notable exception being Judith Shklar's *The Faces of Injustice*. The chapters in this volume consider some contemporary injustices, revealing their presence in ways that help to explain current issues that range from inequities in food access to the dangers of Christian nationalism, from better understanding how to conceptualize international law, to income disparity and the tax code.

In her Storrs Lectures at Yale Law School the eminent political theorist Judith Shklar proposed that "none of the usual modes of justice offer an adequate account of injustice" and that traditional the approach to comprehending justice "inclines us to ignore passive injustice, the victim's sense of injustice, and ultimately the full, complex, and enduring character of injustice as a social phenomenon."[1] She goes on to offer explanations as to why injustice has rarely itself been the direct subject of political theory and when it has, the philosophizing has usually been wide of the mark principally because it has missed the victim's point of view.

An earlier work spoke of the facets of the *sense* of injustice interchangeably using the term aspects.[2] Lawyer and philosopher, Cahn was concerned with "demands for equality, desert, human dignity, conscientious adjudication, confinement of government to its proper functions, and fulfillment of common expectations.... crooked legislation, crooked administration, or crooked police

[1] See Shklar (1990), pp. 8–9. Her manuscript presents and expands on those lectures. See Cahn (1964), pp. 22, 190. Cahn was concerned with "demands for equality, desert, human dignity, conscientious adjudication, confinement of government to its proper functions, and fulfillment of common expectations."

[2] See Cahn (1964), pp. 22, 190.

G. A. Babst (✉)
Department of Political Science, Chapman University, Orange, CA, USA
e-mail: gbabst@chapman.edu

G. A. Babst, W.-c. Lee (eds.), *Contemporary Facets of Injustice*, AMINTAPHIL: The Philosophical Foundations of Law and Justice 13,
https://doi.org/10.1007/978-3-031-93783-5_1

work."[3] Like Shklar, Cohn sought not to build theory, but to enlighten the path the better to see injustices and identify their origins and courses in people's lives.

Victims of injustice may be individuals, groups, societies as a whole, or humanity at large, and they tend to have no trouble at all grasping the injustice that besets them. Individuals may personally experience injustice, fall victim to a majority's injurious point of view, even when that view is religious in nature or seeks to further a religious point of view, be on the losing end of a structural injustice such as those disadvantaged for reason of their inadequate access to the necessities of life such as food, or be victimized by overall poor approaches to settling pointed differences in a just way such as between international foes. With the exception of the last form an injustice might take, Shklar treats each of those purviews in her short but excellent work. A structural injustice, where "the real enemy is an entire society" as in the case of systemic racial discrimination, is a social phenomenon that betokens power relations the perception of which requires an empathetic sensibility sensitive to the indignities and injuries of injustice.[4] She argues that injustice, especially passive injustice that may go unnoticed by the public at large, is more likely perceived and dealt with in a constitutional democracy where the people may give expression to the injustices that victimize them.

The chapters in this volume treat contemporary injustices related to undeserved distributive advantages, income and wealth, taxation and citizen self-respect, and access to basic necessities, followed by chapters focused on religion as a factor in furthering contemporary injustices alongside majoritarian democracy, which may amplify them, and concluding with two chapters theorizing how to handle injustice and its perpetrators at the international level and a final chapter on the increasingly thorny ethical if not metaphysical issues prompted by AI.

The following chapter by Wade L. Robison links taxpaying behavior to inequalities, finding that the wealthy through successful political engagement win favors in the tax code for themselves, while the poor needs must rely on advocates for tax-funded services that might give them a leg up. Jonathan Schonsheck continues the inquiry into undeserved economic advantages connected to the tax code from the perspective of their effects on citizen self-respect, on who benefits and who is carrying a disproportionate burden. Jochen Bojanowski seeks to contribute to the foundations of citizenship, arguing that the basic scheme of cooperation and the political value of fraternity within a citizenry have consequences for attitudes toward undeserved distributive advantages and what might be done about them. The last chapter relating to economic injustice by Joan McGregor examines the harmful outcomes of the food system, how it is structured to disadvantage some communities.

The next three chapters focus some attention on injustices as may obtain between a country's majority and a minority within it. Emily R. Gill questions the position of contemporary Christian nationalists as concerned to represent a minority, seeing them as instead avowedly on path to impose on minorities under cover of neutrality.

---

[3] Ibid.

[4] See Shklar (1990), pp. 97, 83.

The next chapter by Imer B. Flores engages in the democratic principles versus constitutional principles debate and relies on the legal thought of Hans Kelsen to scrutinize the thorny issue of whether a consenting majority is entitled to enforce its rule on a dissenting minority, or whether the majority rule is justly limited by constitutional principles. My chapter interrogates ever allowing legal discrimination on the basis of religious belief and provides an illustrative example of how doing so may facilitate complications that further advance discrimination, rather than express our better inclinations against it.

The last three chapters move outward into the international arena and into cyberspace, or at least its regulation. Win-chiat Lee examines the basis for universal jurisdiction in matters of international criminal law as law in the strict sense, arguing that a certain vigilantism must be accepted for it to work. Rodney C. Roberts proposes that within a theory of rectificatory justice there is no right to be forgiven for perpetrators of injustice whose victims have the right to an acknowledgement of the wrongdoing, but upon whom no obligation to forgive may be laid. Finally, our last chapter by Yi Deng outlines why the moral responsibilities of AI voice generators need to come under regulation the better to ward off unjust manipulation of the citizenry.

In each chapter the author moves beyond common assumptions to see what principles are at stake, with many identifying ways individuals or societies are held back by the injustice under discussion, how we perceive it, and whether our tools to understand and respond to it are adequate.

References

Cahn E (1964 [orig.: 1949]) The sense of injustice. Indiana University Press, Bloomington
Shklar JN (1990) The faces of injustice. Yale University Press, New Haven

The Injustice of Inequalities in Wealth and Income

Wade L. Robison

Abstract The disparities between those with the most income and wealth and those with the least in the United States are huge, with whites far better off than other races. It is difficult to see how any theory of justice can justify such disparities. In any event, we are faced with an unprecedented social and political problem that recent Supreme Court decisions have aggravated. *Citizens United* permits those with great wealth to give enormous amounts of money to those running for office, and it does not take much imagination to see how at least the implicit condition for obtaining money is that once elected, they are not to vote to raise taxes, thus creating greater inequalities.

> Two wealthy men in leather armchairs at their club
>
> The poor are getting poorer, but with the rich getting richer it all averages out in the long run. (Mankoff 2004, p. 521)

The disparities in wealth and income in the United States are staggering, with the top 10% having 51.45 trillion dollars and the bottom 50% having only 3.64 trillion (Board of Governors). Such disparities in wealth are not new in societies. "Rich Romans had a lifestyle that was luxurious by any standards, ancient or modern" (Beard 2015, p. 435). The problem seems to lie in part at least with the kind of beings we are.

Bonobos, for instance, are egalitarians to the core. From food to sex, they share equally, with everyone having an equal opportunity to get an equal share. When given an opportunity to keep food for themselves rather than share it, bonobos will go out of their way to share it and share it equally. In one experiment, one bonobo was given a pile of food while another bonobo in a cage was not given any. The first bonobo opened the cage door to ensure that the caged bonobo got an equal share (Hare and Kwetuenda 2010).

Children may seem to be anything but little bonobos. You need not spend much time at a playground to hear one child say to another, "That's not fair!" It can be said with such frustration that it is hard to imagine the child as a sharing bonobo, but, in

W. L. Robison (✉)
Rochester Institute of Technology, Rochester, NY, USA

G. A. Babst, W.-c. Lee (eds.), *Contemporary Facets of Injustice*, AMINTAPHIL: The Philosophical Foundations of Law and Justice 13,
https://doi.org/10.1007/978-3-031-93783-5_2

fact, toddlers as young as 15 months seem to prefer equitable distributions over inequitable ones (Kelsey et al., p. 10), and by the time they are four or five, egalitarianism rules. They are so committed to equality that when faced with inequalities, they act like bonobos and "attempt to correct these" (Cooper 2015).

That preference continues into the later years of childhood, with six-to-ten-year olds opting for egalitarianism. They make no exception for themselves. As one child said, "Because there's no reason I should have more than the others" (Forsé et al. 2016, p. 24). Self-interest does not override their commitment to egalitarianism.

What does override that commitment is their ethically admirable provision of more than an equal share to those they perceive as needy in some way. A child will be given more than an equal share who "doesn't have anything…because her parents don't have enough money" (Forsé et al. 2016, p. 28). That is the only exception. It turns out that toddlers are egalitarians like bonobos and that "equality is a choice that becomes more firm and stable with age" as toddlers become six-to-ten-year olds (Forsé et al. 2016, p. 26; Welsh, 2011).

But beyond that? Somewhere between being a child and a grownup, we humans come to see inequalities as perfectly acceptable, and we provide reasons that supposedly justify inequality. It is not at all unusual to hear people say that those who work harder and do more get more, and those who did more to get more do not need to share with those with less who must have done less. Inequalities simply reflect what people deserve, it is claimed, and so they are to be applauded, not rectified.

We will first look at how wealth and income are distributed in our society and then, in Part 2, examine whether the distribution is just. In Part 3 we will see that fostering more equality by empowering those with less requires some fundamental changes to our educational system, among other factors, changes that are not likely to occur anytime soon. But meanwhile, as we shall see in Part 4, the rich are subverting our democratic principles of equality, causing real harm to our Constitutional order.

Unfortunately, we cannot readily use the political system to change the distribution. We will examine in Part 5 why our political system makes it difficult to redistribute income and wealth so that the rich have less and the poor have more, and in Part 6 we will consider the difficulties of changing the distribution. We seem to have entered into a faux democracy, a system that appears to have all the features of a Constitutional democracy, a representative one, and yet the oligarchs and corporations have significant say in what gets proposed for legislation and what gets passed, making it all but politically impossible to raise taxes. "Democracy of the people, by the people, and for the people" begins to ring hollow.

1 Disparities in Income and Wealth

When we examine the changes in income since the late 1940's, we find that until 1980, every family gained income at roughly the same amount. But then we began to see significant differences, splitting families into the three groups, those at the

95th percentile, those in the lower 20th percentile and those in between. This Fig. 1 shows the changes from 1947 to 2018 (Center on Budget and Policy Priorities).

Another perhaps more striking way to see these differences is to look at how as of 2017 pre-tax income was distributed among the top 1% with the top .01% getting far, far more than the rest (Congressional Research Service, see Fig. 2).

Other data shows that the top 10% got half of the increase in pre-tax income, leaving 90% of American families to split the other half. Another measure of the huge gap in income is that after the economic collapse of 2008, 93% of the income gains in the next year went to the top 1% (Mayer 2017, p. 441).

The dramatic differences in pre-tax income mirror the striking differences between the top 0.1% and the bottom 50% in terms of the distribution of wealth. These are the percentages for the third quarter of 2023. If we add the percentages for all those between 90 and 100%, we get 66.6%. The top 10% of the population has two-thirds of the wealth whereas the bottom 50% has only 2.6%. So the top 1% has many times the total amount of wealth of the bottom 50% (Statista 2024, see Fig. 3).

The disparities have changed somewhat since 2019 when total family wealth in the United States was calculated to be 96.1 trillion dollars. Of that, the top 10% owned 76%. That group consisted of 12.9 million families. The middle 40% owned 22% of the wealth. That covered 51.5 million families. And the bottom 50% owned

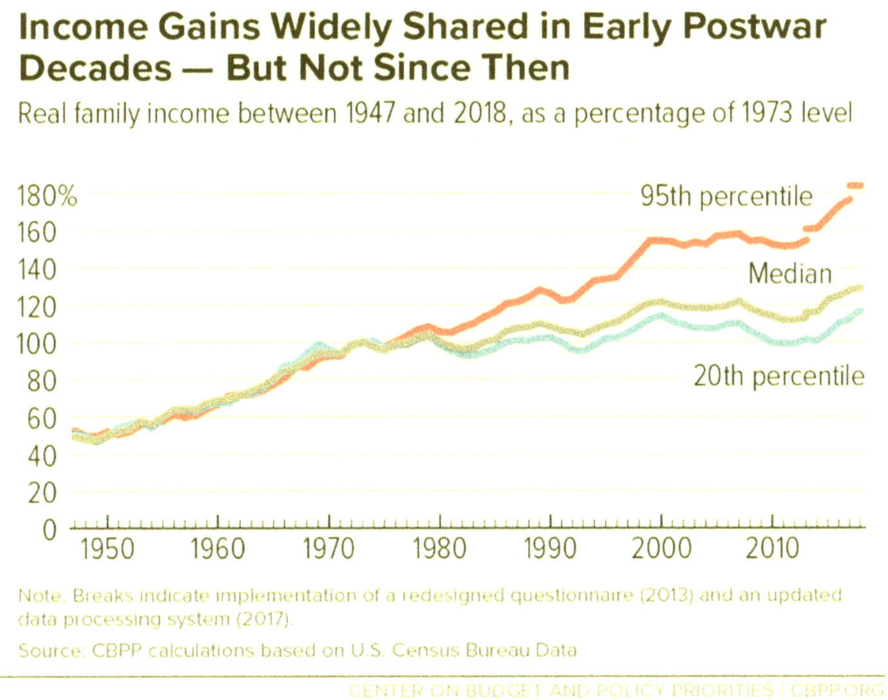

Fig. 1 Disparities in income

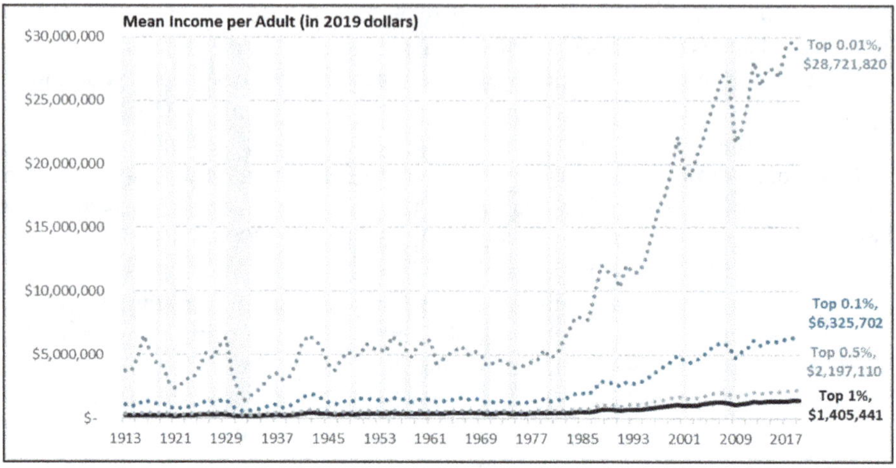

Fig. 2 Pre-tax income

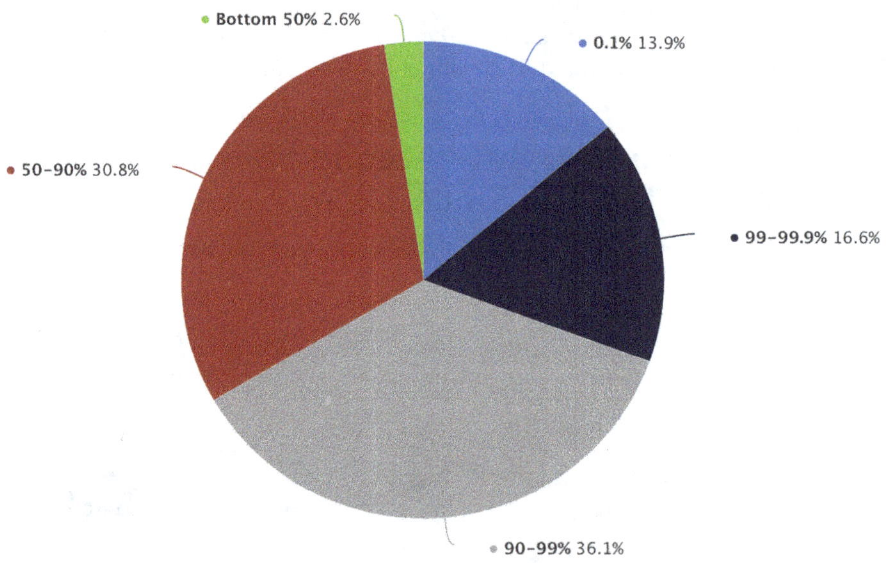

Fig. 3 Differences in pre-tax income

just 1%. That covered 64.3 million families (Kent and Ricketts 2020). These disparities are staggering indeed. The top ten percent owned three-quarters of all the wealth while the bottom fifty percent owned one one-hundred. The rest of the wealth belonged to the middle forty percent.

If we break the top 10% down further, we find that the top 1% had nearly two-fifths of all wealth. Put another way, the top 1% of families owned roughly 39 trillion, and the rest of the top 10% owned more than 34 trillion. Roughly 20 trillion was left for the 90% of families left, and of that amount, the bottom 50% got only 1 trillion.

These are rough figures, made a bit rougher by the passage of years since 2019, but however rough, they indicate huge differences between those at the top and those at the bottom, the bottom consisting of half the population of families.

These disparities are only getting worse for at least two different reasons. First, there are more billionaires than ever. In 2024, there are at least 141 more billionaires than in 2023 and "26 more than the previous record set in 2021." Every billionaire under 30 in 2024 inherited their wealth (Neate 2024), and the number will only increase as more billionaires die and pass their money onto their children. It pays to be a child of the super-rich.

Second, the billionaires are "richer than ever - with a collective wealth of $14.2tn" (Demsey 2024). Having more than enough money to pay for basic necessities means that that extra money can be put to work for you. It is startling that the net worth of Jeff Bezos increases by roughly $59,000 every minute, slightly less than the average yearly salary in the U.S. of $59,384 (Emba 2024). So the latest from Forbes is that 2024 billionaires are "255% richer than a decade ago." As an editor of Forbes said, "Even during times of financial uncertainty for many, the super-rich continue to thrive" (Demsey 2024)

If these vast inequalities in income and wealth were not sufficient to raise an ethical red flag, the way in which the inequalities are distributed between different sorts of families should surely raise such a flag. "The average Black and Hispanic or Latino households earn about half as much as the average White household and own only about 15 to 20 percent as much net wealth" (FEDS Notes 2021).

I will not get into the bushes to lay out in great detail the disparities between the various kinds of households or examine in any detail the disparities between those families with two parents and those with only one, the latter generally being a woman with children without any financial support other than what she can bring in while caring for her children. I will not get into the details because the broad strokes are enough to raise ethical concerns. How can any of these disparities be justified?

2 What Could Justify Such Disparities?

The inequalities are so vast that it is difficult to see how any theory of justice could justify them. If we could justify the inequalities through some theory of justice, we would find ourselves in an uncomfortable situation if we tried to explain to those at the bottom 0.01% or even the bottom 10% that, well, everything is fair. Indeed, if the inequalities were justified by some theory of justice, we should question the theory. There is too much to too few to make it just that so many get so little.

It is possible that the current distribution of wealth and income does provide the most good for the most people, what an utilitarian calculus would require, but if so, so much the worse for utilitarianism. It is surely hard to square a distribution that tells those who are impoverished—homeless without any idea where the next meal is coming from—that they are impoverished so as to maximize the good, including their own. We can easily imagine a distribution with those on the top having less so those on the bottom would have more. We can easily imagine a distribution that gave those on the bottom enough to rise to or above the poverty level. That we can imagine it does not make it just, of course, but illustrates the contingency of the current distribution. There is no necessity that wealth and income be distributed as they are.

The usual counter to such a claim is that those with more deserve more and those with less deserve the little they have. It would certainly be unjust, on this view, to shift wealth and income from those who have made it to support those who have not been able to make it within the current system. If the current distribution is fair, that is, we cannot justify taking from those who deserve what they have to give to those who have so much less and, on this view, deserve having as little as they do.

The theory of justice that underlies the claims about desert is Nozick's (Nozick, 2009). We exchange our labor and goods for other things, and if no exchange is coerced, any resulting inequality is just. A friend of mine had a very large collection of penknives, including some rarities famous among collectors. I asked how he could afford them, and he said he had not spent a dime for his collection. He had one he got as a child, went to the local flea market every Saturday morning, and traded knives for knives. His one penknife netted him two, and the two became the start of his collection. The advantages he had were his relatively intimate knowledge of penknives, which ones were valuable and which routine, and his persistence in ensuring that he always got better than he gave. He never traded down, that is, and though that slowed him in obtaining acquisitions, it explains why he ended up with such a valuable collection.

He exemplified Nozick's theory, that is. The large disparity between his collection and my one penknife is not unjust, on this view, but the just result of transferring ownership, willingly, without coercion. Those he traded with ended up the poorer, measuring their well-being by the number and quality of their penknives, but he was not at fault given that he and those he traded with acted voluntarily.

It is this theory, I suggest, that drives those who say the rich deserve more because they work harder and the poor deserve less because they do less. And when we see it exemplified in miniature, as it were, that seems exactly right. Not much is at stake in the world of penknives, and successes and failures in acquisitions and losses do not reverberate through a collector's life, changing their life's prospects in any significant way. In short, in a constrained setting Nozick's theory seems just right.

That is why games like Monopoly are deemed fair. Everyone starts out with exactly the same amount of money. No one can inherit anything from a previous game. The money has to be doled out anew, and equally, for each game. And then there is the way the game starts.

Being first is an advantage in the game since whoever is first will most likely be the first to land on property that can be bought. So in all versions of the game, who goes first is determined by chance, by throwing a die, high die going first. In some versions of the game, property cannot be purchased until the player who went first goes around the board twice. The idea is that any advantage gained from going first will be mitigated as luck, good and bad, takes effect for all the players as they roll the dice going two times around the board.

Starting out equal and ensuring that no one starts on Boardwalk makes the game start fairly. Provided that each player takes a turn, in turn, and moves without interference or coercion from the other players or outsiders, the game continues to be fair.

If nothing about the procedure skews the results in any way, and there is no cheating and no coercion, we cannot know ahead-of-time what the result of the procedure will be. The procedure is not designed to produce a particular result, but to produce a result that is unquestionably fair because each move has been voluntary, without coercion or interference. So if the proper procedure was followed by all the players, the one who ends up with a monopoly deserves it.

Yet the design of the game encourages, and rewards, certain personality traits that at the least strain our social bonds. A player who wants to help a fellow player by not buying a piece of property the other covets will be viewed as a patsy. Monopoly is not a team sport like basketball where cooperative behavior is crucial for a winning team. Monopoly depends upon each of the players striving to get the most for themselves. If you can prevent someone who has purchased Kentucky and Indiana from completing the duo by adding Illinois, you have a huge incentive to do that. You then prevent that player from building houses on any of the properties and so save yourself money should you land on them. Altruism is not a virtue for a player.

What are virtues are the knowledge and skills essential to recognize and take advantage of a competitive situation along with the drive to continue in the face of bad odds. Some individuals seem to have what we may call a game-sense, an understanding of how to win, and, in any event, some individuals are simply more skillful than others at calculating the odds for buying Illinois, for instance, or bypassing it for another property. Those differences, natural or learned, will make a difference in the outcome of games. Although they have the same amount of money and throw the same dice, the players are different and different enough to make all the difference to winning or losing, barring bad luck, of course.

It is not true, that is, that everyone starts out equally situated. Some, by their native knowledge and skills, or by their experience having played Monopoly, are significantly better positioned to succeed even if they have no more money than any of the other players and start from Go and not Boardwalk.

So Nozick's theory is not value neutral in the way in which the lottery, say, is value neutral. I once read of a man with almost no money who was asked why he spent any of it on a lottery ticket, and his response was telling. He said, in effect, "It's the only thing in life I've ever done where I had an equal chance." That he was Black and in the United States helps explain his response. But if the lottery is an instance of pure procedural justice, one those at the bottom can properly perceive as fair, Monopoly is not pure. Anyone who can buy a lottery ticket—and that need is a constraint on its providing an equal opportunity to everyone—has as much chance as anyone else to win. But we can rank the likelihood of winners and losers in

Monopoly by noting, among other things, what they know, what skills they have, or whether they have a game sense.

In any event, as I have argued elsewhere (Robison 1997), our world is no Monopoly board. On the one hand, we permit, and our tax laws encourage, parents to pass on their wealth to others, giving those a leg up on those whose parents are poor and can leave no inheritance. So we do not start out equally situated. Those new billionaires under 30 are significantly better off than the rest of us. They can live lives that the rest of us can only dream about—vacationing whenever and wherever they wish, eating and drinking whatever they desire, seeing whatever in the world they wish to see, living wherever they wish to live in whatever kind of abode they wish. They did not earn this kind of life; they inherited what makes this kind of life possible.

Is that fair? The current distribution of wealth and income is hardly the result of pure procedural justice. We know full well that some individuals have cheated and coerced and thus that the resulting distribution of wealth and income cannot be just on Nozick's view (Marantz, 2023). If my friend had helped himself to a penknife to enrich his collection, the resulting distribution of penknives in the world would be unfair. It takes only one cheat to skew a pure procedure since the theory of justice as transfer depends upon each transfer being voluntary. Had my friend helped himself to another person's penknife, that person could hardly be said to have relinquished the knife voluntarily, and it is hardly reasonable to suggest that the current distribution of wealth and income in the United States has come about through purely voluntary exchanges. The thieves in Los Angeles who made off with at least 30 million on Easter Sunday, 2024, changed the distribution of wealth and income without getting the consent of any of those who had stored the money (Winton 2024). Far more than 30 million has changed hands without the consent of any of those who previously had the money. By Nozick's theory, the current distribution of wealth and income is unjust.

None of us have any idea how our situation in life has been affected by involuntary transfers. We are born into a social position, a position determined in part by how much money and wealth our parents had. They were each born into a social position determined in part by how much money and wealth their parents had. None of us has any way of tracking how our social position came to be what it was, but at some time or other one or more of our ancestors was no doubt the beneficiary or victim of an involuntary transfer. A robbery would suffice to change in some measure the trajectory of our ancestors' lives and ours. We all have been affected by a history of involuntary transfers.

The result is that no theory of justice, of any sort, can justify a redistribution of whatever the current distribution is. Whatever it is, the current distribution is tainted by that history, and so redistributing it will pass on the injustice of those involuntary transfers. The result is that no theory of justice can justify some having a leg up on others because their parents gave them $200,000 a year starting when they were three years old so that they were a millionaire by the time they were eight (Smith 2018). Even if, by some stretch of the imagination, we thought a three-year-old child deserved such largresse, the gift is still tainted by its past.

That is as true of those who inherit billions as three-year-olds. As has been said, "Some people are born on third base and go through life thinking they hit a triple." On the one hand, there is no merit being born to rich parents and, on the other, no merit inheriting wealth tainted by its past.

I should add that, in any case, those who become billionaires at less than thirty are proof enough that not all the wealthy deserve their wealth, and those who are born to poor parents and lack the opportunities necessary to succeed can hardly be said to deserve their fate. As Thomas Gray said of the poor buried in a churchyard, "Some mute inglorious Milton here may rest," muted by "Chill Penury" (Gray).

3 Real Equality of Opportunity

Just as not all who are rich deserve their wealth, to make a more modest claim, so not all who are poor deserve their poverty. Having as many citizens living in poverty as we do harms them and harms us. It harms them because their meager means cuts to the core of their capacities to pursue their interests, develop their talents, and fulfill what they consider a good life. The contrast is almost as striking for the average American. How can we not be struck by Bezos making every minute what the average citizen has to work a year to achieve? Bezos can afford whatever he wishes and the rest of us must measure out what dollars we have to get what we need and having little more, if any, to fulfill our dreams.

With hard work, intelligent choices, and good luck, the ideal goes, anyone can parlay their personal riches into great wealth and income. But that ideal cannot be achieved for those born into poverty if they are not supported in ways that encourage them. Among other factors, we need educational systems throughout the country that graduate students with the skills they need to be full members of society, that allow children to develop their talents and encourage them in ways that will benefit them and society.

Such a system would provide the conditions for real equality of opportunity. I am not referring to formal equality of opportunity, that positions in society that provide access to increased income and wealth be open to all applicants. We can have formal equality of opportunity in a society with such disparities in education that only the children of the wealthy can in fact obtain such positions.

We have real equality of opportunity when those with similar talents and a similar willingness to use them have "the same prospects of success regardless of their initial place in the social system" (Rawls 1999, p. 63). But such a possibility depends upon having access to the same sort of education, for instance, a far cry from what we have here in the United States.

As I have argued elsewhere (Robison 2022), our educational system fails to provide even the most basic requirements for having an educated public able to compete on equal terms with anyone else. In a high school in Detroit, for instance, 98.2% of eleventh-graders were functionally illiterate. There is a standard test for proficiency in English in Michigan, and only "1.8% of eleventh-graders" passed the test (Gary B., et al. v. Whitmer, p. 12). That is worth repeating. It means that over 98% of the students at this high school who had completed ten years of schoolings were unable to pass the standard test for literacy. We can hardly expect any of them to be competitive in hunting for a job, for instance. They cannot read job advertisements, and they cannot read any instructions if they get a job. There is no way they can really have an equal opportunity with those who are literate, let alone those who have gone on to college.

Without a massive commitment to change the educational system, we cannot have a fully productive citizenry. We will continue to have a society that, however productive it may be, will fail to reach anywhere near its full potential because too many of the poor will be foiled in getting out of poverty. The amount of wealth and income the rich have obscures how much more our society could have were the poor able to be more productive. We have many a story of those who go from rags to riches, the Horatio Algers who make it out of poverty, but that we tell such stories tells us that success is far more rare than it need be.

It is not just individuals who are harmed, who fail to pull themselves out of poverty. We are harmed as well. The body politic is impoverished when 50% of its citizens get only 1% of the total wealth and income in the country and when the bottom 20% are significantly worse off. Like those eleventh graders, they are condemned to remain in or close to the bottom.

That is a loss to the rest of us because it means a good portion of our population is not as productive as it could be. The argument is purely practical. Benjamin Franklin might well have said, “A healthy country is a wealthy country.” A country is more productive the more of its citizens are able to work rather than hobbled by illness. Just so, a country is more productive the more of its citizens have the capacity to develop their capacities. The fewer inglorious Miltons we have, the better for all of us. We harm ourselves by not ensuring real equality of opportunity with what else is needed to allow citizens to realize their potential.

4 Our Constitutional Ideals

We fail to reach our full potential as a country when so many of our citizens are unable to realize their potential, but there is a far more serious harm that comes from having citizens with such huge amounts of wealth and income. These are the harms the wealthy inflict on the fundamental principles that undergird our Constitutional order. It was founded on the egalitarian principle that we are one another’s equals, morally and politically. We possess “equal standing and access to political life—the right to vote, to hold office, to hold leaders accountable, to form political associations that shape politics, to be represented” (Guelzo 2024, p. 10). We can see how the rich can subvert that principle by examining how great wealth can affect voting and equality under the laws.

Consider voting. It has been suggested that those with more should have more votes, with the billionaire Tom Perkins saying,

> You don't get the vote if you don't pay a dollar in taxes. But what I really think is it should be like a corporation. You pay a million dollars, you get a million votes (Whitaker 2014).

Such suggestions have not garnered much support. They cut against the ideal expressed by one person/one vote, a foundation of our democratic system, one purposefully without the aristocracy of the English, designed to ensure that no one person's vote has any more weight at the ballot box than anyone else's.

There is an obvious practical reason to reject "the Perkins system," as he calls it. I pay taxes, but the few votes I would have would count for little against those who pay much more. They could elect anyone they wish, and elections would consist of those who pay the most taxes facing off over different candidates. We poor citizens could vote, but our votes would have no practical effect. We take it so seriously that each citizen is entitled to only one vote that it is against federal law to vote more than once, with significant penalties (Corasaniti and Saul 2020).

One person/one vote would seem to level the playing field for candidates. That egalitarian principle would require that candidates have positions that appeal to a majority of the voters, but our electoral system is driven by money—to advertise, hire people to knock on doors, maintain offices with staffers and their desks and phones, and all the other paraphernalia required. Every avenue for reaching voters has a toll. So the more money a candidate can raise, the better positioned the candidate is to win, and the inequalities of wealth and income affect the electoral system because those with more can give more and help elect their preferred candidate. Perkins and other billionaires have the wherewithal to make their voting preferences count for far more than most of the rest of us.

Well-funded candidates can dominate the airwaves, television and social media, and box out their opponents, giving them an often insurmountable edge in an election. Billionaires can provide far more funding to candidates than any of the rest of us, and that funding goes with implicit but real strings attached.

In *Citizens United v. Federal Election Commission* (558 U.S. 310 (2010)), the Supreme Court "ushered in massive increases in political spending from outside groups, dramatically expanding the already outsized political influence of wealthy donors, corporations, and special interest groups" (Lau 2019). Those with outsized amounts of wealth and income can have a much greater say in who is elected, giving some of their bounty with the implicit message that the chosen candidate is to support the position of the donor. Those being elected have very good reasons, for instance, not to raise taxes on those who are showering them with the money they need to be elected.

In the same way, we are all supposedly equal under the law, but wealth and income make the system anything but just. The rich can afford the best lawyers, well-trained and seasoned by trial experience, but the poor cannot hire the best lawyers or any lawyer at all, having to make do with whomever the state appoints to defend them. Worse, many of the poor cannot afford bail, and although the rich are by no means responsible for the bail system, the poor are hobbled by it. "Our jails swell with poor people never convicted of anything" (Marshall 2016). They simply cannot "come up with $2,500 -- or less, in many cases" and so must wait in jail for the trials in which they may well be found innocent (Ehrenfreund 2015). The stay in jail may cost them their jobs, among other things. So it is not a minor harm.

But far worse for the poor is that they cannot afford the lawyers who might convince a jury to find them innocent. Brian Dorsey was executed by Missouri, the governor refusing to grant clemency even in the face of 70 of Dorsey's prison guards asking for it because Dorsey was, to their minds, completely rehabilitated. It is certainly arguable that he received the death penalty because he could not afford a lawyer. He said he was in "a drug-induced state of psychosis" when he committed the crime, but his lawyer, paid a flat rate by the state, failed to make the case for leniency (Romero 2024). Had he had the wealth of Bezos, he would not have had this problem.

Equality under the law is an ideal, of course. If we had a system of perfect procedural justice, we could achieve that ideal. Those who committed a crime would be found guilty and those falsely accused would be declared innocent. But the best we can do is design a system of imperfect procedural justice. We could tilt the system one way by presuming guilt, forcing those accused to defend themselves, or by presuming innocence, forcing the state to prove them guilty. The former puts all defendants at a disadvantage vis-á-vis the state; the latter puts the state as a disadvantage vis-á-vis the defendants. The aim of tilting it in favor of defendants is to minimize as best we can the number of innocent found guilty.

But our system of justice, even with that tilt, will find some innocents guilty, and the one variable that seems to make the most difference is the amount of money a defendant has. Like our electoral system, our system of justice runs on money, and that ensures that the wealthy are in a far better position than the poor to affect the outcome. They have whatever funding is necessary to hire the best lawyers, ensure that all the necessary research has been done, hire a company to vet potential jurors, and so on. Had Dorsey had the wealth of Bezos, he would have had a far better chance of escaping the death penalty.

Even if there were not the disparities of wealth and income we have here, we would not be able to achieve equal justice under the law or ensure that the electoral system was not skewed in any way. The funding now necessary for elections and trials ensures that we will not realize our Constitutional ideals even if some citizens did not have the immense wealth they now have. Because their immense wealth allows them far more leverage over elections and trials than the average American and especially the poor, the rich do not further our Constitutional ideals, but slowly and insidiously subvert them.

5 Tying Down the Rich

We might compare the rich to Gulliver and the rest of us to Lilliputians (Swift 2001). The rich loom large over the social and political landscape. There is no escaping their presence. They dominate everything, the culture, the news, the politics, leaving us Lilliputians way behind.

We have examined some of the harms they cause to our Constitutional order, but that concern understates the political risk such massive inequalities present. Any social system depends upon at least the acquiescence of its members to its structure, allocation of power, and distribution of social goods. Even the alpha male in a chimpanzee troop depends upon the females supporting him. One of his tasks is to ensure the troop's security by intervening when there is an altercation and quieting things down so the troop remains united. But he is to do that fairly, not showing any favoritism to those with whom he is most close, for instance. If he does his task properly, the females will hoot and holler in support, and if he fails through discriminating between members, they will remain silent, showing him that he no longer has their support. He will soon be replaced by another male (deWaal 1982).

The general point is true for any society, and we must consider whether it is possible to moderate the disparities to minimize such a risk. The most obvious remedy is some form of taxation that would increase the taxes on those with high incomes and great wealth enough to decrease the inequalities to some reasonable level. What is considered reasonable will be a contentious matter, but the argument for such taxes is hardly contentious. Those with billions depend upon the existence of a system which provides them with police protection, with protection from potential foreign invaders, with an educational system, successful enough whatever its failures, to produce enough proficient workers, and so on. They succeed in acquiring and maintaining so much because they live in a country that creates the opportunity to acquire that much with the social stability necessary to keep it.

What kind of tax would be best? Someone, somewhere, must have said that everything can be taxed. There are, after all, head taxes where just being a person makes one an object of taxation. Such a tax has the advantage of treating each citizen equally: all are taxed the same amount. A government checks its list of citizens, determines who has died since the last time the tax was administered, and sends out tax bills to all the rest.

Such a tax is thus easy to administer and difficult to evade, two features a government would want to have in a tax. That is why governments opt for taxes on sales. Collecting the taxes goes along with making a purchase. Customers have no choice but to pay the tax if they want to purchase something. Sellers have to collect the tax and turn it over to the government, of course, a process that opens the door to abuse, but the general point still holds: a tax should be easy to collect. A sales tax could be avoided by trading something to the person from whom we want something, but in our corporate world, most of what we want comes from corporations, and trading is not an option.

Unfortunately, no tax that is easy to administer and difficult to avoid will work to collect money from the wealthy. We might think we could raise the income tax rate. The top rate has fluctuated over the years from its start in 1913 at less than 10% to almost 80% by 1918, only to dip again by 1925 and then rise yet again to 90% and more in the early 1940's. It has fallen from those heights down to its present effective rate of 40.8% (Bradford). So Congress has raised and lowered the top rate over the years, and one might think that raising it again back up to 80 or 90% would solve the problems created by the disparities in wealth and income. After all, 90% of billions would provide a lot of money for the government and certainly chop off much of the wealth of the rich.

Unfortunately, any set of rules can be gamed. One way to avoid the income tax is not to have income. One may well wonder how anyone could be a billionaire and not have to pay income taxes, but the answer is obvious: make sure you have no taxable income. "Over several years, billionaires Elon Musk, Jeff Bezos, and Michael Bloomberg, among others, paid no federal income taxes at all," and "[a]t least 18 billionaires received stimulus checks in 2020, because their tax returns placed them below the income cutoff" (Kim 2024).

The rich, in short, have a myriad number of ways to avoid or lower their taxes. They have money to spend because they can borrow against their stock portfolios. Given their wealth, "those with $100 million or more could get interest rates as low as 0.87 at Merrill Lynch" (Kim 2024). So the wealthy keep their money and live off their low-interest loans.

The tax code is so complicated that it is easy to find ways for the rich to ensure they pay as little as possible in taxes. They can lower their taxes by making sure everything is a business expense. Have a private plane? It is for business. Own race-horses? Well, "six owners of thoroughbreds at the 2021 Kentucky Derby had taken a combined $600 million in tax write-offs on their horse racing operations" (ProPublica). You are rich and had gains that would be taxable? Make sure that you have losses sufficient to offset the gains (Kim 2024).

We could go on about how porous the tax code is and how much the wealthy are able to hide and so avoid paying taxes (Guyton), but the main problem is an effect of a problem we have already noted. Because the wealthy have an outsized role in electing candidates, they have an outsized role in affecting legislation. Their contributions to candidates carry the implicit rider that the candidates are to return the favor by lowering the taxes on the wealth. Trump's tax cut thus "sent $1 billion in tax savings in a single year to just 82 ultrawealthy households" (Kim 2024).

So a change to the income tax will not provide us with a tax that is easy to collect or difficult to avoid. There are other possible taxes, but all will face the same problem any legislation faces that affects the wealth of the wealthy.

For instance, one possible solution would be to tax transfers of money (Klein 2020). That would not be a wealth tax, but a tax on every financial transaction. Over twelve trillion dollars moves daily on the Nasdaq, and a tax of, say, even .01% would raise an enormous amount of money which could help skim off resources for those at the lowest level of our society. Such a tax would hit all of us. So depositing a pay check would cost us, but not much in comparison with what we would gain from the trillions transferred daily in the stock market and other financial markets. We could raise trillions of dollars we could put to education, for example, and also trim the top layer of distribution significantly.

But, again, passing legislation for such a tax would, well, tax the political system, and that is the nub of the problem. That is why we seem to have entered into a faux democracy. We can hardly have a government responsive to the will of the majority when the rich can skew the democratic process by funding candidates who will then not tax them.

6 Were We Bonobos

It is difficult to see a way out of this problem. Were we bonobos, we would not have it, but we mature into acquisitive beings with a selfish nature not found in bonobos. So the question is how we are to create a structure that provides incentives that satisfy that nature while not causing such inequalities as we now find.

It would be easy to be thoroughly pessimistic. It does not seem likely that any new generation of humans will be any less acquisitive than past generations. It seems no more likely that we can change the system of buying and selling that created the same problem for the Romans, and it seems no more likely that in our current political climate we will have any significant changes in the ways in which income and wealth are distributed.

We should not be overly pessimistic, however, even though we now live in a society where it is not amiss for a single person to be wealthier than some nations. Cultural change is possible, sometimes occurring very quickly. It was not so long ago when interracial marriage was illegal in some states and thought immoral by many or when gays had to keep in the closet. Times have changed, and cultural mores have changed. So a time may yet come when we find vast inequalities in the distribution of wealth and income unacceptable.

It is also true that the political landscape has changed over time. In our current political climate no bill that raises taxes is likely, and it is possible it might change in a way to meet this problem. A huge impediment, however, is our Constitutional structure. That structure ensures that a minority can always thwart the majority (Levitsky and Ziblatt 2023). The electoral college guarantees that the candidate with the most votes will not always win. Having two senators for each state, regardless of their populations, guarantees that senators representing a much smaller segment of the population can scuttle legislation favored by the majority. The result is that even if the bottom 90% of the population were to favor changing the distribution of wealth and income, our Constitutional structure makes it extremely unlikely that would happen.

We might think that our judicial system would serve as a check on distortions in our political system because judges and justices are to be impartial, but they are not. *Citizens United* is just the most egregious example of how the judicial system reinforces rather than restrains the worst excesses of our Constitutional structure. The bias that thwarts majority rule infects the judicial system as well. It matters whether a judge or justice was appointed by a Republican or a Democratic president, with those appointed by Republican presidents far more likely to rule in favor of the seemingly stronger party while those appointed by Democratic presidents are more likely to rule with the seemingly weaker party. They may not be political hacks, but judicial outcomes turn on party affiliation far more often than they would were the judicial system above politics (Cohen).

We should remember, however, before succumbing to deep pessimism, that Constitutional changes are possible, given time and a concentrated commitment just by even a few. It took from the 1840's until 1918 to get an amendment that gave women the right to vote, a long time, indeed, but that is what it took to get enough men to change the way they viewed women, as equally capable of choosing who should represent them. So Constitutional change is possible, however unlikely it may now seem.

We also have examples of how the buying and selling of goods and services does not have to lead to great disparities in income and wealth. After all, Adam Smith was describing what we do in *The Wealth of Nations*, not proscribing what we ought to do and not noting what we must do (Smith 1982) what Smith described are not immutable economic laws. There is no necessity about them. It is true that invisible hands will continue to buy and sell whatever constraints we put on the system. That is why Prohibition failed, after all. But we have examples readily at hand of how to design economic structures that do not lead to great disparities. Employee owned businesses and cooperatives are but two examples (Romeo 2024).

So perhaps we should not be deeply skeptical, but we are entering an era that could test our democracy to its core. We have just been through one and may have yet another as a result of the 2024 election, but however that works out, we need to face up to the problems the inequality of wealth and income present to the foundations of our democracy.

References

Beard M (2015) SPQR, a history of ancient Rome. Liveright Publishing Corporation, New York, p 435

Board of Governors of the Federal Reserve System. https://www.federalreserve.gov/releases/z1/dataviz/dfa/distribute/chart/. Accessed 1 Feb 2024. See also FRED, the St. Louis Fed. https://fred.stlouisfed.org/release/tables?eid=813668&rid=453

Bradford Tax Institute. https://bradfordtaxinstitute.com/Free_Resources/Federal-Income-Tax-Rates.aspx — Bradford Tax Institute

Center on Budget and Policy Priorities. https://www.cbpp.org/income-gains-widely-shared-in-early-postwar-decades-but-not-since-then-3

Cohen A The pervasive influence of political composition on circuit court decisions. National Bureau of Economic Research. https://ssrn.com/abstract=4528999

Congressional Research Service. The U.S. Income Distribution: trends and issues, p 14. https://sgp.fas.org/crs/misc/R44705.pdf

Cooper D (2015) Children have an innate sense of restorative justice. News in Science, ABC Science, July 19, 2015. https://www.abc.net.au/science/articles/2015/06/19/4258170.htm

Corasaniti N, Saul S (2020) Is voting twice a Felony? New York Times, September 9, 2020. https://www.nytimes.com/article/voting-twice.html

Demsey J (2024) Taylor Swift joins world's richest on billionaire list. BBC, April 2, 2024. https://www.bbc.com/news/business-68711921at_campaign_type=owned&at_link_origin=BBCWorld&at_format=link&at_bbc_team=editorial&at_ptr_name=twitter&at_link_type=web_link&at_link_id=3A0F6A70-F0FF-11EE-8F23-97C64B3AC5C4

deWaal F (1982) Chimpanzee politics: power and sex among Apes. Johns Hopkins Press, Baltimore

Ehrenfreund M (2015) How bail punishes the poor for their poverty. The Washington Post, February 13, 2015

Emba C (2024) What would society look like if extreme wealth were impossible? The Washington Post, April 1, 2024
FEDS Notes (2021) Aladangady, Aditya and Forde, Akila. Wealth Inequality and the Racial Wealth Gap. October 22, 2021. https://www.federalreserve.gov/econres/notes/feds-notes/wealth-inequality-and-the-racial-wealth-gap-20211022.html
Forsé M, Richardot S, Frénod A, Lafaye CG, Parodi M (2016) The sense of distributive justice in children from 6 to 10. Eur J Soc Sci 54(1). https://journals.openedition.org/ress/3403
Gary B. v. Gretchen Whitmer, No. 18-1855 (6th Cir. 2020). https://law.justia.com/cases/federal/appellate-courts/ca6/18-1855/18-1855-2020-05-19.html
Gray T. Elegy Written in a Country Churchyard. The Poetry Foundation. https://www.poetryfoundation.org/poems/44299/elegy-written-in-a-country-churchyard
Guelzo AG (2024) Our ancient faith. Alfred A. Knopf, New York
Guyton J et al. Tax evasion at the top of the income distribution: theory and evidence. IRS. https://www.irs.gov/pub/irs-soi/23rptaxevasiontopincomedist.pdf
Hare B, Kwetuenda S (2010) Bonobos voluntarily share their own food with others. Curr Biol 20(5):R230-1. https://www.sciencedirect.com/science/article/pii/S0960982209022015
Kelsey L, Pospisil J, Sommerville JA. Fairness informs social decision making in infancy. PLos ONE, p 10. https://journals.plos.org/plosone/article?id=10.1371/journal.pone.0192848
Kent AH, Ricketts LR (2020) Has wealth inequality in America changed over time? Here are key statistics. Federal Reserve Bank of St. Louis, December 2, 2020. https://www.stlouisfed.org/open-vault/2020/december/has-wealth-inequality-changed-over-time-key-statistics
Kim W (2024) The billionaire's guide to doing taxes. Vox, March 13, 2024. https://www.vox.com/money/2024/3/13/24086102/billionaires-wealthy-tax-avoidance-loopholes
Klein A (2020) What is a financial transaction tax? Brookings Institute. March 27, 2020. https://www.brookings.edu/articles/what-is-a-financial-transaction-tax-2/
Lau T (2019) Citizen united explained. Brannan Center for Justice, December 12, 2019. https://www.brennancenter.org/our-work/research-reports/citizens-united-explained
Levitsky S, Ziblatt D (2023) The tyranny of the minority. Crown Publishing, New York
Mankoff R (ed) (2004) The complete cartoons of the New Yorker. Black Dog & Leventhal, New York, p 521
Marantz A (2023) Behind every great fortune is a great crime, according to an adage attributed to Balzac. The New Yorker, August 14, 2023
Marshall R (2016) America's bail system is a war on the poor. Let's get rid of it. Vox, August 24, 2016. https://www.vox.com/2016/8/24/12590060/doj-bail-unconstitutional
Mayer J (2017) Dark Money. Anchor Books, New York
Neate R (2024) All billionaires under 30 have inherited their wealth, research finds. The Guardian, April 3, 2024. https://www.theguardian.com/business/2024/apr/03/all-billionaires-under-30-have-inherited-their-wealth-research-finds
Nozick R (2009) Anarchy, State and Utopia, Revised edition. Basic Books, New York
Rawls J (1999) A theory of justice, 2nd edn. Belknap Press, New York
Robison W (1997) Monopoly with sick moral strangers. In: Minogue B, Palmer-Fernandez G, Reagan JE (eds) Reading Engelhardt: essays on the thought of H. Tristram Engelhardt, Jr. Kluwer Academic Publishers, Dordrecht, pp 95–112
Robison W (2022) The right to an education. In: McGregor J, Navin M (eds) Education, inclusion, and justice. Springer, Heidelberg, pp 45–58
Romeo N (2024) The alternative: how to build a just economy. PublicAffairs, New York
Romero D (2024) Missouri executes convicted murderer despite prison staff's campaign to save him. NBC News, April 9, 2024. https://www.nbcnews.com/news/us-news/brian-dorsey-missouri-execution-rcna147113
Smith A (1982) The wealth of nations. The Liberty Fund, Indianapolis
Smith A (2018) Trump was reportedly earning $200,000 in today's dollars by the time he was 3 years old. And he was a millionaire by age 8. Business Insider, October 2, 2018. https://www.businessinsider.com/trump-tax-fraud-fred-inheritance-millionaire-by-age-8-2018-10?op=1

Statista (2024). https://www.statista.com/statistics/203961/wealth-distribution-for-the-us/
Swift J (2001) Gulliver's travels. W. W. Norton, New York
Welsh J (2011) Babies as young as 15 months grasp fairness. LiveScience, October 8, 2011. https://www.livescience.com/16460-babies-grasp-fairness-sharing.html
Whitaker M (2014) Billionaire suggests rich should get more votes. MSNBC, February 14, 2014. https://www.msnbc.com/politicsnation/billionaire-rich-should-get-more-votes-msna267621
Winton R (2024) In one of L.A.'s largest cash heists ever, burglars steal as much as $30 million from vault. Los Angeles Times, April 3, 2024

On Various Injustices in the United States Tax Code, and How They Eviscerate the Bases of Citizen Self-Respect

Jonathan Schonsheck

Abstract John Rawls argues that citizen self-respect is the most important primary social good; I fully concur. In consequence, we ought to be deeply concerned about policies that undermine, or even eviscerate, self-respect. Especially important among these threats are various injustices in the income tax code. Complex and arcane provisions—treating hedge fund profits as "carried interest," the "stepped-up basis" for assessing capital gains, the operation of "family offices" designed to preserve excessive wealth and power—are indefensible. The tax burden on ordinary citizens is unjustly increased, to lighten the load on the UltraWealthy, and consequently the institutions that enhance self-respect are woefully underfunded. Citizen cognizance of these injustices leads to divisiveness, disillusionment, anger and despair.

1 Introduction & Overview

It would be quite impossible, in a paper of this length, to even *enumerate*, much less fully discuss, the myriad injustices in the United States federal income tax code.[1] Thus, one must be selective. On what criterion? My focus herein: those injustices which have the effect of eviscerating the bases of citizens' self-respect. For I shall be endorsing the position argued by John Rawls—that self-respect is the most

[1] My principal concern in this paper is with injustices internal to the tax code itself, and less so with the injustices of tax *evasion*—the failure of some citizens to pay what they owe, as demanded by that tax code. Since this is a matter of mere criminality, it is of (comparatively) less *philosophical* interest. Nonetheless, I will discuss it briefly when appropriate, indicating tax evasion's role in undermining citizen self-respect.

J. Schonsheck (✉)
Department of Philosophy & Madden School of Business and Economics, Le Moyne College, Syracuse, NY, USA
e-mail: schonsjc@lemoyne.edu

G. A. Babst, W.-c. Lee (eds.), *Contemporary Facets of Injustice*, AMINTAPHIL: The Philosophical Foundations of Law and Justice 13,
https://doi.org/10.1007/978-3-031-93783-5_3

important "primary social good," absolutely indispensable to human flourishing. In consequence, injustices in the tax code merit particular philosophical scrutiny, and thereafter legislative reform.

The place to begin is with an understanding of the essentials, the dynamics of our economy; that is the context of our system of taxation and expenditures, of revenues collected, and revenues dispersed. To that end, I propose we think in straightforward terms of *flows* of resources. In particular, resources flow *from* various "Entities" (to be defined), *to* the United States Treasury; resources flow *from* the Treasury, *to* various "Entities." All of these flows are appropriately subjected to moral assessment—and in particular, to the demands of defensible principles of justice.

In Sect. 2, I further explain the crucial dynamic of "flows of resources," as well as the fairly intuitive concept of various "Entities." In Sect. 3, I provide a brief overview the Internal Revenue Code, ending with the crucial question, "Who benefits" from this monstrosity? Unsurprisingly, it does not work to the benefit of "We-the-People," but rather—decidedly—it works *contrary* to the welfare of We-the-People, and *to* the obscene benefit of the "Ultra-Wealthy." I pose in the trenchant question: "How has this come about?" And in Sect. 4, I offer, and defend, an answer: "An unholy synergism between the Congress of the United States, and the Supreme Court of the United States." Members of Congress have a voracious, insatiable appetite for "flows of resources" from an array of interested parties. The Court, in deciding a series of cases, has been facilitating these corrupting flows of resources. In previously published work, I have argued that this entire line of decisions is profoundly misguided. Section 5 is devoted to a number of particular provisions and practices by which the UltraWealthy advance their financial interests by constricting their flows to the Treasury. I address two topics regarding the Internal Revenue Service in Sect. 6. First, I criticize the expressions of "owing money to the IRS," or "Uncle Sam," as they disguise the fact that resources are actually owed to an array of Entities essential to civil society. Second, I detail the consequences of underfunding the IRS, *viz.*, facilitating tax evasion. I argue for the transcending importance of citizen self-respect in Sect. 7. To motivate it, I begin with a Parody, "I am a Self-Made Man," intended to shame resistance to reforms. I then argue for reform directly, extoling the value of fully funding (by flows of resources) the various social institutions necessary to create Rawlsian "Fair Value of Opportunity," and show the ways in which the injustices of our current tax regime eviscerate the bases of self-respect. I summarize the overall argument in Sect. 8.

2 Visualize the Economy as Extraordinarily Intricate "Flows of Resources" (et sequelae)

I propose that we think of "the economy" as incredibly intricate *flows of resources.* Most obviously, resources flow from employers to employees; we call these "wages." Resources flow from employees (and others), as consumers, to various retail outlets ("shopping"), and various creditors and utilities ("paying the bills"). And of course there are incredibly many flows of resources from "business-to-business:" to and from suppliers, shippers, retailers, etc.

However, let us focus our attention on some particular participants in the economy, and some particular flows.

Most importantly, resources flow from citizens to various governmental entities—what we call "taxes." Resources flow from residents to local governments, typically in the form of property taxes, for the services of first responders, and in support of public education, and for the removal of trash and snow, etc. In most states, there are flows from various Entities to the state itself—for additional first responders, higher education and licensures, etc.

And then there is the federal government: resources flow from businesses and individuals into the Treasury; resources flow from the Treasury to various Entities. Some of these are Domestic, are internal: Resources flow to various social institutions (Education, Energy, Commerce, etc.), the many "alphabet" agencies (EPA, FDA, CDC, etc.). Some of these institutions are external, or International (Department of Defense, Department of State, etc.).

Abstractly, we must apply principles of justice to these flows; abstractly, there are four points at which *in*justices might be found: too *little* from an Entity to the Treasury, too *much* from an Entity to the Treasury; too *much* from the Treasury to an Entity, too *little* from the Treasury to an Entity. Causally, in this order, we call too little from an Entity to the Treasury a failure to pay one's "fair share." Too much from an Entity to the Treasury is called the imposition of an unwarranted burden on the taxpayer. Too much of a flow from the Treasury to an Entity is called wastefulness, an unwarranted enrichment. Too little a flow from the Treasury to an Entity is to "shortchange" that Entity. Most importantly, when that Entity is a social institution, we call it "underfunded:" it lacks the resources to effectively perform its designed functions.

Also abstractly—but crucial to our inquiry—are these implications: Whenever the flow from an Entity to the Treasury is too small, then either social institutions will be underfunded, or else—if we believe that the institutions *must* be fully funded—the shortfall will have to be made up by *shifting* that burden, i.e., by *increasing* the flows from some *other* Entities.

This phenomenon will prove crucially important in the arguments that follow. For ease of reference, let us give it a name; let us call it the "Shortfall Dilemma." We are confronted by this dilemma whenever the resources that flow into the Treasury are not adequate to sufficiently fund our institutions, whether Domestic or International. We are compelled to choose between "burden-shifting," or "institution crippling"—or, obviously, both. This, despite the fact that "Americans overwhelmingly say the wealthy and corporations don't pay their fair share in taxes. This view is, er somewhat at odds with Republicans' plans to grind down these groups' tax rates even further." (Rampell 2024).

In a similar vein: Whenever the flow to some other Entities is too great, then either social institutions will be underfunded, or, if funding must be maintained, then *other* Entities will be forced to increase their respective flows, to make up for that unwarranted largesse. Again, we face the dilemma of choosing between "burden shifting," or "institution crippling."

Now as we move forward, we will be focusing our attention more narrowly on two particular sets of resource flows: First, we should scrutinize the flows *into* the Treasury from various Entities, principally individuals and businesses, principally (of course) by taxation of various sorts. Second, we should scrutinize the flows of resources *out of* the Treasury, and *to* various Entities—principally to individuals in entitlement programs, and also to an array of social institutions—these by means of various appropriations.

3 The Federal Income Tax Code

Let us consider United States Title 26—the Internal Revenue Code. It runs some 6,871 pages. But do not stop there. As any competent accountant, any competent tax lawyer will assure you, it is not possible to determine one's tax liability—whether ordinary citizen, or business of any size—without consulting additional IRS regulations, tax guidance, and voluminous case law. While no one knows precisely, all told these will add some 75,000 pages to your mandatory reading list (Iris 2020).

In my considered judgement, to call the current income tax law of the United States a "dumpster fire" is to insult and demean dumpsters (which play important social roles), and to insult and disrespect Prometheus, the god who brought fire to humankind. In its stead, I propose to label this gargantuan unwieldly and loop-hole-ridden tax code "a Fetid and Putrefying Quagmire."

This leads, quite naturally, to a crucial question asked by biologists in search of explanations: *Qui bono?* Who benefits? Beyond all doubt, this Quagmire does *not* benefit We-the-People, We-the-99%. It is essential to fully comprehend the fact that nearly three quarters of taxpayers take the Standard Deduction, i.e., do not file even a Schedule B, itemizing deductions. Their tax returns consist of but a few pages; they rely upon only a miniscule *fraction* of the IRS code. So what can, what *must* be said about the *other* tens of thousands of pages of regulations? More pointedly: who but the Ultra-Wealthy can afford to engage the CPAs and tax lawyers required, in order to take advantage of the tens of thousands of remaining obscure provisions, all components of the Quagmire? For they provide legal permission to constrict their flows to the Treasury, or enhance the flows from the Treasury to themselves.

4 Creating, Maintaining and Expanding the Quagmire

How has this happened? Who is responsible for developing and maintaining—and indeed expanding—this Fetid and Putrefying Quagmire? Succinctly, it is an ongoing and unholy synergism between the U.S. Congress, and the Supreme Court of the United States. Let us see how this is so.

4.1 Consider First the Supreme Court

In a line of cases, it has thwarted virtually all attempts to reform our current arrangements for funding political campaigns. As I have already published an extensive critique of this, a very brief synopsis will suffice for present purposes (Schonsheck 1981, 2000, 2010, 2014).[2]

Beginning with *Buckley* v. *Valeo*, through *Belotti* v. *First National Bank*, and culminating (at least for now) in *Citizens United* v. *FEC*, the Court has moved from the obviously correct position that exercising one's right to freedom of speech in the context of political campaigning can cost enormous sums of money, to the ludicrous position that money *is* speech. And since speech should be unfettered, money too should be unfettered. Furthermore, the Court has held that the right to freedom of speech is not limited to biological individuals, but extends to corporations and other organizations: they are "people" as well. Thus, all can direct virtually unlimited flows of Resources (in our language) into political campaigns: those troughs into which (almost) all candidates—incumbents and challengers alike—plunge their greedy snouts, to lustily gobble it up.

4.2 Consider Now the Congress

If you remember anything at all from your years in middle school, it is likely to be the topic "How a Bill Becomes a Law." The orthodoxy: a member of Congress, perceiving a problem which can be solved by federal legislation, crafts a bill; by dint of persuasive powers in the cloakroom, or on the floor, convinces one's colleagues to vote in its favor ....

This now seems so precious. For we have come to know that members of Congress spend approximately 30 hours/week fundraising for their next campaign, not drafting legislation (Ratliff 2021). Bill-writing is done predominately by "experts" in the employ of special-interest groups, e.g., the lobbyists known collectively by their favored Washington, DC address: "K Street." Lobbyists vastly outnumber our 538 Legislators; there are 12,644 of them.[3] (Statistica 2023) Thus "model legislation," favorable to the interests of the lobbyists' clients, is delivered to Congressional offices—along with political campaign contributions.

Yet matters get (far) worse than the mere crafting of legislation. Consider a truly insidious practice, discussed in an investigative piece published in *The New York*

---

[2] As I argue there (2014), in order to secure the *values* that Freedom of Speech is intended to promote—principally individual autonomy—restrictions on campaign contributions are not merely permissible, but indeed are absolutely *required*. Otherwise, whenever there are vast disparities in resources, the monied side will overwhelm, will drown out, the impecunious side.

[3] Research on some of the effects of this, conducted by *The Washington Post*, appears under the headline "When lobbyists and legislators socialize, lobbyists are more likely to get what they want." (Sadhwani et al. 2022) Ya *think*?

Times under the headline "How Accounting Giants Craft Favorable Tax Rules From Inside Government."

> The largest accounting firms have perfected a remarkably effective behind-the-scenes system to promote their interests in Washington. Their tax lawyers take senior jobs at the Treasury Department, where they write policies that are frequently favorable to their former corporate clients, often with the expectation that they will soon return to their old employers. The firms welcome them back with loftier titles and higher pay ....

Indeed, "Even some former industry veterans said they viewed the rapid back-and-forth arrangements as a big part of the reason that tax policy had become so skewed in favor of the wealthy, at the expense of just about everyone else." (Drucker and Hakim 2021) The authors provide numerous, quite specific examples of the operation of this "revolving door."

Essential reading on all these issues is Jane Mayer's thoroughly researched and deeply documented *Dark Money: The Hidden History of the Billionaires Behind the Rise of the Radical Right* (Mayer 2016). But let us now turn to extricating some of the "provisions" from the Quagmire, vividly illustrating (very) serious injustices in flows of resources, that have become operative since the 2016 publication of *Dark Money*.

5 Some Particularly Galling Examples

5.1 *Vast Resources Given in Support of Right-Wing Causes: To Be Dispersed* Anonymously

As if right on cue, we have just witnessed a genuinely terrifying set of developments. *ProPublica's* headline serves as an informative introduction: "How a Secretive Billionaire Handed His Fortune to the Architect of the Right-Wing Takeover of the Courts." The "secretive billionaire" is Barre Seid, described as a "manufacturing magnate." His fortune is estimated to be $1.6 billion. The recipient is the Marble Freedom Trust, a nonprofit, a so-called 501(c)(4). In so donating, "Seid avoided up to $400 million in state and federal income tax ...." (Once again, we know that the burden of that constricted flow of resources will have to be borne by We-the-People.) The Marble Freedom Trust is controlled by Leonard Leo, co-chair of the Federalist Society. According to *ProPublica,* "The Marble Freedom Trust is a so-called dark money group that is not required to publicly disclose its donors. It has wide latitude to spend directly on elections as well as on ideological projects such as funding issue-advocacy groups, think tanks, universities, religious institutions and organizing efforts." For example, "In 2005 Leo and his allies formed a dark money network to rally support for George W. Bush's Supreme Court nominees, John Roberts and Samuel Alito." More recently, "... it led a campaign to block Obama Supreme Court nominee Merrick Garland's confirmation." Bringing together the two components of (what I have called) the Unholy Synergism, "Seid's

$1.6 billion donation is a landmark in the era of deregulated political spending ushered in by the Supreme Court's 2010 Citizens United decision." (Perez 2002) This is an absolutely stupendous flow of resources, further enriching the Ultra-Wealthy, and also confounding Progressive efforts to reform taxation in accord with justice.[4]

5.2 *Hedge Fund Profits Treated as "Carried Interest"*

An appallingly obvious example of too constricted a flow from an Entity to the Treasury is the treatment of hedge fund profits as a "carried interest," so that they are not taxed at the "income" rate, but at the (substantially lower) "capital gains" rate. Even if there is some justification for a difference in rates of taxation between regular income, and investment income (which is a separate issue), no reasonable principle of justice would countenance *this* particular differential. This obscure provision in the tax code is the workings of lobbyists, not justice.

Now an effort was launched to rectify this injustice in President Biden's Inflation Reduction Act of 2022. But Senator Krysten Sinema (D-AZ) threatened to vote against the entire bill—which would have resulted in its defeat—unless that provision were deleted. So in order to secure her vote, and thus to secure the passage of the bill, it was in fact deleted. Writing in *The New Republic*, Timothy Noah asks rhetorically, "Who's Shocked that Krysten Sinema Went to Bat for Hedge-Funders?" and notes that she "has collected $2.2 million overall from the financial sector since 2017, and much of that is a likely payoff for opposing repeal of the carried interest loophole." (Noah 2022) (Sorkin et al. 2022) So this wholly unjustified enrichment of a few of the Ultra-Wealthy, granting legal permission to reduce their flows to the Treasury (and so the inescapable burden-shifting, or else social institution underfunding), *endures*.

5.3 *The Exchange of Campaign Contributions for Favorable Tax Legislation*

ProPublica has published a report about the nefarious activities of Senator Ron Johnson (R-WI) during the writing of (then) President Donald Trump's tax legislation of 2017. He insisted upon the inclusion of a provision that greatly benefitted two of his constituents: Dick and Liz Uihlein of Uihlein packaging, and Diane Hendricks of ABC Supply. "The expanded tax break Johnson muscled through netted them $215 million in deductions in 2018 alone, drastically reducing the income they owed taxes on. At that rate, the cut could deliver more than half a billion in tax

[4] A book-length treatment covering this ground more extensively can be found in Sheldon Whitehouse's *The Scheme* (2022).

savings for Hendricks and the Uihleins over its eight-year life." (Glauber 2021) And as we know, of course, "tax savings" in this context means constricted flows to the Treasury—and *that* means either the shifting of the tax burden to the rest of us, or the underfunding of certain Entities (e.g. social institutions), or both. Now this did not go unnoticed by Wisconsin Lt. Gov. Mandela Barnes, who was harshly critical of Johnson's actions, asserting that it was "disgraceful that Senator Johnson used his office to enrich some of the wealthiest political donors while raising taxes on the middle class – and widening the income equality gap across our state" (Glauber 2021). Perhaps it's just a coincidence, but these two beneficiaries of said deductions contributed some $20 million to Johnson's reelection campaign.

5.4 An Egregious Injustice with the Obscure Name "Stepped Up Basis"

> Billionaires can defer taxes on their capital gains for decades or forever as income tax is due only upon the *sale* of assets. When gains are realized, they are taxed at a preferential top tax rate of 20% (instead of 37% for ordinary income). If assets are bequeathed, *no tax is ever due on gains* (Saez and Zucman 2021). (Emphases added)

So capital gains tax is due on the increase in value of the assets—the difference between the acquisition cost of the assets, and the value realized when sold. But what if the assets are not sold? What if they are passed down? Well, capital gains tax will indeed be owed, when the inheritors sell the assets. However, the capital gain to be taxed will be the difference between the selling price, and the value of the assets *at the time of the inheritance*, and *not* their value when initially acquired by the person bequeathing. Thus, *all* the gains in asset value, from acquisition to inheritance, *are never taxed*. The "basis" used for determining the gains that are subject to taxation has been "stepped up," from the value at acquisition, to the value upon inheritance.

Robin Kaiser-Schatzlein details the effects of this as follows:

> For a select few families with vast fortunes amassed over many generations, it means that they can pass down millions or billions of dollars in stock, investments or real estate without having to pay income or capital gains taxes on many decades, or possibly a century or more, of gains. The windfall grows each time the money is transferred, endowing those families with disproportionate power for generations to come.

He continues, "... the children of today's oligarchs ... stand to inherit unthinkable sums of money, further concentrating wealth and political power away from the rest of society, including small businesses and farmers." And his conclusion is directly on point, as regards the central thesis of this essay: "Wealth easily buys political power. The longer we fail to constrain inherited wealth, the sooner the dream of a democratic society dies." (Kaiser-Schatzlein 2021).

Of course We-the-People *could* take advantage of this tax provision. Step One: amass generational wealth ....[5]

5.5 *The "Family Office:" Preserving Wealth and Power*

The final topic regarding the Unholy Synergism between the Congress and the Supreme Court is the institution known as a "family office."[6] Arguably this is the pinnacle of the efforts to constrain the flows of Resources from the Ultra-Wealthy to the Treasury.[7] As baldly stated by *Investopedia,*

> A family office is a private wealth management advisory firm that serves ultra-high-net worth individuals. Family offices are different from traditional wealth management shops in that they offer a total solution to managing the financial and investment needs of an affluent individual or family.... Besides financial services, family offices can provide various kinds of planning, charitable giving advice, concierge services, and other comprehensive services.... The family office can also handle non-financial issues, such as private schooling, travel arrangements, and miscellaneous household arrangements (Hayes 2023).

To put it in our terms, the "family office" is a set of tax experts devoted to constricting as tightly as possible that client family's flows to the Treasury. These people paw through the aforementioned 75,000+ pages of IRS code and cases, searching for obscure and arcane provisions that have nothing to do with justice, but might give plausible legal cover for even tighter constrictions of the client family's flow. This typically involves highly technical treatments of their "incomes" and wealth.

And as we know, the more "successful" are these various strategies, the more *other* taxpayers must compensate for the revenue shortfalls they have created, or else put up with the pain of underfunded social agencies.

6 "Nobody Owes Nothin' *to the IRS!*"

Resources, principally in the form of taxes, flow from Entities into the Treasury. (And from there, of course, to various Entities, principally social institutions.) *Specifications* of the various flows into the Treasury is the province of the United

[5] I have a very vivid image of a particular cartoon, despite the fact that the image is decades old. (It might be the work of Charles Rodrigues, though I have not been able to verify this.) The scene is a county morgue; on the slab is the corpse of an elderly gentleman. Standing by his side is an elderly woman, apparently his wife, wearing a babushka, and clutching the handles of her purse with both hands. The coroner asks her, "Would you like a paper bag for his estate?" The vast majority of us are closer to needing a paper bag, than being able to avail ourselves of the "stepped up basis" for calculating the capital gains tax upon the sale of inherited assets.

[6] This is not to be confused with the "home office" deduction taken by ordinary taxpayers who operate a business from their residence.

[7] To anticipate a bit: this is diametrically opposed to the Rawlsian conception of justice in taxation.

States Congress. The *management* of the flows into the Treasury—in contrast to their *specifications*—is the responsibility of the Internal Revenue Service. It is the absolutely indispensable "collection agency" of the Treasury.

Perhaps this is too obvious to mention. But perhaps not. All too often, in various contexts, this fundamental fact is obscured by a trope that is deeply misleading and profoundly destructive: that citizens owe money (taxes) *to the IRS*. Citizens are required by law to flow resources *to the Treasury*, for its myriad disbursements to the agencies and institutions that benefit the commonweal. Put more starkly: citizens are required by law to flow resources to the *citizenry*, and *not* "to the IRS" *per se*. To speak of "owing money to the IRS" is not only inaccurate (false), it creates an adversarial relationship between citizens and the institution that is vital, but is nonetheless merely the *collection agency* for the *Congress*—which is, of course, the institution that actually *specifies* the taxes owed.

However, since it is the IRS that is in immediate and frequent contact with taxpayers, it is the IRS (and not so much the Congress) that is the continuous target of citizen rage. Indeed, it is safe to say that no politician has ever lost an election for excessively bashing the IRS. So the IRS gets characterized as a fiscal "black hole." Money is withheld from our paychecks, or submitted with our filings, or *both*. And then it seems to disappear; it's just *gone*. And since we would all (in general) prefer to keep more of that money, whatever anyone can do to remit less rather than more might *seem* to be a good thing: "Hey, I beat the tax man!"

This is dangerous nonsense. For as we have seen, when understanding the economy as the flows of resources, "beating the tax man" entails revenue shortfalls to the Treasury. The consequences of those shortfalls: an underfunding of social institutions, or additional borrowing (increasing the federal deficit), or the wrongful shifting of that burden to other Entities, i.e., to other taxpayers—in the current fiscal year, or to subsequent generations in subsequent fiscal years.

This point can be wonderfully, vividly illustrated by considering businesses devoted to tax negotiations. Due to its ubiquitous television commercials in America, Optima Tax Relief is a splendid exemplar. Their commercials begin with an ominous voice-over: "Do you owe the IRS $10,000, or $30,000, or $65,000, or even more?" Unless stifled by my spouse, I scream at the screen: "No! Nobody owes nothin' to the IRS! It's just a collection agency![8] You don't owe that money to the IRS,[9] but to the Treasury, to *us*, your fellow citizens. If you don't pay what you owe, then the rest of us will suffer: either compelled to make up your shortfall, or by

[8] Albeit a highly effective one—as the commercial is quick to point out.

[9] Imagine you have just completed your weekly grocery shop. A voice booms over the loudspeaker: "Do you owe the checkout clerk $200?" What? Of course I *do* owe the *supermarket* $200 for the victuals I shall be taking home. But it is profoundly confused to say that I owe the *clerk*—who is just a low-paid individual who merely scans and bags—anything at all. (Except basic civility, and perhaps a compliment if the job has been well done.) It is entirely out of place to disrespect, or to vilify, the person who is merely accepting your form of payment. (If you believe that grocery prices are too high, perhaps due to gouging, you should take it up with the owner, or with management, but not the hapless clerk.)

coping with the pain of underfunded institutions!" The commercials continue with testimonials by various clients—how much they owed in taxes, and how much less they actually paid, in a settlement. And, as we know, that payment, albeit reduced, is a flow *not* to the IRS *per se*, but to the Treasury. And again, this results in the wrongful shifting of their burdens to the rest of us, or else our having to endure the pain of underfunded institutions.[10] These commercials end with the testimonialists saying how much better they now feel, with their tax problems resolved. The point of these, obviously, is to encourage others with tax problems to contact Optima, for tax relief. I find these particularly galling; *I*, for one, feel neither empathy nor sympathy for them. I don't *want* them to feel relief. Indeed, I feel outraged at their cheating, knowing that their new-found "peace of mind" is coming at *my* expense.[11] Would that they feel remorse, guilt even about what they have (not) done; would that they resolve to be conscientious in the future, flowing their fair share of resources to the Treasury, to *us*.

In a similar vein, one often encounters the expression that taxes are "owed to Uncle Sam." This brings to mind a picture of a very tall, very elderly man, wearing striped pants and a starred top hat. He seems more doddering than fearsome. Why should we be giving money to *him*, and what's he going to do about it if we don't? For example, according to Catherine Rampell, lowering tax rates is "not the only way the GOP hopes to reduce their tax payments. It would also defund the tax police, making it easier for rich people to shortchange Uncle Sam." (Rampell 2024) Of course I am in complete agreement with her sentiment here—but reject her reference to "Uncle Sam." In my judgment, we ought to adamantly reject this flippant expression. For it trivializes what constitutes a serious transgression. It is *we*, the *conscientious* taxpayers, who are being "shortchanged," who are being cheated. And as discussed above, we are compelled to confront the "shortfall dilemma," forced to choose between coping with underfunded institutions, or shouldering an additional and unjust burden—in the present, or in the future due to increased federal debt.

Our concern to this point has been the many ways that the Ultra-Wealthy have been designing, and continue to design, the federal tax code, in order to further restrict their flows to the Treasury—i.e., to the rest of us. Philosophically, these are the more interesting issues. However: even more outrageous is tax *evasion*, i.e., the Ultra-Wealthy not paying even *that* amount, not shouldering even their wrongfully *lightened* tax burden. In an interview, then IRS Commissioner Charles Rettig acknowledged that "We do get outgunned' when trying to enforce taxes on wealthy." Furthermore, Rettig said that "The tax gap between what corporations and the

[10] Imagine, as vividly as you can, your last expedition to the Department of Motor Vehicles. Now imagine what your experience would have been like if the DMV were underfunded—that it had, say, *half* as many clerks. Bring a sandwich, a good book, and a blanket.

[11] This is not to say that I *oppose* this IRS program of resolving these matters; I can accept the maxim "Half a loaf is better than none." What I *do* oppose is the meme that the tax liability is owed *to the IRS*, when in fact it is owed to the rest of us, the actual tax *payers*, whose burden they have thereby made heavier.

wealthy should be paying in taxes versus what the IRS is collecting could approach and possibly exceed $1 trillion per year." (Tsekova 2021).

Yet even more galling, as detailed in the *Washington Post*: "Thousands of millionaires haven't filed tax returns for years, IRS says." Furthermore, "As Congress slashed the IRS's funding in the last decade, the agency's shrinking staff did less to enforce compliance …." According to current IRS Commissioner Danny Werfel, the wholly missing returns "represent hundreds of millions of dollars in unpaid taxes, on more that $100 billion of income." He described this as "one of the clearest examples of the need to have a properly funded IRS." (Weil 2024) A portion of that funding would be devoted to hiring more experienced auditors, so that they would no longer be "outgunned."

It is a consistent and persistent theme of Republicans in Congress to cut the funding of the IRS. "Since 2010, the IRS has lost 21,000 employees and its budget has declined around 20% when taking inflation into account." (Tsekova 2021) Once again, we must ask: Who benefits? Their wealthy constituents, their wealthy "benefactors," constricting their flows to Treasury, i.e., to the rest of us, We the People, to whom it is owed. In speaking of money "owed to the IRS," or "owed Uncle Sam," to that doddering old man, they deflect attention from the fact that resources are owed to *us*, to (actual) "tax*payers*," with the inevitable consequence of inflicting upon us the "Shortfall Dilemma," inflicting on us either "burden shifting," or "institution crippling."

We might well feel that we are being played for fools. That feeling is veridical; we are.

7 Of Transcending Importance: The Fully Adequate Funding of the Institutions of Rawlsian "Fair Equality of Opportunity"

Of paramount importance here, in my judgment, is the flow of resources to the set of social institutions that create and maintain Rawlsian "fair equality of opportunity." These include (but are not limited to) supplying the basic necessities of food, clothing and shelter (a "social safety net"); good education from preschool through high school (at least), vocational training and apprenticeships for those with the requisite aptitudes, and (some degree of) college for those with the requisite aptitudes. Furthermore, these flows should *not* be considered "expenditures," but rather "investments"—enabling *these* citizens to augment overall social wealth, not unlike their genetically and culturally more fortunate fellow citizens, including some of the Ultra-Wealthy (Rawls 1971, 2001).

Now I believe that this position has powerful intuitive appeal. But not to everyone, I readily acknowledge. My strategy for defending it proceeds as follows. First, I offer a Parody: "I am a Self-Made Man!" This is intended to poke fun at those who seek to take personal credit for everything they have become, and everything they have achieved. They do this seeking to justify an entitlement to all the resources they have accumulated. This sense of entitlement is the foundation of their resistance to taxation of their income and wealth, *beyond* merely funding their fair share of essential social goods, e.g. first responders and national defense. Second, I support the fully sufficient funding of the array of the institutions essential to fair equality of opportunity, which is itself essential to the preeminent social good, self-respect.

7.1 I Am a Self-Made Man! A Parody

I am a self-made man; who I am, and what I possess, is a direct result of numerous great decisions that I have made, over a lifetime.

First, I chose a genetic endowment which would form the basis of aptitudes and abilities that I could develop into marketable skills in my chosen economy. This was really challenging; I had to scrutinize and assess my mom's ripening egg each month, and subsequently choose the one-and-only optimal sperm to be the strongest swimmer. (No one would choose an egg or a sperm that would combine for any of a vast array of birth defects, or limited potential for developing marketable skills.)

Second, I chose to be born into a family with substantial fiscal resources and social advantages that make for financial success, and the professional networks so important for advancement. Additionally, I would choose a family from which I could anticipate a significant inheritance. (No one would choose a broken, dysfunctional or impoverished family, or a family isolated from persons of prominence, or a family bereft of generational wealth.)

Third, I had to choose a historical time-period. I decided upon an era of advanced technology, including medical technologies that have conquered childhood/communicable diseases. (No one would choose a primitive period, with all the grave perils of pestilence.)

Fourth, I chose a private-property-owning democracy. I chose this for the opportunity to amass great personal wealth. (No one would choose to live in an impoverished society, or to live under a dictatorship.)

Fifth, I chose to be born in a nation-state with an advanced educational system—from Pre-K through graduate and professional programs. (Given the importance of education in taking advantage of the opportunities for amassing great wealth, no one would choose to live in a society with only a rudimentary educational system.) I attended prestigious institutions, networked extensively, and graduated without the onerous burden of student loans.

Finally, I chose to be born in a nation-state with a strong and stable central government, able to protect the state from external aggression, and able to maintain strong internal institutions—e.g. police and other first-responders, a system of courts to maintain the rule of law, and the stability and rectitude of financial markets. (Preserving one's life, and one's assets, requires stability and protection—no one would choose to live in a nation where one's fortune, one's very life, is in constant peril.)

I have managed to amass great wealth due to the marvelous choices I have made, from the particular sperm & egg, to family and social circumstances, to economic and historical period, and social institutions. Thus I have earned it all; I deserve it all! I am a ***self! ade! man***!

Two pretty obvious conclusions should be drawn from this Parody.

First, it is ludicrous to suggest that people somehow exist as individual, rational agents, even prior to conception, and that they could possibly make *any* of the aforementioned "choices." And, it is even *more* ludicrous to claim *entitlement* to wealth and privilege *based upon* one's supposed making those advantageous choices.

Second, it is even more ludicrous—if that's even possible—to presume that those who find themselves in *dis*advantageous family or social circumstances, or with a disadvantageous genetic endowment, have made stupid or idiotic decisions or choices, and thus are individually responsible for their current social and financial impoverishment, and thus their bleak life prospects.

When once we survey the vast terrain of factors relevant to "success" and "failure" and every station in between, we are compelled to acknowledge the incredibly important role of mere chance—to acknowledge that it's not a matter of "deserving" at all. No claim of "entitlement" to wealth or status can be founded on this good fortune; no condescension towards those who have had ill luck in the natural and social lotteries is warranted.

So: What *should be* the societal response to this realization? A large dose of humility: "There, but for the grace of God (or a different sperm, or egg, or family, or economy, or epoch, etc., etc.,) go ***I***." And following that, a commitment to a significant degree of social solidarity.

Thus, a conception of social justice broadly, and more narrowly justice in flows of resources—must be founded upon the bedrock reality that no one "deserves" one's natural endowments and social starting position, whether these are exceptionally advantageous, exceptionally disadvantageous, or somewhere in between (i.e., where most of us are to be found).

7.2 Fair Equality of Opportunity & Self-Respect

The appropriate societal response to the Parody, I contend, begins with a commitment to solidarity—that we are all, indeed, in this together. Those individuals with fortunate draws in the natural and social lotteries should be encouraged to develop their marketable talents and skills, and thereby to augment the overall wealth of society—not to be "trickled down," but to be subjected to principles of justice in distribution. That encouragement will be monetary; to be sure, this will result in *some* disparities in income and, over time, disparities in wealth—but we will *all* be better off due to their creativity and industriousness.

However, there will be many individuals who *could* in fact make similar, significant contributions, if only they could receive some social assistance in overcoming natural or cultural *dis*advantages—and again, those disadvantages are not their responsibility, much less their choice. John Rawls, in *Justice as Fairness,* advocates "fair equality of opportunity," which requires "… not merely that public offices and social positions be open in the formal sense, but that all should have a fair chance to attain them." (Rawls 2001, p. 43) What might undermine a person's "fair chance?" Having been born into a family with limited financial resources, and limited social/political connections. This, especially in light of the magnitude of such resources that is essential if one is to be a competitive candidate for elective political office—at least under current campaign finance arrangements. Furthermore,

> To specify the idea of a fair chance we say: supposing that there is a distribution of native endowments, those who have the same level of talent and ability and the same willingness to use these gifts should have the same prospects of success regardless of their social class of origin, the class into which they are born and develop until the age of reason. In all parts of society there are to be roughly the same prospects of culture and achievement for those similarly motivated and endowed (Rawls 2001, pp. 43–44).

Now if we were to accept "*fair* equality of opportunity" as the goal, the next question is how this "fair chance" is to be *achieved.* Again relying upon Rawls,

> … background institutions must work to keep property and wealth evenly enough shared over time to preserve the fair value of the political liberties and fair equality of opportunity over generations. They do this by laws regulating bequest and inheritance of property, and other devices such as taxes, to prevent excessive concentrations of private power (Rawls 2001, p. 51).

Quite straightforwardly, this requirement of justice is explicitly, precisely violated by the institution of the "family office." For its very *raison d'etre* is to *preserve*, and not to "prevent excessive concentrations of private power." Put another way: the Fetid and Putrefying Quagmire in general, and the "family office" and the "stepped up basis" in particular, inevitably have the consequence of obliterating "fair equality of opportunity." Now this is not to claim that such is an explicit intention of the Ultra-Wealthy. For most (excepting Leona Helmsley), I suspect that their focus is narrowly on preserving their wealth and power—ignoring, or oblivious to, the devastating impact of these tax provisions on their fellow citizens.

Why this emphasis on "fair equality of opportunity?" Because of its essential connection to the "most important primary social good:" **self-respect**.

> We may define self-respect (or self-esteem) as having two aspects. First of all … it includes a person's sense of his own value, his secure conviction that his conception of the good, his plan of life, is worth carrying out. And second, self-respect implies a confidence in one's ability, so far as it is in one's power, to fulfill one's intentions (Rawls 1971, p. 440).

One's "ability to fulfill one's intentions" requires fully funded, fully functioning, institutions that create fair equality of opportunity. For on the contrary,

> When we feel that our plans are of little value, we cannot pursue them with pleasure or take delight in their execution. Nor plagued by failure and self-doubt can we continue in our endeavors. It is clear then why self-respect is a primary good. Without it nothing may seem

> worth doing, or if some things have value for us, we lack the will to strive for them. All desire and activity become empty and vain, and we sink into apathy and cynicism. Therefore the parties in the original position would wish to avoid at almost any cost the social conditions that undermine self-respect (Rawls 1971, p. 440).

Let us now shift from the abstractions of the rational legislators in the original position, to current progressive politics. Shouldn't *we*—vociferously, forcefully—advance this position, *rejecting,* "at almost any cost the social conditions that undermine self-respect"? And to the extent that we are successful, could that not ameliorate the deep and widespread political disaffection that plagues our country? Justice in the flows of resources from Entities to the Treasury, and from the Treasury to the institutions that advance the commonweal, would enhance self respect, and address the genuine grievances that have led, and continues to lead, so many citizens to (rather mindlessly) become fervent disciples of a relentlessly narcissistic, thoroughly corrupt, anti-democratic and indeed dictatorial cult leader like Donald J. Trump?[12]

8 Concluding Summary

The transcending concerns of this paper are these: citizen self-respect as essential to human flourishing, its foundation of fair equality of opportunity, and (some of) the threats to that foundation—principally those embedded in the contents of the federal tax code, and its enforcement—or non-enforcement.

We began with the conception of our economy as Extraordinarily Intricate "Flows of Resources;" this to indicate its extreme dynamism. Quite quickly, we narrowed our focus to flows of Resources from Entities to the Treasury, and from the Treasury to Entities. These flows, whether excessive or deficient, are appropriate sites for philosophical scrutiny, and the application of principles of justice. We took note of the gargantuan size and complexity of the federal tax code; we took note of the fact that the vast majority of tax payers rely upon just a few of the Forms and Schedules. Only the Ultra-Wealthy can avail themselves of the obscure and arcane provisions of the remainder—in the attempt to maximally constrict their flows to the Treasury. This monstrosity, which we defined as a "fetid and putrefying quagmire," has arisen from an unholy synergism between the Supreme Court of the United States, and the Congress of the United States. In a series of catastrophic decisions, the Court has permitted virtually unlimited flows of resources, anonymously, into political campaigns. And members of Congress have developed insatiable appetites

[12] In an earlier piece, I labeled some (not all, but many) of those Trumpists "GINs:" "Gullible, Ignorant, Noncritical." We can add to those descriptors "devoid of self-respect." And we can attribute that to the thoroughgoing destruction of the *bases* of self-respect. This renders them incredibly susceptible to a leader who—regardless of how preposterously—claims to identify with them, and promises "retribution," "retaliation" against the perceived enemy, the SERTs: "Skeptical, Educated, Rational Thinkers." (Schonsheck 2020).

for that filthy lucre—more or less transparently in exchange for legislation benefiting their contributors. This results in the "Shortfall Dilemma"—the choice between "burden shifting" from the Ultra-Wealthy to the rest of us, or "institution crippling," hampering the myriad institutions which lack the resources to function effectively to create fair equality of opportunity.

As all of the following have been discussed above, I merely mention them here. The billions of dollars given to Federalist Society/Marble Freedom Trust to influence the judiciary, the "carried interest" provision that allows capital to be taxed at a lower rate than labor, the stepped up basis that allows gains in family fortunes to be under taxed, or to never be taxed at all, the institution of the "family office," which is designed to preserve generational family wealth and power: the effects of all these provisions are in direct contradiction to one central function of just taxation, which is to *prevent* such consolidations of wealth and power. It is misleading to speak of owing money to the IRS, or to "Uncle Sam;" it is owed to fellow citizens. And then there are those who totally shirk payments, not bothering to even file tax returns.

I sought to reject, by means of a parody, the idea of the "self-made man" who preposterously believes his privileged position is the result of his prudent "choices" (which it is not), unmindful of the vast, nearly infinite array of factors totally outside one's control—all matters of serendipity, not rational choice. I endorsed self-respect as the most important primary social good, and the essential role of fair equality of opportunity—and the array of social institutions that create and maintain that indispensable equality—fully funded by a just system of taxation.

References

Buckley v. *Valeo*, 1976. 424 U.S. 1

Citizens United v. *Federal Election Commission*, 130 S. Ct. 876 (2010)

Drucker J, Hakim D (2021) How accounting giants craft favorable tax rules from inside government. The New York Times, 9/20

First National Bank of Boston v. Belotti 435 U.S. 765 (1978)

Glauber B (2021) Ron Johnson defends pass-through tax provision as Democrats accuse him of doing the bidding of his top donors. Milwaukee Journal Sentinel, August 11

Hayes A (2023) What is a family office and do you need one? investopedia.com/terms/f/family-offices.asp

Iris (2020). irisreading.com How many pages is the tax code? January 16

Kaiser-Schatzlein R (2021) This is how America's richest families stay that way. The New York Times, September 25

Mayer J (2016) Dark money: the hidden history of the billionaires behind the rise of the radical right. Doubleday, New York

Noah T (2022) Who's Shocked that Krysten Sinema Went to Bat for Hedge-Funders?" The New Republic, August 5, 2022. See also, "A Tax Loophole's Powerful Defender: Senator Krysten Sinema had one main request before she would support a key spending bill: Preserve a tax loophole that mainly benefits people in private equity," NY Times, August 5, 2022

Perez A, The Lever, Kroll A, Elliott J (2002) ProPublica, August 22

Rampell C (2024) The law-and-order party defunds the IRS. Again. Washingtonpost.com, June 7

Ratliff A (2021) The congressional fundraising treadmill, July-September 2021. Issue one. https://issueone.org/articles/the-congressional-fundraising-treadmill-5-key-numbers-to-know-from-the-newest-house-and-senate-campaign-finance-filings/

Rawls J (1971) A theory of justice. The Belknap Press of Harvard University Press, Cambridge, p 440

Rawls J (2001) In: Kelly E (ed) Justice as fairness: a restatement. Harvard University Press, Cambridge

Sadhwani S, Lopez P, Grose C, Yoshinaka A (2022) When lobbyists and legislators socialize, lobbyists are more likely to get what they want. The Washington Post, January 12

Saez E, Zucman G (2021) How to get $1 trillion from 1000 billionaires: tax their gains now. Econometrics Laboratory. https://eml.berkeley.edu › SZ21-billionaire-tax. April 14

Schonsheck J (1981) 'Hobbling Ideas and Unfettered Expression': First Amendment Rights and Restrictions. Proceedings of the Creighton Club (New York State Philosophical Association), Spring 1981

Schonsheck J (2000) A Hard Look at 'Soft Money': Does Prohibiting Soft Money Campaign Contributions Violate First Amendment Rights? Invited address, the first in the series "Celebrate the Humanities: Presentations on Political Issues with Ethical Implications," sponsored by the New York Council for the Humanities. Rochester Institute of Technology, October 2, 2000

Schonsheck J (2010) The 'marketplace of ideas:' a siren song for freedom of speech theorists. In: Golash D (ed) Freedom of expression in a diverse world. The philosophical foundations of law and justice book series. Springer International, pp 27–37

Schonsheck J (2014) A Tsunami of Filthy Lucre: how the decisions of the SCOTUS Imperil American Democracy. In: Cudd AE, Sally J (eds) Philosophical perspectives on democracy in the 21st century. Scholz, Springer International, pp 159–174

Schonsheck J (2020) In: Navin MC, Nunan R (eds) The lethal synergy corroding American Democracy: who are the "GINs" – and why is it that they can't "Quit Trump"? Democracy, populism and truth, Springer International, pp 219–223

Sorkin A, Giang V, Gandel S, Hirsch L, Livni E, Gallagher (2022) A Tax Loophole's Powerful Defender: Senator Krysten Sinema had one main request before she would support a key spending bill: Preserve a tax loophole that mainly benefits people in private equity. The New York Times, August 5

Statista Research Department, April 5, 2023

Tsekova D (2021) IRS commissioner: "We do get outgunned" when trying to enforce taxes on wealthy, yahoo!money. aol.com/finance

Weil J (2024) Thousands of millionaires haven't filed tax returns for years, IRS says. Washingtonpost.com/business/2024/02/29

Whitehouse S (2022) The scheme: how the right wing used dark money to capture the Supreme Court. The New Press, New York

Chance, Greed, and Fear: Why We Need the Value of Fraternity to Register Distributive Injustices

Jochen Bojanowski

Abstract "Fraternity" and the often synonymously used concept "solidarity" are usually understood as ideals or values that go beyond justice. It is no surprise that the liberal tradition has found it difficult to fully embrace fraternity as a political value. Fraternity as an expression of our moral motivation is beyond the sanctioning power of the liberal state. I will defend a different conception of fraternity in this article. Taking the feminist slogan "The personal is political" seriously, I'll interpret fraternity as a foundational political value. Fraternity does not go beyond justice but is one of its constitutive elements. I do not use the term in the broad sense of "unconditional love." The intended narrower meaning is based on the idea of a luck egalitarian interpretation of reciprocity or mutuality. This narrower notion of fraternity takes its initial clue from what I will call Rawls's luck egalitarian insight. According to my interpretation, we take a fraternal attitude towards each other **if** we don't demand undeserved distributive advantages and agree to a scheme of cooperation in which brute luck differences are not reflected in such a way that they lead to distributive advantages.

1 Introduction

1.1. "Fraternity" and the often synonymously used concept "solidarity" are usually understood as ideals or values that go beyond justice. According to a widespread view, there can be a right to freedom as non-interference but no right to fraternity. Good Samaritans do not make their help dependent on whether a needy person deserves help or whether helping would be just; they help victims unconditionally. Fraternity, understood as unconditional Samaritanism, is supererogatory; it is permissible, even praiseworthy, but it necessarily goes beyond what we are required to

J. Bojanowski (✉)
University of Illinois, Urbana, IL, USA
e-mail: job39@illinois.edu

G. A. Babst, W.-c. Lee (eds.), *Contemporary Facets of Injustice*, AMINTAPHIL: The Philosophical Foundations of Law and Justice 13,
https://doi.org/10.1007/978-3-031-93783-5_4

do. A state that tried to enforce fraternity would be trying to force us to love each other. Moreover, as a just state, it would have to treat the interests of its citizens with equal concern and their choices with equal respect. Guaranteeing help to its citizens unconditionally would seem to violate these justice constraints.

It is no surprise that the liberal tradition has found it difficult to fully embrace fraternity as a political value. Fraternity as an expression of our moral motivation is beyond the sanctioning power of the liberal state. This is not to say that fraternity or solidarity are not significant ingredients of the "cement," as Emile Durkheim puts it, of a liberal society (Durkheim, "On Institutional Analysis," 1978, p. 234). However, to stay with Durkheim's metaphor, they are not ingredients that give this "cement" its binding force. It is therefore understandable that within the value triad of the French Revolution, "fraternity" has received comparatively less attention than equality and liberty. The concept remains a stranger in the liberal theory of the state. Rawls's and Dworkin's theories of justice are paradigmatic examples of this tendency (Dworkin 2011; Rawls 1999b). The institutional application of the concept of fraternity seems limited to permissible but merely voluntary communities, to so-called fraternities, sororities, or other communities of mutual support. Here, people promise each other mutual help and support in good and bad times. Their reasons for entering such a union are likely to be more prudential than moral: Such unions serve as insurance one can fall back on in an emergency. In return, one helps other members in need. The central principle of these unions is thus one of reciprocity: If you help me, I'll help you.

1.2. I will defend a different conception of fraternity in this article. Taking the feminist slogan "The personal is political" seriously, I'll interpret fraternity as a foundational political value. It goes without saying that I don't want to reconnect to the nationalist and gender-biased sense of this term. "Fraternity" is not supposed to express a relation between French male citizens, as the term *fraternité* in the Declaration of the Rights of Man of the French Revolution did. I take for granted the gender-neutral meaning of the word, which the German term *Geschwisterlichkeit* adequately captures. What is controversial and provocative about my interpretation of fraternity, however, is that it is to be understood as constitutive of the concept of justice. According to my political interpretation, fraternity is what we owe to each other. State institutions are unjust to the extent that they do not sufficiently reflect this value.

My theory is a radicalized version of Jerry Cohen's attempt to make the egalitarian ethos part of a political theory of justice. I believe that the value of fraternity is constitutive of justice. I do not use the term in the broad sense of "unconditional love." The intended narrower meaning is based on the idea of a luck egalitarian interpretation of reciprocity or mutuality, i.e., luck egalitarian mutuality. This narrower notion of fraternity takes its initial clue from what I will call Rawls's luck egalitarian insight. I take it to be a platitude that we deserve neither our biological predispositions nor the social conditions in which we are born. To the extent that distributional advantages depend on these unchosen differences, these advantages qualify as unjust. In other words, our native endowments and the social contexts into which we are born do not constitute a good reason for distributional differences. I will argue that the idea of justice can only be adequately brought into view if it reflects our ability to recognize and respect this insight. Despite its bad reputation, luck egalitarianism, adequately understood, is an articulation of the ideal of fraternity. As I interpret it—and to use John Rawls's early formulation—fraternal justice hinges on sharing "one another's fate" (Rawls 1971, p. 102). This formulation did not make it into the revised second edition of *A Theory of Justice* (Rawls 1999a, p. 88). In the later "restatement" of his theory, *Justice as Fairness*, Rawls removed the concept of fraternity entirely (Rawls, p. 105 ff.; Rawls 2001, -). He became convinced that the idea of fraternity has no role to play in a theory of justice.

I want to reconnect with the idea expressed by the early Rawls: We owe it to each other "to share each other's fate." If social institutions sufficiently reflect this idea, then fraternity will be the "form in which we may execute our freedom" (Honneth 2017, p. 123, my translation). The fraternal attitude that I take to be constitutive of justice can be defined as follows:

> *x* and *y* have a fraternal attitude towards each other iff *x* and *y* don't demand undeserved distributive advantages and favor a scheme of cooperation in which brute luck differences are not reflected in such a way that they lead to distributive advantages.

The justice of our social institutions and our economy is to be judged against the backdrop of our capacity for fraternity thus understood. They are deficient from a justice point of view if they are not sufficiently fraternally embedded.

Three further qualifications can prevent possible misunderstandings. First, my concept of fraternity should not be understood in a particularistic or clannish sense. Fraternity as a political idea reflects the normative ideal that all human beings relate to one another as brothers or sisters. This sense has no room in my universalist conception. Secondly, as I understand it, fraternity differs from solidarity as it expresses the primordial and inescapable nature of this commitment. We do not choose to be sisters or brothers, yet we have obligations in virtue of this unchosen relationship. Solidarity, by contrast, is often understood as a bond into which we voluntarily enter, and it is this voluntary choice that creates the obligation (Metz 1998, p. 176; on the semantics of both concepts and their history, see Brunkhorst 2016, pp. 7–110; Metz 1998; Bude 2019, pp. 20–44; Wildt 1998). Finally, unlike strong forms of altruism, in the here-intended political sense, fraternity entails not that we must subordinate our interests to the interests of others but that they are to be treated *equally* (Nagel 1970, p. 79). The concept of equality, however, receives its specifically fraternal meaning once it is interpreted in light of what I call the luck egalitarian insight.

1.3. This paper is divided into two parts. In the first part, I will introduce three paradigmatic cases to articulate my idea of fraternal justice. The first case, *Fraternal Sharing*, is a paradigm case of fraternal justice. It will reveal the high bar to which fraternal justice commits us. The second, familiar case, *Harrison Bergeron*, is often taken to be a counterexample to the principle of equality. This case will help us to more clearly articulate the kind of equality that fraternal justice deems valuable. The last case, *Gross Negligence*, will show the limits of fraternal equality and determine the scope of just inequality.

In the second part, I will confront my idea of fraternal justice with three possible objections: I first want to argue that my attempt to avoid the absurd consequences of *Harrison Bergeron* by introducing *Gross Negligence* does not entail throwing the equality baby out with the desertist bathwater. Luck egalitarian commitments deeply inform fraternal justice and preserve the equality compatible with justice. Secondly, I want to show why the impracticality of my desertist position should not lead us to abandon fraternal justice as the bar of justice. The impulse to abandon it is based on what David Estlund calls a "practicabilist" confusion. Finally, I'll try to show, against socialist critics, how my view can account for exploitation and why justice can get us much closer to the value of community socialists cherish (Estlund 2019).

2 Fraternal Justice

2.1. This section will introduce three paradigm cases that will bring the idea of fraternal justice more clearly into view: *Fraternal Sharing*, *Harrison Bergeron*, and *Gross Negligence*. I will consider each of these cases in turn. Let us assume that Paul and Anton work together doing the same job. Unlike Anton, however, Paul was born with only one arm. Let us further assume that Paul is half as productive as Anton precisely because he can only work with one arm. Therefore, Paul's lower productivity results from an unchosen misfortune. I take it to be true that it would be *unjust* for Paul to receive less pay than Anton. Since Paul's lower productivity is fully explained by his bad brute luck compared to Anton, Anton does not deserve to earn more than Paul.

Now suppose Anton proposes a "deal" to Paul. In this deal, Anton makes his cooperation conditional on receiving 65 percent of the profits. Cooperating would still be a strong Pareto improvement; not only is no one worse off and at least one better off, but *everyone* is better off. Paul might agree to this deal, for without Anton's contribution, he'd be worse off even if they did not share the profits fraternally. Fraternal justice, by contrast, requires that both share their profits equally. Let me call this paradigmatic case of fraternal justice *Fraternal Sharing*.

2.2. With *Fraternal Sharing*, one does not commit oneself to what Derek Parfit calls "telic egalitarianism" (TE) (Parfit 1997). According to telic egalitarianism, an outcome is necessarily better if it is equal rather than unequal. Fraternal sharing leaves room for inequalities that count as just or better than strict equalities. If, for example, the difference in Paul's and Anton's productivity were due not to a biological coincidence but to the fact that, given equal assets, they each chose a different work-leisure balance in life, unequal pay between Paul and Anton would be deserved. This income difference would be based on another egalitarian idea: "Equal work, equal pay." *Fraternal Sharing* reminds us that, from the standpoint of justice, the expression "equal work" need not be identified with "equal productivity."

We have devised various means of measuring our actual output levels. Determining the influence of brute luck on our output/productivity levels is a more complex enterprise, however. To identify a just distribution, we need to know how much brute luck influences performance levels. In *Fraternal Sharing*, it is simply stipulated that the difference between Paul's and Anton's productivity is due solely to a difference in brute biological luck. As a matter of fact, we lack the epistemic tools to identify pure effort levels or choice, and we are also not in a position to reliably track those factors that are not due to our choosing. We might, then, in the spirit of Rawls's "method of avoidance," pragmatically use productivity levels to determine differences in income (Rawls 1999b). However, we must not change or lower our *ideal* of justice simply because we are currently unable to tell whether some instance counts as a realization of that ideal.

2.3. Let me contrast the egalitarian idea of *Fraternal Sharing* with the egalitarian notion of Kurt Vonnegut's well-known but often misunderstood satirical dystopian short story "Harrison Bergeron." This story is popular among anti-egalitarians because it supposedly provides us with a paradigmatic case for the worthlessness of egalitarianism. The presupposed notion of equality, however, is somewhat limited. Contrasting my conception with Vonnegut's colorful, poetic descriptions will help us to see more clearly the unattractiveness of a certain kind of equality:

> The year was 2081, and everybody was finally equal. They weren't only equal before God and the law. They were equal every which way. Nobody was smarter than anybody else. Nobody was better looking than anybody else. Nobody was stronger or quicker than anybody else. (Vonnegut, "Welcome to the Monkey House," 1968, p. 7)

In Vonnegut's state, people are not simply treated as equals before the law; their abilities are made equal. Vonnegut's state presupposes objective standards of intelligence, beauty, and strength. If people happen to be born with different physical and intellectual traits, these differences are themselves equalized. Less talented people are not empowered to achieve equality; rather, more talented people are "leveled down" so that their performance level drops, mentally, physically, and aesthetically. We can call this ideal "equal performance through leveling down" (EPLD). In Vonnegut's story, this leveling-down equality is guaranteed by the constitution and enforced by an authoritarian state in the person of a so-called "handicapper general."

To achieve equal performance, Vonnegut's egalitarian state takes extreme measures. People with above-average intelligence must, for example, wear radio transmitters that send out loud and distracting sounds, preventing them from thinking clearly. At best, the notion of "average" remains underdeveloped in Vonnegut's story. If it were based on the natural distribution of talents, the egalitarian state in "Harrison Bergeron" would require the leveling up of less able people. Vonnegut doesn't address this more attractive idea but focuses exclusively on leveling-down equality. Physically stronger citizens must wear bags filled with lead weights that make it more difficult for them to move. These kinds of handicaps are required to prevent any competitive advantage. The goal is equal performance, and the means to achieve it is the forced neutralization of people's natural differences. Those who attempt to free themselves of their artificial impairments, such as by removing lead balls from the lead bags, are punished (Vonnegut 1968, p. 9). The story focuses on the extreme case of Harrison Bergeron, the tragic hero and villain of the egalitarian dystopia. Harrison's abilities are so outstanding that he must be impaired more severely than anyone has been before: "In the race of life, Harrison carried three hundred pounds," such that he "look[ed] like a walking junkyard" (Vonnegut 1968, p. 11). Instead of a small radio transmitter in his ear, he must wear headphones and, in addition, glasses that not only make him blind in one eye but also cause him headaches (ibid.).

Notice that the goal of EPLD is to eradicate the differences in ability themselves. While leveling up seems permissible, or in some cases even obligatory, leveling down seems wrong (for cases in which leveling down may be permissible see Peña-Rangel 2023). By contrast, our fraternal account of justice does not entail that Anton owes it to Paul to cut off his arm. Anton and Paul can differ with regard to their productivity or their output. Fraternal egalitarianism adequately interpreted does not oppose the unequal exercise of our unequal capacities. It merely entails that insofar as a difference in productivity or output reflects brute luck differences, it does not merit a difference in compensation. Our fraternal account of justice does not eradicate the talent differences themselves. Equality is instead directed at the impact these brute luck differences have on the distribution of social benefits and burdens. We can call this equality the equality of brute luck conversion (EBLC). EBLC differs from EPLD in that it does not alter the natural abilities themselves but the compensation or reward given in light of these natural abilities.

Notice that there might still be something desirable from a justice point of view about a world in which Anton and Paul are no different with regard to their natural abilities. Admitting this, however, does not commit us to the idea that we should take measures to bring about this kind of equality. As Larry Temkin correctly argues, although it is perfectly plausible that leveling down would make the world better in one respect, by no means would any such improvement take priority over the harm done to Anton (Temkin 2000). In Vonnegut's story, the government harms Harrison not only because he performs above average. He is also suspected of trying to start a revolution.

For this reason, he is taken away from his parents and put in prison. In this "egalitarian state," even suspicion is apparently enough to get thrown in jail. These are all very unattractive features of this state. However, they don't relate to the value of EBLC. Instead, this example powerfully illustrates the disvalue of EPLD.

2.4. Vonnegut's thought experiment is based on the following consideration: What would a state look like if the more talented could only exercise the same abilities as the untalented, despite their different talents? More generally, Vonnegut dismantles the idea that equality is a value that overrides all other values. To make people perform equally, they are deprived of their freedom and individuality, weakened and dumbed down, and forced to live a dull and monotonous life based on fear and envy. Because of these equalizing measures, no one knows who they are or who they could be. They also cannot really know their fellow citizens. Anti-egalitarians take Vonnegut's story to confirm their belief that equality is of no particular value. However, Vonnegut's satire only shows the worthlessness of a certain kind of egalitarianism. The narrative makes it possible to see why the idea of a society where the talented are leveled down by force is a nightmare scenario, not a society we would value. The story leaves us with the task of uncovering the actual value of equality. The question is whether our conception of fraternal justice can articulate equality such that it can legitimately be called a value. We need to be clear about what we value about equality. Only then will we be in a position to distinguish between the kind of equality that has value and the kind that does not.

In Vonnegut's narrative, the realization of equality leads to coercion, conformism, envy, and monotony. These features obscure the intrinsic value of equality. There might be something desirable about the fact that people are equally capable, but the way in which equal capability is achieved in *Harrison Bergeron* makes equality worthless. However, this does not mean that there is no respect in which it would be better if people all performed with equal ability. Conceding this much does not entail that equal ability is always the overriding value and desirable regardless of how it is achieved. In Vonnegut's dystopia, the value of this kind of equality is muted by other values. These other values might include, for example, the person's integrity, individuality, self-realization, freedom, privacy, prosperity, and efficiency. Even if the value of a certain kind of equality doesn't override all other values in at least most contexts, however, this does not mean that equality, fraternally understood, loses its intrinsic value (cf. Frankfurt 1987).

2.5. Our fraternal account of EBLC leaves room for what I take to be the kernel of truth of seemingly anti-egalitarian concerns. Anti-egalitarian concerns are best appreciated as justice concerns: the anti-egalitarian is usually concerned about fraternal institutions being abused by greed, negligence, and laziness. People rely on other people's help. In doing so, so the anti-egalitarian claims, they not only exploit other people but also lose the ability to help themselves. When examined more closely, however, this seemingly anti-egalitarian concern is ultimately the other side of the fraternity coin. This becomes clear when we consider a third thought experiment.

Suppose Oscar lives in a small, poor pre-industrial farming community. If one of the workers in this community stops contributing, malnutrition will be the result. Oscar is fully able to participate in the production process. Every worker in this community contributes to the best of their abilities. However, Oscar has a hobby that causes him to recklessly risks his productive power. After work each day, he jumps off a 50-foot cliff into the sea. Oscar is aware of the danger; he has already slightly injured himself a few times. He knows that each of his jumps poses a significant health risk and is very likely to lead to food shortages for his fellow villagers. Oscar is fully aware that his behavior towards his fellow villagers is irresponsible and unacceptable. Suppose Oscar injures himself so severely that he is no longer able to work productively. There is no insurance in the village. Oscar can no longer contribute to the social product. The loss of his labor leads to food shortages, and he must receive his food from the villagers. Let us call this case *Gross Negligence*.

How should *Gross Negligence* be assessed, from the standpoint of fraternal justice? Does our conception of fraternal justice reward Oscar's negligent behavior because society owes him compensation? Not quite. Oscar regularly puts the elementary conditions of the other villagers' wellbeing at risk. At the very least, his behavior expresses indifference to the fate of the other villagers. He thereby displays a genuinely unfraternal attitude. The villagers may rightly say, "Such a person does not *deserve* help." Admittedly, whether Oscar deserves the help of the other villagers also depends on other factors. But if gross negligence is Oscar's distinguishing feature, Oscar makes himself unworthy of the other villagers' help. Notice that even his ability to work productively for a certain period of his life depends not only on him but on his caretakers in his childhood.

We might still find refusing to help Oscar "cruel," since he can no longer help himself. We might endorse the general principle "We ought to help those who cannot help themselves." In Oscar's particular case, however, this principle is defeated by the fact that others will carry the same significant burden for which Oscar is responsible. The degree of sanctioning measures in these cases depends on the prosperity of the society in question. An affluent society may allow more room for mistakes to foster individuality and personal development than Oscar's poor village community. In a more affluent context where everyone's basic needs are secured, considerations of individual desert can take a back seat. However, regardless of how we would, in fact, act in cases of gross negligence, in no context does an action like Oscar's *deserve* the help of others. *Gross Negligence* demarcates the limits of fraternal justice and the transition to charity or mercy. It is meant to capture what I take to be a justified anti-egalitarian concern: In cases where people are compensated for the disadvantages that arise from the choices they make (even under ideal choice conditions), those who have to pick up the tab for irresponsible and reckless choices are the victims of exploitation. Rightly understood, the anti-egalitarian concern is a concern about exploitation. More precisely, it concerns telic equality through exploitation (TEE).

Gross Negligence is no less problematic if no actual exploitation results from the agent's choice due to the contingency of the realization conditions of actions: Anton, who makes the same choices as Oscar, might *contingently* escape a fatal injury. His choice is still in violation of the principle of fraternity. Neither Anton nor Oscar *deserve* help. But, *ceteris paribus*, Anton also does not deserve to be better off than Oscar. The difference between them is a difference that is not due to their own choice. Since it is easier to demarcate and to track actual failure rather than potential or character failure, it will be challenging to design rules of regulation or policies that hold both Oscar and Anton equally accountable. However, this fact ought not to mislead us into thinking that, from a justice point of view, there is a difference between Oscar's and Anton's behavior. Anton's choice even if without harmful consequences is normatively no less problematic than Oscar's. Some believe the fact that Oscar does not escape the fatal injury does make Oscar's act worse than Anton. According to this view, "the badness of this act is partly up for grabs; it depends on what happens in the world. It follows that the badness of acting on malicious intentions is partly fixed retrospectively, depending on whether the aim embodied in the malicious agent's act was successfully realized" (Lang 2021, p. 70). I admit that I don't find this intuition in me. I can understand why in Oscar's case the consequence is worse than in Anton's case, but Anton's character (as his causal potential that is under his control) is in the relevant respect not any different from Oscar's.

Again, it might be institutionally apt to treat the two cases differently, but this does not make them morally distinct.

3 Objections to Fraternal Justice

3.1. In the previous section, I attempted to determine the scope and limits of the conception of fraternal justice: *Fraternal Sharing* was an attempt to articulate the normative core of this conception. *Harrison Bergeron* articulates a common worry leveled against egalitarian accounts like *Fraternal Sharing*. We saw that fraternal justice neither entails leveling down nor commits us to the goal of equal performance. Yet *Harrison Bergeron* leaves us with the important task of explaining which inequalities are legitimate. This is how *Gross Negligence* comes into play. It is a paradigmatic case of inequality compatible with fraternal justice.

In this section, I want to focus on three crucial objections to my view: The first objection holds that in my attempt to avoid the absurd consequences of *Harrison Bergeron*, in *Gross Negligence* I throw out the equality baby with the desertist bathwater. Fraternal justice seems to make welfare support dependent on whether an individual is deserving of it, thus reintroducing the distinction between the "deserving" and the "undeserving poor." In addition to being moralizing (Anderson 1999, pp. 310–311, 327), this distinction is divisive and discriminatory; it is the opposite of fraternal and paves the way for the "abandonment" of society's weakest members. Hence Elizabeth Anderson's "abandonment objection"—which is considered by many to be the knock-down objection to luck egalitarianism—also translates to my fraternal account of justice. We can restate Anderson's argument as follows:

(1) The state should only compensate for inequalities if they result from unchosen luck.
(2) Oscar's unequal situation, from which he cannot extricate himself, is due to his own calculated decision (bad option luck).
(3) So, the state ought to deny Oscar emergency assistance.

3.2. The conclusion of this argument is counterintuitive. It is supposed to bring out the cruel implications of luck egalitarianism. What went wrong in this argument? Premise (2) merely asserts a fact. Since the argument is valid, something must be wrong with the content of premise (1). It appears that (1) is simply a formulation of the principle of luck egalitarianism. However, this view is what David Estlund might call a "practicabilist" confusion. Luck egalitarianism is a theory of justice, not a theory of state action. There may very well be reasons other than justice for state intervention. Premise (1) needs to be reformulated accordingly. Avoiding the practicabilist confusion, it would simply state:

(1)* Inequalities are unjust if they are the result of unchosen misfortune.

We may then conclude:

(3)* Helping Oscar would be unjust.

Nevertheless, it does not follow from (3) that the state should not help Oscar, because charity considerations may trump justice considerations. Anderson would be unhappy with this solution because it turns justice into something cruel and malicious (Anderson 2010, p. 39). She would probably say it is just to help Oscar because it preserves the conditions of "equal citizenship" (Anderson 1999, p. 332). However, my pluralist analysis seems better to capture the ambivalence of our natural response to Oscar's behavior. According to my conception, Oscar as described in *Gross Negligence* does not deserve the help of others. He does not deserve support because he negligently brought about his own and other people's suffering. He put his and their well-being on the line for the mere thrill of a life-threatening experience. However, this does not mean that Oscar should not receive help for reasons of charity or beneficence. It is a very long way from the assertion "Oscar doesn't deserve to be helped" to the assertion "we ought to make the government's welfare allocation dependent on whether someone is 'deserving' or 'undeserving.'" The abandonment objection equates "justice" with an "unconditional right to assistance." But "justice" must distinguish between deserved and undeserved differences. Luck Egalitarianism does not fall prey to.., as what we should do, all things considered, is a more complex question. The question "What should the state do?" or "What ought to be done" and the question "What is just?" must be kept distinct. Justice is one important consideration, but it does not necessarily trump all other concerns.

In *Gross Negligence*, Oscar's culpability is an established fact. This fact alone does not have normative force. It is relevant only against the backdrop of our fraternal principle of justice. If culpability is uncertain, withholding help becomes even more problematic. Since basic living conditions are at stake, even libertarians ought to be willing to apply the principle *in dubio pro paupero* to this case. However, social policy-making is not only a question of comparative distributive justice. Could it ever be appropriate to invade people's privacy to determine compensation levels? Does distinguishing between different compensation levels based on people's bad choices lead to the stigmatization of poverty? Fear of being exposed and of being stigmatized may conceal real existing poverty. This might then make it impossible to help people in need. These are important considerations, and they should caution policymakers against overemphasizing comparative justice.

3.3. Even if one accepts that in Oscar's particular case he doesn't deserve to be helped, one might still wonder whether the notion of desert is misplaced in political theory. This is one way to understand Anderson's objection against the distinction between the deserving and the undeserving poor. The liberal tradition has rejected the notion of desert mainly for two reasons. First, we don't have epistemic access to the desert level of each individual. Secondly, there is no general agreement on how we should measure desert. Both reasons make the notion of desert "impracticable" (Rawls 1971, p. 312; Rawls 2001, p. 73). However, even if the notion of desert is "impracticable," this hardly makes it the case that it does not play a crucial role in our thinking about justice. Finding appropriate measures and assessing individual desert may be epistemically challenging, but to give up on this notion entirely is to give up on individual justice. Resorting to a non-individual notion of "entitlements" according to which we are all generally entitled to some fundamental rights and some form of welfare equality merely blocks the hard question of justice: "What do we deserve as individuals?" The fact that it is difficult to answer this question *in concreto* does not mean that we cannot articulate the relevant criteria formally and abstractly. The luck egalitarian answer to the hard question is, in short: We deserve what we have chosen under conditions that are sufficiently conducive to making our choices our own.

We can distinguish between a comparative and a non-comparative dimension of desert. Non-comparative desert concerns the essential living conditions we deserve in virtue of being free and equal people, capable of happiness and fraternity. This non-comparative dimension makes room for the sufficentarian intuition that our basic functions as free and equal beings, capable of happiness and fraternity, take priority over comparative considerations of justice. Comparative considerations become significant once basic living conditions have been met. Thus, fraternal justice should not be considered a plea to abolish unconditional subsistence rights. On the contrary, fraternal justice is a radically humanist theory. It considers us as fundamentally equally deserving. Moreover, it not only requires us to acknowledge the deep contingency of our lives but also to share this contingency equally. I will refer to these two aspects of my fraternal account of justice—i.e. its comparative and non-comparative aspects—as the "dual conception of desert" or "dual theory of justice."

Those who are convinced that *Gross Negligence* is the rule and that people's existential hardship is usually due to individual, grossly negligent decision-making will have little sympathy for welfare state institutions. Fraternal justice, by contrast, rests on the platitude that our abilities are essentially dependent on our genetic predispositions and social circumstances. Even in the context of our life history, our success is crucially dependent on contingent circumstantial conditions. The degree to which this is true in the individual case is an empirical question. Social legislation should be somewhat interested in answering this question so that aid does not fall into the wrong hands. To give a clear-cut example, the luck egalitarian insight has not been adequately reflected in social policy-making if Jeff Bezos receives $4,000 in tax relief for his children (Eisinger et al. 2021).

To make this even clearer, consider the following dialogue from Paul Auster's novel *4321*, in which Archibald Ferguson, the main character, criticizes his mother's notion of desert:

> If we have more money than we need, then we should give it to someone who needs it more than we do. A starving person, a crippled old man, someone with no money at all. Spending it on ourselves isn't right. It's selfish.
>
> Don't be difficult, Archie, his mother replied. Your father works harder than any two men in this town. He deserves every penny he's made, and if he wants to show off a little with a new house, that's his business. (Auster 2017, 1.4)

Against his mother's conception of desert, Archibald seems to defend the famous Marxian principle of "need": "From each according to his abilities, to each according to his need" (Marx, KGP, MEW, Bd. 19, 21). With our dual account of "desert," however, we need not let Archibald's mother spin the notion in a right-libertarian direction. Under normal conditions, the starving person and the crippled man are not (entirely) responsible for the position they find themselves in. They don't only "need" help; they *deserve* it. They deserve it by being cooperating members of a society of free and equal people, capable of happiness and fraternity. The fact that Archibald's father "works hard," on the other hand, hardly makes it the case that "[h]e deserves every penny he's made." To mention only some of the many obvious factors that Archibald's mother fails to consider: There was a time in Archibald's father's life when he was dependent on caretakers. Their care, at least in part, made him the responsible, hard-working person he is. It should be equally evident that it is a matter of circumstantial luck that he was in a position to build the business he owns. How many "pennies" he ultimately deserves is a function of his own and his fellow citizens' brute luck balance. From a fraternal standpoint, if his father "wants to show off a little with a new house," it is precisely not "his [own] business." This attitude would seem to reflect his father's unconcern for the fate of his fellow citizens, and Archibald rightly calls it out as "selfish." Conversely, if everything were up to us, then it would be just to let others live the lives they've freely chosen, no matter how wretched. This only sounds cruel because, for good reason, we don't think anyone in their right mind would make such a choice.

Marx was certainly skeptical of the justice talk I invoke here. But even Marx would admit that a communist society would be more just than a capitalist society in the twofold sense I'm trying to defend: On the one hand, undeserved class differences would be abolished in the communist state, and thus nobody would be undeservedly worse off (the relational sense). On the other hand, the material conditions would be such that all people could live a decent life (the non-relational sense). Marx was right that societal transformation requires more than ideal political philosophy. However, he was wrong to think that his theory had normative force without presupposed moral convictions (see Geras 1984, p. 60; Cohen 1983; Elster 1983, 1986, pp. 79–102). What is ultimately problematic about capitalism is the fact that "some [the capitalists] satisfy their needs at the expense of others [the proletariat]" (Marx, "Ideologie," MEW, Bd. 3, 417); this is a paradigmatic case of selfish behavior.

3.4. Still, fraternal justice faces opposition from the socialist camp. According to Jerry Cohen's powerful account of socialism, it consists essentially of two principles: the principle of socialist equality of opportunity and the principle of community (Cohen 2009a). Only the first is a principle of justice. The principle of community, by contrast, goes beyond what justice requires. Cohen believes that since cases of bad option luck are to be counted as just, they cannot be compensated for on grounds of justice; instead, they must be compensated for because they violate the principle of community. When, in the well-known fable of the grasshopper and the ant, the grasshopper decides to be lazy all summer while the ant chooses to work, the grasshopper cannot legitimately complain if it does not have any food when winter comes. Justice does not require the ant to share its goods with the grasshopper. For Cohen, this is where the principle of community kicks in and demands compensation.

I share with Cohen a general luck egalitarian orientation (Cohen 2008). However, I believe that he misunderstands his own theory. Socialist equality of opportunity already requires a fraternal or communal disposition. We are willing to share our fate with our fellow citizens if we don't demand distributional advantages based on social or biological differences grounded in brute luck. If the grasshopper knowingly counts on the ant's generosity when it lazes about all summer, it violates the fraternal spirit. A theory of justice needs to register this behavior for what it is: A breach of the fraternal or communal bond. Community requires the grasshopper to do its part when it can. It is generosity that lets the grasshopper off the hook, even when he doesn't cooperate fraternally, i.e., according to his personal abilities.

3.5. At first blush, my analysis of *Gross Negligence* and the fable of the grasshopper and the ant might sound like a claim from a right-libertarian playbook: The poor "exploit" the wealthy with their leisurely lifestyle. However, appearances are deceptive. I take it to be a strength of my principle of fraternity that, in contrast to Marx, it brings the concept of exploitation properly into view. For Marx, capitalists exploit the proletariat because they pay them only enough to reproduce, while entirely withholding surplus value. Exploitation consists in appropriating the value created by the workers' labor. On a superficial level, it looks as if the capitalist and the worker trade value for value, but Marx's labor theory of value supposedly reveals that the capitalist steals what is not his. Thus, Marx's theory of exploitation crucially depends on his labor theory of value. Since his labor theory of value is controversial, to say the least (von Böhm-Bawerk 1896; Cohen 1988; Elster 1985, 1986; Roemer 1981), his theory of exploitation is equally problematic.

However, one does not need such a controversial theory to recognize exploitative relations as such. Exploitation can be understood in general terms as the denial to workers of a fair share of the fruits of their labor. In *Fraternal Sharing*, I have attempted to explain the general idea of what would count as fraternal sharing and why this is what we owe to each other. As in Marx, our account will deem the permissibility of taking unrestricted advantage of private property in the means of production as an explicit license to exploit others. In contrast to Marx, however, the luck egalitarian insight also makes other sources of exploitation visible, such as the possession of our natural talents and the social conditions in which we grow up. More generally, according to fraternal justice, exploitative relations exist if it is permissible to transform brute luck differences into distributive advantages over others. I thereby try to accommodate the concept of exploitation within the framework of distributive justice.

Not everyone agrees with this approach (see Wood 1995; Vrousalis 2014, 2017). Luck egalitarian approaches in general are thought to be unable to account for exploitation. A distributional disadvantage might be chosen and hence not the result of misfortune, yet it might still be exploitative. Exploitation and undeserved misfortune will therefore have to be distinguished: If Paul falls into a pit and Anton, the "greedy savior," helps him only on the condition that Paul works for him in his sweatshop, then Paul, insofar as he has consented, has chosen the distributive difference himself (Vrousalis 2014, p. 157; Vrousalis 2017, p. 92 f.).

I believe that my fraternal account can still explain the "exploitative" character of this difference. We don't need to locate the exploitation in the "deliberative act" of the exploiter or the exploited (e.g., Cohen 2009b, p. 97). We can, in some proximity to Marx, call institutions and social practices exploitative if they promote the transformation of brute luck differences into distributive advantages. The permission rules of institutions and practices themselves (or, if you will, the permission rules of "the system") can count as "exploitative" if they don't adequately reflect fraternal justice. Exploitation hinges on the notion of taking advantage of someone. "Taking advantage of someone" does not necessarily mean breaking existing rules (see Arneson 2016, p. 28). Even if one assumes that Paul has chosen to jump into the pit in the supposed "greedy savior" counterexample, our fraternal principle still deems unjust the institutional rules that allow Anton to turn Paul's vulnerability into a distributional advantage. For even if Paul's vulnerability is self-inflicted, and thus no "involuntary" or "unjust steps" have led to it (Vrousalis 2014, p. 157), the resulting distributional differences must not exceed appropriate sanction or compensation payments. In this way, we can reconcile the notion of exploitation with the idea of undeserved misfortune, against the "greedy savior" counterexample (see Barry 2006, p. 94 f.; for a detailed reply to Wood and Vrousalis, see Arneson 2016).

3.6. Let me point out one final difference between Cohen's principle of socialist equality of opportunity and our principle of fraternity. Socialist equality of opportunity views as just certain inequalities that cannot count as just under our principle of fraternity. For Cohen, inequalities that result from option luck are just if we could have avoided engaging in the relevant gamble. If Anton and Paul agree to gamble, the resulting inequality is just if both could have walked away from the wager. Let's say they agree to throw the dice. Anton wins $1000. According to Cohen's principle, Anton's being $1000 better off than Paul is just. Again, Cohen does not hold that this kind of inequality should be permitted in a socialist state. But he needs the principle of community to explain why this result is undesirable. Economic differences, even if just, make it the case that we cease to share a common world with each other. Thus, if Anton lives in a mansion and Paul in a shack, Anton can hardly complain to Paul about his pool heater.

What Cohen says about community is true here. However, we do not need to rely on the principle of community to recognize what's wrong with option luck differences. Even if we willingly engage in option luck gambles, their outcome is not necessarily justice-preserving. Consider a more extreme case. Anton and Paul decide to go out in icy weather, and they both know that the probability of their being involved in an accident is 10%. Only Paul, however, not Anton, has an accident and is injured. It seems wrong to say that Anton's being better off than Paul is just. They both made the same decision. The reason why one is better off than the other is luck. This is problematic from our fraternal point of view. In this view, all mere luck differences are problematic (see Segall 2007, Ch. 3). Whether we should always compensate people for their bad option luck is a different question.

We would perhaps like to live in a world where our gambles and decisions under uncertainty make a difference, but calling the resulting inequalities *just* would be a mistake.

4 Conclusion

In this paper, I have attempted to interpret fraternity as a value that is constitutive of distributive justice. Following the idea of the early Rawls, I hold that we owe it to each other to "share each other's fate." I have tried to sharpen this idea by presenting three paradigmatic cases. The upshot of the *Fraternal Sharing* case is that if Anton is to share his fate with Paul fraternally, his good brute luck cannot be transformed into advantages over Paul. Moving from the personal to the institutional level, I claimed that institutions satisfy the demands of fraternal justice if and only if they prevent the conversion of bad brute luck into distributional disadvantages. This does not entail that talent differences must be eradicated, as in *Harrison Bergeron*. The target of equality is the impact that differences have on the distribution of social benefits and burdens. I call this kind of equality the equality of brute luck conversion (EBLC), and I have tried to explain why it differs fundamentally from the equality rightly ridiculed in Kurt Vonnegut's short story: equal performance through leveling down (EPLD). To emphasize the connection between choice and luck, I introduced my final case, *Gross Negligence*. It shows that fraternal justice leaves room for the kernel of truth that lies in seemingly anti-egalitarian concerns: the idea that fraternal institutions are unjust because they promote greed, negligence, and laziness. *Gross Negligence* makes it clear that fraternal justice is not to be equated with "unconditional benevolence" and that reckless choice (under certain conditions) might result in the forfeiting of any claim on others to share one's fate. In the second part of the paper, I dealt with three objections to my view. In response to the objection that it is a desertist and not an egalitarian position, I tried to show why any viable theory of justice ought to account for both desert and equality and why fraternal justice's minimal concession to libertarians is necessary to account for justice. In response to the objection that my view is unable to account for exploitation, I tried to show that exploitation is to be found not in the mere bad brute luck people happen to have but in the social practices and institutions that promote the transformation of brute luck differences into distributive advantages. In response to the final objection, I freely admit that my theory of fraternal justice is, as it stands, "impracticable." This does not make it false, however, nor does it mean that we won't someday develop applied theories that can track desert proxies that appropriately take the luck egalitarian insight into account. Even if we could succeed in this regard, however, it remains to be seen to what extent we still want to live in a world in which bad brute luck can be converted into distributive advantages, i.e., to what extent justice is overridden by other considerations

References

Anderson E (1999) What is the point of equality? Ethics 109(2):287–337
Anderson E (2010) The fundamental disagreement between luck egalitarians and relational egalitarians. In: Macleod CM (ed) Justice and equality. University of Calgary Press, Calgary, pp 21–39
Arneson RJ (2016) Exploitation, domination, competitive markets, and unfair division. South J Philos 54(S1):9–30
Auster P (2017) 4 3 2 1. Faber & Faber, London
Barry N (2006) Defending luck egalitarianism. J Appl Philos 23(1):89–107
Brunkhorst H (2016) Solidarität. Von der Bürgerfreundschaft zur globalen Rechtsgenossenschaft. Suhrkamp, Frankfurt am Main
Bude H (2019) Solidarität. Die Zukunft einer großen Idee. Hanser, München
Cohen GA (1983) Wood, A. W. 'Karl Marx'. Mind 92(367):440–445
Cohen GA (1988) History, labour, and freedom: themes from Marx. Clarendon Press, Oxford
Cohen GA (2008) Rescuing justice and equality. Harvard University Press, Cambridge
Cohen GA (2009a) Why not socialism? Princeton University Press, Princeton
Cohen GA (2009b) Reply to Michael Otsuka's Justice as Fairness. Luck Egalitarian, Not Rawlsian. Partially published in Vrousalis, N The Political Philosophy of G. A. Cohen. Back to Socialist Basics. Bloomsbury, London, p 97
Durkheim É (1978) Émile Durkheim on institutional analysis, edited, translated, and with an introduction by Mark Traugott. University of Chicago Press, Chicago
Dworkin R (2011) Justice for Hedgehogs. Belknap Press of Harvard University Press, Cambridge
Eisinger J, Ernsthausen J, Kiel P (2021) The secret IRS files: trove of never-before-seen records reveal how the wealthiest avoid income tax. In ProPublica - Journalism in the Public Interest. Retrieved from Propublica: https://www.propublica.org/article/the-secret-irs-files-trove-of-never-before-seen-records-reveal-how-the-wealthiest-avoid-income-tax
Elster J (1983) Exploitation, freedom, and justice. Nomos 26:277–304
Elster J (1985) Making sense of Marx. Cambridge University Press, Cambridge
Elster J (1986) An introduction to Karl Marx. Cambridge University Press, Cambridge
Estlund D (2019) Utopophobia: on the limits (if any) of political philosophy. Princeton University Press, Princeton
Frankfurt HG (1987) Equality as a moral ideal. Ethics 98(1):21–43
Geras N (1984) The controversy about Marx and justice. Philosophica 33(1):33–86
Honneth A (2017) Die Idee des Sozialismus: Versuch einer Aktualisierung. Suhrkamp, Berlin
Lang G (2021) Strokes of luck: a study in moral and political philosophy. Oxford University Press, Oxford
Metz KH (1998) Solidarität und Geschichte. Institutionen und sozialer Begriff der Solidarität in Westeuropa im 19. Jahrhundert. In: Bayertz K (ed) Solidarität. Begriff und Problem. Suhrkamp, Frankfurt am Main, pp 172–194
Nagel T (1970) The possibility of altruism. Clarendon Press, Oxford
Parfit D (1997) Equality and priority. Ratio 10(3):202–221
Peña-Rangel D (2023) Economic inequality and the permissibility of leveling down. Ethical Theory Moral Pract 26(5):803–832
Rawls J (1971) A theory of justice. Belknap Press of Harvard University Press, Cambridge
Rawls J (1999a) A theory of justice. Revised edition. Belknap Press of Harvard University Press, Cambridge
Rawls J (1999b) Justice as fairness: political not metaphysical. In: Freeman S (ed) John Rawls, Collected Papers, vol 1999. Harvard University Press, Cambridge, pp 388–414
Rawls J (2001) Justice as fairness: a restatement. Harvard University Press, Cambridge
Roemer J (1981) Analytical foundations of Marxian economic theory. Cambridge University Press, Cambridge

Segall S (2007) In solidarity with the imprudent: a defense of luck egalitarianism. Soc Theory Pract 33(2):177–198
Temkin LS (2000) Equality, priority, and the levelling-down objection. In: Clayton M, Williams A (eds) The ideal of equality. Macmillan Press, Houndmills, Basingstoke, pp 126–161
von Böhm-Bawerk E (1896) Zum Abschluss des Marxschen Systems. Pierer, Altenburg
Vonnegut K (1968) Welcome to the Monkey House. Rosetta Books, New York
Vrousalis N (2014) G. A. Cohen on Exploitation. Polit Philos Econ 13(2):151–164
Vrousalis N (2017) The political philosophy of G.A. Cohen: back to socialist basics. London: Bloomsbury Academic
Wildt A (1998) Solidarität – Begriffsgeschichte und Definition heute. In: Bayertz K (ed) Solidarität. Begriff und Problem. Suhrkamp, Frankfurt am Main, pp 202–216
Wood (1995) Exploitation. Soc Philos Policy 12(2):136–158

Structural Injustices and the Harms of the Food System

Joan McGregor

Abstract How do we account for the harmful outcomes of the food system, in particular, the differential distributional effects of it? Are those disadvantaged by the food system merely suffering the consequences of their bad choices, or are the disadvantaged merely misfortunate? Rejecting both these accounts, I will argue that there are structural impediments that limit individuals' capacities to simply "make better choices" and consequently the disadvantages are not just a matter of misfortune and certainly not merely attributable to bad choices of the individuals in those communities. I will argue that the inequalities in the food system are perpetuated by unjust social structural background conditions. Those background conditions severely diminish the opportunities of some individuals and communities in our society. Since these background structural conditions are products of human creation or maintenance and they undermine the capabilities for social freedom, there is a shared responsibility for rectifying these structural injustices.

The harms caused by the food system have come to the attention of the wider public, largely fueled by the work of popular writers such as Michael Pollan (*Omnivore's Dilemma, Food Rules*) and films such as *Food Inc., Supersize Me*, and *Fast Food Nation*. These popular portrayals exposed the problems with the growth and ubiquity of "big-ag," with its monocultures cheapening the price and the quality of food, leading to an abundance of low-quality food fueled by government subsidies, in turn causing a burgeoning health crisis of obesity, cancer, and heart disease. Beyond the direct detrimental health consequences of this diet, industrial agriculture's reliance

This paper was presented at the AMINTAPHIL conference in Chicago Ill in 2023. I am grateful to the participants for their comments. The framework of the paper, based on structural injustices, I developed and used in my previous paper: "Structural Injustices in the Educational System, Inequality, and its Effects on Democracy." Understanding structural injustices will make visible many of the invisible structures that lead to injustices in our society.

J. McGregor (✉)
Arizona State University, Tempe, AZ, USA
e-mail: J.McGregor@asu.edu

G. A. Babst, W.-c. Lee (eds.), *Contemporary Facets of Injustice*, AMINTAPHIL: The Philosophical Foundations of Law and Justice 13,
https://doi.org/10.1007/978-3-031-93783-5_5

on artificial fertilizers, herbicides, and pesticides results in devastating effects on the environment, including driving climate change. Additionally, modern animal agriculture produces cheap meat but at the cost of horrendous cruelty to animals, and the production methods, for example CAFOs (concentrated animal feeding operation), are destructive to the environment and exacerbate GHGs (greenhouse gases) leading to more climate change. There are other harms perpetrated by the food system to people who work therein, from low paid farm workers who are often migrant laborers without safety protections to others in food production, meat packers, restaurant workers, and so on. Out of this attention to the harmful effects of the food system grew a robust nationwide food movement, focused on healthy, local, and organic foods that are good for people and the planet (Werkheiser and Noll 2014). This food movement aimed at local foods, however, is largely populated by the white upper middle class who have resources and the ability to access healthy, environmentally friendly alternatives. With this movement we have witnessed an explosion of farmers' markets, CSAs (community supported agriculture), community gardens, and farm-to-table restaurants.

While this movement is bringing needed attention to the food system, the attention has not been on the social inequities in and around the food system, and the barriers faced by low income and minority communities that preclude them from participating in the food movement's proposed solutions.[1] Much of the food movement has been focused on changing individual people's behavior, on helping people make better *choices*, and not acknowledging the structural and other interrelated problems that make individual choices and market solutions very difficult or not viable at all in these communities (Guthman 2008; Gilson 2014; Alkon and Mare 2012). For members of low-income and minority communities the proposed solution, such as Pollan's "Eat mostly plants, especially leaves" (Pollan 2009), is not necessarily possible. The incomes of the poor have been steadily declining since the 1970s (Pew 2015), and sadly, if the inner-city poor have access to fresh vegetables in their neighborhoods, they tend to be cost prohibitive, even more expensive than in predominately white suburban neighborhoods (Chung and Meyers 1999).

The impact of the food system on the poor (many of whom are single women with children) and minorities is widely known; for example, the poor and minorities have a much higher rate of obesity, hearth disease, diabetes and the diseases related to it (Neff et al. 2009). Many of these same communities have high rates of food insecurity, with lack of regular access to sufficient nutritious food (Odoms-Young 2018), including farm workers who have the highest of levels of food insecurity in

[1]Another food movement, the food justice movement emerged addressing the inequities of the food system. "Food justice" is defined as "communities exercising their right to grow, sell, and eat [food that is] fresh, nutritious, affordable, culturally appropriate, and grown locally with care for the well-being of the land, workers, and animals" (Aldon and Agyeman 2011). The food justice movement's attention is to issues of affordability, access, community participation, and the effects of the food system on class, race, and gender. The food justice movement is making important contributions to the understanding of the food system's problems through the lens of people without access, money or power.

the nation (Ip et al. 2015). Many low-income minority communities are "food deserts" (Dieterle 2015), areas without reasonably close access to grocery stores with fresh foods (Bower et al. 2014). Food deserts are most prevalent either in inner cities with high concentrations of low-income and minority populations, or in rural areas, such as agricultural areas and tribal nations. As noted above, the current industrial food system results in not only devastating health effects from consuming unhealthy foods, but in environmental damage as well, such as soil toxicity and depletion, chemical runoffs in streams and other waterways, leading to loss of biodiversity (Nesheim et al. 2015). Those damaging effects on the environment in turn have effects on the communities around them. The industrial agriculture system, moreover, has a substantial impact on the amount of global greenhouse gases in the atmosphere, somewhere between 30 and 40% of the total amount (Natasha 2012). Excessive carbon in the atmosphere will harm future generations and is already having effects on current populations, often the most vulnerable ones, unfortunately, in those subject to the problems with the food system and the environment degradation caused by it.

How do we account for the harmful outcomes of the food system and the differential distributional effects of those harms? Are those harms injustices, and if so, who or what is responsible for them? Arguably, there are two dominant accounts for the harms of the current food system and the responsibility for those harms. The first is the popular view that individuals are responsible for their own choices, and consequently those suffering harms from the food system are merely suffering the consequences of their bad choices (Gilson 2014). The second account is that those suffering with bad health related to diet are merely suffering misfortunes. In terms of political philosophy, the first account aligns with libertarians' theories of justice and the second is endorsed by contemporary egalitarian theorists. Rejecting both these accounts, I will argue that there are social structural impediments that limit individuals' capacities to simply "make better choices," and consequently the harms are not just a matter of misfortune and certainly not merely attributable to bad choices of the individuals in those communities. Building on the work of Iris Marion Young and Elizabeth Anderson on the nature of justice and responsibility (Young 2010; Anderson 1999) and the work of Erin Gilson on the problems of the model of consumer choice, I will argue that the inequalities in the food system are perpetuated by unjust structural background conditions. Those unjust background conditions severely diminish the opportunities of some individuals and communities in our society. Those diminished opportunities in the current food system result in harms to those who are mostly poor, mostly women, and mostly people of color. Inequalities of opportunities falling on some due to race, gender, and/or class are the subject of an egalitarian account of justice (Anderson 1999). The subject of egalitarian justice, Anderson reminds us, is eradicating oppression which results from unequal opportunities. At minimum egalitarian justice attempts to ensure that individuals have equal opportunities over essential capacities and to advocate the equal moral worth of persons (Anderson 1999, p. 312). What I will argue is that many suffer from inequalities of opportunity in the food system that result from background structural conditions and constitute injustices. That they are injustices is difficult if not impossible to see. No obvious person or policy necessarily causes the limitations on their opportunities, and hence sometimes the limitations are without wrongdoers—specific individuals or groups—perpetrating them. Nevertheless, these structural injustices limit the opportunities to access quality food, and thereby perpetuate harmful outcomes for the poor and minorities. That is not to deny that some of the harms or the nexus of opportunities that any individual faces may result from government policies and practices and corporate agents—they do. I will argue that individuals who find themselves with these restricted opportunities, not because of their choices, that affect their health and well-being, suffer a dignitary harm as a result. Because of the network of background circumstances limiting their "opportunity set" (Young 2010, p. 19), they are not able to stand up as equals with other citizens who live without these limitations on the social conditions of freedom. Moreover, given that their restrictions often result from invisible background circumstances, their loss of agency is even more pernicious without obvious wrongdoers perpetrating wrong against them. This paper is focused not merely on the issue of structural injustice but on who should take responsibility, and why—this is the politics of responsibility. I argue that since these structural conditions are a result of social and political forces, they are all of our responsibility to eradicate them.

1 Who's Responsible for the Harms?

The so-called "obesity epidemic" and health disparities in poor and minority communities in the United States are met with concern, but not as injustices (Guthman 2011; Petersen et al. 2019).[2] More often than not in the popular media and society in general, the health conditions of the poor are addressed as consequences of individual or market choices, and not the product of government or corporate actors' decision-making and control. Much of the societal discussion about the health outcomes of the food system is to hold responsible those who have bad health conditions for their decisions about food (Thomson 2015, pp. 80–106). This popular understanding of the problem is the *personal responsibility model* and implicitly what food commentators like Pollan are endorsing (Gilson 2014). Under the personal responsibility account, individuals are responsible for their food choices and the resulting outcomes. The assumption of the model is that we are all free actors with the same or roughly the same capability to make better or worse choices, and consequently it is no one's fault but the individual's if they make choices that lead to bad health outcomes. It is the behavior of individuals, it is argued, that puts them at relative disadvantage, or in harm's way, not, therefore because of an injustice against them. Relying on the personal responsibility model, there are not widespread calls to address the food related health crisis in poor and minority

[2] I do want to acknowledge the problematized understanding of obesity and race, see Strings (2019) and consequently, too much focus on obesity may play into this narrative. A better framework might be the healthy outcomes from the food system.

communities as an issue of social injustice. Doubling down on the personal responsibility model, we have seen calls for the obese to pay higher health insurance premiums; they should have to internalize the consequences, such as higher costs of medical care, of their actions (Schmitz 1998). If having diet related poor health is merely a matter of actively choosing foods that lead to poor health, the argument goes, then those individuals are responsible for that outcome of those choices.

Holding adults responsible for their decisions is a critical aspect of respect for individual agency and autonomy. The personal responsibility model can be seen as protecting that important value. States that do not value individuals' autonomy dictate what people do without regard to individuals' decisions and their own perceived interests. Treating adults as children as paternalism does—not competent to make choices, without real agency—is another way of not respecting autonomy.[3] That said, it is only intelligible to hold individuals responsible when their decisions and options are to some extent in their control. To what extent does it make sense to claim low-income inner-city minorities, or rural farmworkers, or Native Americans living on remote reservations have the capability to make autonomous food choices when there are extremely limited accessible options and other structural obstacles?

Consider Dolores Bateman, a single mother of five children, who lives in South Memphis, a predominately African American neighborhood without a supermarket accessible on foot to most of the area's residents (Jones et al. 2019; Kitch et al. 2021). Dolores is a janitor at a local elementary school who must rely on public transit to and from her job and the grocery, a store which is a 45-minute bus ride from her home. Many low-income children like those of Dolores get their meals covered by the federal free breakfast and lunch programs at school. While those school meals include key nutrients, they tend to be high in sugar, fat, and salt, and consist mostly of refined processed foods. This places their children at risk for type-two diabetes (Almarshad et al. 2022). Lack of public amenities, parks, or playgrounds due to redlining further exacerbates their health risks. A history of underinvestment means that low-income minority neighborhoods have few commercial outlets. Dolores's neighborhood is a "food desert" (Karpyn et al. 2019), a situation often referred to more aptly as "food apartheid," a term for human-created systems of segregation that relegate certain groups but not others to food deprivation (Penniman 2018, p. 4; Unshared Bounty: How Structural Racism Contributes to the Creation and Persistence of Food Deserts 2012). These background conditions, most of which are not of Dolores's choosing, limit her food options. Entrenched social norms, for instance, about gender roles, mean women are usually the sole caregiver for children. These norms also track women into low-paid work (Schieder and Gould 2016). This is not to say that Dolores has no agency in her food choices. She may well want healthy food options and public spaces for her children to safely play, but long work hours, constrained transit options, geographically limited access to healthy foods and playgrounds, and a low income, minimize her options. Social

[3] Taxes on sugary foods and drinks are opposed on grounds that it undermines individuals' autonomy. See Véliz et al. (2019).

structures lock her into a constrained set of choices. Dolores is not in the same "choice" situation as middle-class suburbanites in the broader Memphis area. She must work harder to create a healthy life for her children. The topology of harms that Dolores suffers are the physical harms to her health and the health of her children that result from an unhealthy diet and little access to exercise options (Bjornstad et al. 2021); the psychological harms that result from her feelings of helplessness about her lack of opportunities—the harm of lack of agency; the moral harm that comes from knowing that she is unequal to other parents in society who can provide better foods and environmental opportunities for their children. And finally, there is psychic harm of society blaming her for the harms that result to her and her children when the opportunities to do otherwise are extremely difficult to achieve or just plain inaccessible.

2 Bad Luck, Injustice, and Responsibility

It is disingenuous and demeaning to claim that individuals such as Dolores are personally responsible for their food choices and the harmful outcomes that result. Since it is widely accepted that individuals should only be responsible for choices and outcomes that are in their control, it is not fair that individuals be blamed for conditions outside their control. The harms of the food system, particularly for low-income individuals living in food deserts, cannot justifiably be fully attributed to the individuals suffering those harms. They are not responsible for those harms given the circumstances of their choices.

Another approach to understanding the harms of the food system and their differential impact on some groups is to conceive of those harms as matters of bad luck. Elements of individuals' situations that disadvantage them but are not in their control should, according to liberal egalitarian theorists, be compensated—they are injustices since they disadvantage vis-à-vis others in society. Egalitarian theorists, such as Ronald Dworkin and others, argue that those attributes or characteristics that disadvantage individuals and are not in their control are matters of bad luck. The poor and minorities, such as Dolores, are stuck in communities without grocery stores, investments in public spaces, economic development, and unequal goods, are simply unlucky. It is no fault of their own as the personal responsibility model would suggest; it is, rather, a matter of bad luck that they find themselves in these circumstances. Being a member of a minority group or even being female are characteristics that can disadvantage individuals, making them "unlucky" in the social system, and thereby receiving less "goods" than others. Luck egalitarians focus on the characteristics or attributes of persons to explain why they are disadvantaged, and the injustice is in terms of the unequal distribution of goods. Their disadvantage might be through disability or not having characteristics that are valued in the social system, being intelligent, attractive, or athletic, for example. According to Dworkin and other luck egalitarians, being disadvantaged in the social system by attributes beyond one's control is unjust (Dworkin 1981).

Does this account of the harms as products of misfortunate make more sense than the personal responsibility model? At least it does not blame the disadvantage for their harms. But does it make sense to focus on characteristics or attributes of individuals that work to their disadvantage and then compensate them for those characteristics or attributes as the luck egalitarian supposes? On this account, the poor and minorities are unfortunate to live in areas without grocery stores and other amenities of healthy lifestyles should be compensated for their misfortune. This view conceives of egalitarian justice as essentially about how goods are distributed in society, how much goods people have in relation to others. Anderson in "What is the point of Equality?" rightly objects to this approach to egalitarian justice focusing on attributes and distributions, since it looks like justice is a matter of "taking pity" on persons with the "bad luck" attributes that disadvantage them. Anderson argues that egalitarianism should be interested in how those distributions affect social relations, making some inferior to others and effect their opportunities. Luck egalitarians suppose that the point of egalitarianism is to ensure that "losers in the natural lottery" not be disadvantaged by those features that are outside their control. Furthermore, it assumes that the "unlucky" attributes will disadvantage, whatever the social situation.

Starting with the second point, that unlucky attributes will disadvantage and limit one's capabilities, whatever the social situation, Anderson points out that "[o]ne's capabilities are a function not just of one's fixed personal traits and divisible resources, but of one's mutable traits, social relations and norms, and the structure of opportunities, public goods, and public spaces" (Anderson 1999, p. 319). Focusing on the attributes as fixed traits that "inevitably" affect one's capacities misses how these other factors can and do affect individuals' capacities. Capacities are a measurement of what one is free to do, what it is accessible for one to do and be, and what opportunities are open to one. For example, consider many disabilities that do not fix individuals' capabilities in the way Dworkin implies. Being wheelchair bound can be ameliorated by ramps and elevators, laws and norms requiring nondiscrimination, and so on; or alternatively, social and environmental structures can negatively impact wheelchair bound persons' lives by limiting their physical opportunities to get access to workplaces and schools and not prohibiting discrimination of the disabled. The background social structures can make an attribute a disadvantage or not. Moreover, as Iris Marion Young rightly notes, Dworkin fails to distinguish "between the causes of relative disadvantage," those that are simply misfortune, and "those that result from social organizations and processes" (Young 2010, p. 28). Many attributes that disadvantage individuals are a result of social organizations and processes; race and gender, for instance, are not immutably disadvantaging. They are attributes which for a variety of social/historical reasons make persons disadvantaged under the current social system. Race and gender are not simply misfortunes as having a serious and extremely debilitating genetic disorder can be. Another related case to be addressed is that of social norms. Given social norms about gender roles of caregiving and appropriate career choices, women are disadvantaged, both from the facts that certain roles are gendered (for example caregiving), and thereby low paying. Pitying women for their disadvantage and compensating them, by giving them SNAP (Supplemental Nutrition Assistance Program) benefits, for instance, does nothing to change the social system that limits them and limits their capacities, nor does it change the position of inferiority they experience in society. Just having a little more money does not change one's capability to access high quality food in one's neighborhood or provide one's children with safe playgrounds; it doesn't change the historical effects of redlining and segregation, nor does it affect the construction of gender roles that lock women in as sole caregivers.

The second objection to luck egalitarianism is its focus solely on the distribution of goods. Egalitarian justice, according to Anderson, focuses on disrupting hierarchical systems of people, some superior and some inferior, that lead to oppression, and on the positive side, seeking social orders where people can "stand in relation of equality" (Anderson 1999, p. 313). On this view of egalitarian justice, it is about destroying systems of privilege and ensuring that everyone has the social conditions for freedom. We would be mistaken to merely focus on the unequal distribution of goods, as Jennifer Szende argues in "Food Deserts, Justice and the Distributive Paradigm" (Szende 2015). Just conceiving the problem as one of minorities, or the poor, or women not getting as many goods, in this case, access to quality food, is not the right target. It should matter that people can stand in relations of equality, not oppressed, or marginalized or exploited. As discussed earlier, one critical way in which individuals can experience inferiority is when they do not have the same opportunities as others to provide decent food and a healthy life for their children. Where there is unequal access to good schools, libraries, outdoor public spaces for one's children, and to grocery stores, that means they do not have the same social conditions of freedom as others in wealthy neighborhoods with that access. "Food deserts are…another form that marginalization with affluent societies may take" (Szende 2015, p. 62). Dworkin's framing of the target misses the social structure and institutional contexts, the social norms within which the distributional inequality occurs and does nothing to change those social conditions. Seeing people as having traits that inhibit what capabilities they have in society and then compensating them, treating them as objects of pity or misfortune, does not address the sources of their lack of capability, nor does it allow them to stand up as equals. Many of the obstacles to individuals' opportunities are structured in the background conditions in which people find themselves. They are "trapped" in relationships of inequality vis-à-vis those with more opportunities who don't face the same structural barriers. Just providing individuals with compensation, but not addressing the social structures that enable and perpetrate these disadvantages, is to perpetuate the cycle of inferiority or inequality in relation to those who do not face those limitations on their opportunities.

The luck egalitarian's answer to responsibility for harms of the food system focuses on the wrong source of inequality—unlucky characteristics—and the wrong target for rectifying the inequality—distribution of goods. Neither focus tackles the social structural conditions that perpetuate unequal outcomes and limit an individual's capacities to be and do things that others in society can.

3 Structural Injustice

Returning to Dolores's situation, what affects her "opportunity set" for food choices, and who or what is responsible for her situation? Dolores's story reflects the unjust social structures in the U.S. that have perpetuated patterns of unequal distribution of harms from the food system. The patterns of unequal distribution of harms such as worse health outcomes, are not necessarily caused by individual wrongdoers. Rather, they result from human-created and maintained societal arrangements and, therefore, constitute social/political wrongs. "Social structures" include the background conditions, rules, policies, practices, and norms which govern individual actions, collective actions, and government actions. When social structures unfairly constrain or limit some people's opportunities and their capabilities vis à vis others in society, they create structural injustices. "Capabilities" refers to the set of valuable functioning—e.g., being well-nourished, having control over some property, being educated—that a person can effectively access. Mere freedom to consider these functionings is not sufficient; the key is effective freedom to choose among them and thereby to choose the life that one values (Nussbaum 2003).

Egalitarian Justice on this account is concerned with equality of capabilities. Of course, egalitarian justice doesn't require that there must be equality of all capabilities. The capability to race cars, be an expert skier, or take vacations to exotic lands are not ones that egalitarians are obligated to ensure. Following Anderson, "[P]eople are entitled to whatever capabilities are necessary to enable them to avoid or escape entanglement in oppressive social relationships…[and] they are entitled to the capabilities necessary for functioning as an equal citizen in a democratic state" (Anderson 1999, p. 316). For Anderson this does cover a wide range of capabilities. She asks us to consider three aspects of individual functioning: "as a human being, as a participant in a system of cooperative production, and as a citizen of a democratic state" (Anderson 1999, p. 317). One's capability to function in these ways can be constrained not only by the distribution of resources but by "social relations and norms, and the structure of opportunities, public goods, and public spaces" (Anderson 1999, p. 319). These constitute the social structure in which individuals' function. Gender norms, for instance, can relegate women to the role of caregivers and provide internal obstacles to choosing more lucrative occupations, undermining their self-confidence in the marketplace. Background structures, such as historical discrimination, redlining or lending disparities, shape the current structure of opportunities for African Americans to create wealth. Another example is implicit bias on the part of employers that limit opportunities for racial minorities even when those employers are not aware of their bias.

Erinn Gilson gives a detailed example of the social structures of the food system behind the concentrated animals feeding operations (CAFOs) leading to disastrous results on many fronts, human health, animal welfare, and ecological damage. And yet with all these deleterious results the system not only persists but is growing. The factor that underlies and motivates the system is efficiency. With a few large meat producers who contract with smaller scale farmers, requiring them to incur debt to build the requisite infrastructure, they must operate in such a fashion that they can produce large qualities of meat at a very low cost. Those farmers "lack the power to object to the required practices or try out alternatives. Market consolidation and sub-contracting are thus structural features of the contemporary food system that remove decision-making from the purview of those directly involved in food production and constrain farmers' autonomy" (Gilson 2014, p. 117). Further, since the meat industry can externalize their cost of waste, for example, the meat industry appears to be efficient when in fact the costs would be much higher if it had to internalize those and other costs. Gilson reminds us that the meat conglomerates and the farmers are all acting within the rules and norms of the market in pursuing their interests. They are not intentionally creating food that leads to diseases or deliberating trying to create dead zones in the Gulf of Mexico from the runoff of animal waste.

Dolores's story is an example where social structures put her in a disadvantaged position vis-a-vis other people in society. These social structures provide her with a very limited opportunity set; consequently, she is not in the same "choice" situation as middle-class white suburbanites. Dolores's ability to function in certain ways to achieve her desires for a healthy life for her children is more limited; she does not have the capability to do so, or at least she does not have the same capability as others in society to function in particular ways. What is limiting her opportunity set are the background social structures. To understand the background social structures that limit her food choices, we need to expose the factors that create the background conditions of the current food system (at least in the U.S.). Why calorie intense and nutrition deficient foods are cheap and abundant in the US goes back to a system of subsidizing commodity crops in the 1930s (Franck et al. 2013). Subsidizing commodity crops led to an overabundance of corn, resulting in the food industry finding new uses for it, for example, the ubiquitous use of high fructose corn syrup which the food industry added to everything from ketchup to soups to salad dressing (Fields 2004). With the prices down, the food industry created new markets for foods loaded with corn syrup and hydrogenated fat. Recent data confirms what has been suspected, that diets of highly processed foods lead to overeating, which leads to obesity, diabetes, heart disease, cancer, and higher mortality rates (Hall et al. 2019).

The food industry continues to manipulate what we eat (Brownell and Warner 2009) from advertising, to influencing the government's dietary recommendations (Nestle 2018), to what goes into school lunches, to manipulating the actual food itself; hence, characterizing food choices as fully voluntary for anyone should be met with incredulity. Furthermore, the food industry has spent billions engineering their food, even hiring neuroscientists to find the "bliss point" where human brains respond to ingredients such as sugar, salt, and fat, making their food "irresistible" (there are similar effects on the brain with heroin) (Harmon 2010). Adding to manipulating the food itself, the food industry spends an enormous amount of money advertising these foods to the public. Recent studies show that childhood obesity would be significantly less if there were less food advertisements directed towards them (Veerman et al. 2009). Industry, with the help of government, has created a food system where there is an abundance of cheap, unhealthy food, misinformation about the quality of the food, and a dearth of reasonably priced alternatives to those foods.

There are, according to Marion Nestle, so many factors that militate against the construction of our food choices as "informed choices." She states:

> We may believe that we make informed decisions about food choice, but we cannot do so if we are oblivious of the ways food companies influence our choices. Most of us, if we choose to do so, can recognize how food companies spend money on advertising, but it is far more difficult to know about the industry's behind-the-scenes efforts in Congress, federal agencies, courts, universities, and professional organizations to make diets seem a matter of personal choice rather than of deliberate manipulation. The emphasis on individual choice serves the interests of the food industry for one critical reason: if diet is a matter of individual free will, then the only appropriate remedy for poor diets is education, and nutritionists should be off teaching people to take personal responsibility for their own diet and health—not how to institute societal changes that might make it easier for everyone to do so (Nestle 2002, p. 60).

Government policies and the practices of the food industry influence the entire food system, and that consequently shapes the background conditions in which individuals make choices about food. Some communities have additional, more directly serious barriers to healthy food choices. Consider the fact that 23.5 million Americans currently live in food deserts. As mentioned earlier, food deserts occur in urban and rural communities when there is no access or very limited access to healthy and affordable food (USDA n.d.). This is the situation in which Dolores finds herself. Lack of access to fresh healthy foods leaves individuals in those communities with little options except to purchase fast, unhealthy food. Fast foods outlets or mini marts are often prevalent in urban poor neighborhoods (Freeman 2007).

Nor can we suggest that the reasons for the composition of the neighborhoods are merely products of market forces and personal choices as they are often characterized. Segregated urban communities grew up in the 1940s when the government, through the FHA (Federal Housing Administration) and VA (Veterans Affairs), provided white middle-class families with home loans, enabling them to move to the suburbs of cities. Richard Rothstein in *The Color of Law* details how the FHA subsidized builders creating suburbs with the requirement that no houses be sold to African Americans (Rothstein 2017). "African American families" according to an ACLU study "were unable to access the same low-interest home loans as white families due to government sanctioned redlining, restrictive housing covenants, and discrimination, and were left stranded in the cities" (ACLU 2010). With the white flight to the suburbs, many businesses moved too, and the development of supermarkets grew with them, leaving the urban areas without reliable sources of affordable healthy foods. By 1970, the demographics of the country had drastically changed, and the typical northern African American was "more likely to live with other blacks than with whites" and…" [c]ities continued to lose supermarkets in the 1980s while, nationally, supermarket openings surpassed closings" (ACLU 2010). It is important to highlight that the "segregated living patterns are not a natural consequence of private choices but have been significantly influenced by government policies" (ACLU 2010).

The personal responsibility model and the luck egalitarian accounts of the harms of the food system ignore these background conditions, created by government policies, corporate practices, and other social practices, within which people act, and how those conditions limit the "opportunity set" of individuals, and how that affects individuals' abilities to stand as equals with others in society. These conditions of the food system structure Dolores's choices. Dolores's agency is affected by her limited attainable choices—fast food outlets that are close and affordable. Agency is having the capability to act, not merely to overcome physical obstacles in one's way but having the physical, financial, geographical, and emotional resources to act in a particular way. The government does have complicity in creating and sustaining a food system of unhealthy foods based more on industry profits than human and environmental health. The food industry has complicity as well, creating foods that taste good but are bereft of nutrition, filled with empty calories, and then aggressively markets those unhealthy foods to children and adults.[4]

The social structures which encompass the rules and norms of society, more severely limit the poor and members of minority groups' freedoms with lack of access and resources. The practical reality is that the existence of food deserts and the higher costs of healthy foods, the decreasing income of the poor, the lack of social mobility, and the on-going racism and sexism all have a greater impact on the poor. The assumption that we are all free actors, with the same opportunity sets, voluntarily making informed choices in markets free from unjust background social structures is belied by the facts about the circumstances in which we act, particularly regarding food. Considering the above facts about why people live where they do, why unhealthy foods are cheap and available in the low-income neighborhoods and healthy foods are not, and why people in those communities "choose" the foods they do, it is not accurate to suggest that those people are fully responsible for their food choices and therefore responsible for the outcomes. When prescriptions for the problems of the food system are focused on individuals taking personal responsibility and making better-informed food choices—"voting with your fork"—there is no recognition of the unjust structural conditions which limit and manipulate a person's range of choices. Though the effects of the food industry and government's actions are on all individuals in society, those with resources, transportation, greater knowledge, and access to fresh foods have many more opportunities to make "better" food choices than low-income individuals in food deserts. Nor is it adequate to suggest that people, minorities, women, and the poor, who find themselves in these restricted circumstances, are just unlucky, and we should only compensate them for their bad luck. These are human created and maintained structures, and people's standing in society will not be changed until the structures are changed.

[4] There is data that taste preferences are formed when we are children and that fast food companies target minority neighborhood children. Khazan (2014).

4 Responsibility for Structural Injustices

Both the earlier considered accounts of responsibility for harm, namely the personal responsibility and the luck egalitarian account, miss the essential focus on the background social structures that perpetuate some individuals' disadvantage in exercising their capacities to function as equals. The alternative account that I am advancing here is that the disadvantages and harms resulting from the food system are largely a result of the social structures which put barriers (which are complex and varied) in individuals' option networks, closing off or not even providing certain options. Structural injustices are created by social structures—laws, rules, policies, practices, and social norms—that are largely products of human creation and maintenance (Haslanger 2012). The COVID-19 virus was a natural occurrence, but the responses to the pandemic—for example, which groups were most likely to get sick and who got treatment—are products of social institutions. The fact that low income and minority populations were disproportionately affected had to do with the fact that those populations are more likely to be in "essential services" roles, whereby they are not able to work from home. Many of them were not provided PPE for those jobs. And they also have less access to early and quality medical care, thereby resulting in worse outcomes.

Social structures can harm individuals in particular groups by narrowing the opportunities open to them, limiting their capacities to do and be various things (Sen 1992). The social structures, however, do not affect everyone the same way. The social structures we have discussed here, for example, those which create food deserts, only affect some, mostly poor and minority populations. Living in a food desert, which was often created by racist redlining and consequent underinvestment, limits food choices making residents unequal to others in society who are not limited by these social structures which created and sustained food deserts. In relation to others in society without limitations, the victims of structural injustices are unequal, their capacities are diminished because of the social structure. The inequalities among individuals in society are socially created and maintained. But recognize that the constrained capacities are not simply products of misfortune, since they are often products of social collective arrangements, even if they are historical byproducts. Unlike being born with an unknown genetic disorder that affects one's opportunities (such a condition is bad luck, let's say), living in a historically redlined neighborhood without grocery stores is a product of social processes and could be reformed.

Although it is correct that individuals do make choices in these constrained circumstances, they are not, for example, coerced, but given their circumstances circumscribed by the background conditions not of their choosing, they are significantly constrained vis-à-vis others in their society. External conditions, for example, no grocery stores or inadequate transportation, and internal conditions, for example, manipulating one's and one's children's preferences by industry advertising and the manipulation of the foods themselves, put constraints on their capacities to function. Those structural obstacles can undermine their agency and their ability to stand as an equal in society. The limited opportunity set that results constrains their essential capacities because they do not have access to sufficient levels of functionings, hence they do not have the social conditions of freedom. Injustice in this sense concerns more than simply the fact that people suffer fates they do not deserve. It concerns how institutional rules and social interactions conspire to narrow the options that many have. Quoting Iris Young:

> Social structures do not constrain in the form of direct coercion of some individuals over others; they constrain more indirectly and cumulatively as blocking possibilities. Part of the difficulty of seeing structure, moreover, is that we do not experience particular institutions, particular material facts, or particular rules as themselves sources of constraint; the constraints occur through the joint action of individuals within institutions and given physical conditions as they affect our possibilities (Young 2010, p. 55).

Why consider these constraints as *injustices* as opposed to disadvantages that the individual is not entitled to have redressed? Egalitarian justice requires not that individuals have the same resources but that individuals have the social conditions of freedom to function as equal citizens. When there are social and political structural barriers, particularly when those barriers are the result of governmental policies and other collective arrangements that prevent people from having the social conditions of freedoms, those limitations on their opportunities are injustices. Social structures that limit opportunities, limit their capabilities and result in perpetuating patterns of unequal distribution of harms are unjust. Those structures also result in some being inferior to others since they don't have the same capacities to live the life they value.

Those injustices are not necessarily, however, perpetrated by individual wrongdoers, but rather are the effects of the collective arrangements of society. Many of the actions of individuals and even the government are not aimed at limiting opportunities or harming groups, they are working within the practices and norms of that structure. This is one of the reasons that it is not always possible to point out specific intentions of racists, for example, when heavy concentrations of pollutants end up in minority communities. The actors involved may well act within the guidelines laid out for the processes of picking a waste site, for instance. The social structures are the largely invisible framework in which we act. The background social structures, however, are products of human agency; for instance, racist motivation led to redlining and disinvestment in inner city minority neighborhoods. And patriarchy supported gendered occupations and the low pay that went with them. Nevertheless, many of these background social conditions are not necessarily supported by active racist or sexist actors. Redlined neighborhoods are no longer redlined but the legacy of those historical injustices persists, including the fact that minority families have much less wealth than white families, due to the consequences of not providing housing loans to black families and investment in minority neighborhoods. Further, there are other government policies and corporate actions, such as the subsidizing of commodity crops that result in an overabundance of cheap junk food swamping minority neighborhoods, which were not motivated by racism but nevertheless do have a disproportionate impact on the poor and minorities. The continuation of those policies in agriculture and food support corporate profits over human health but were not created to target harm to minorities or the poor. In that way they differ from directly racist or sexist policies. But they do have a differential impact on the poor and minorities leading to injustices.

5 Responsibility for Wrongs

Most theories of responsibility look for specific agents or collectives to hold responsible for the harm. As noted above, with these harms that result from the social structures, there are not necessarily identifiable wrongdoers who we can hold responsible for these injustices. There is not one identifiable person or group of persons who did some action that resulted in the harm and are thereby blameworthy for the harm. Many accounts of responsibility, particularly in the legal framework of criminal or tort law, are what are known as "liability" models (Young 2010, p. 97). There is a causal connection between someone doing or failing to do something that results in a harm to another person, that makes someone liable for blame for the harm. Who can we blame for there being no grocery store easily accessible to Dolores? Is the grocery store chain blameworthy for not locating a store in her neighborhood? Or is it the executives of banks and insurance companies who perpetrated redlining but are now long gone who are to blame? What about Dolores's lack of education, resulting in a low-paying job; or her being a single parent which is a result of an even more complex set of factors, including social gender norms, unequal funding of school and childcare, etc.? These harms are not necessarily caused by any agents' intentional actions, consequently there is no individual or group responsible to hold accountable. If your theory of justice and responsibility only pertains to individual wrongdoings, then these structural cases go unaccounted for.

Theories of responsibility that focus on the guilty party who caused the harm or is liable for harm are backward-looking, assigning blame based on fault or liability to harm. But we also talk about "taking responsibility" for the future to ensure that harm or injustices do not occur. That approach doesn't ask whether anyone intended harm or injustice. Accounts of this type of responsibility are offered by Young, what she calls the "social connection model" (Young 2010, p. 96), and Darrel Moellendorf calls "social responsibility" (Moellendorf 2014, p. 152-ff). Both require us, as members of a political order, to collectively assume responsibility for changing the social structures that produce and reproduce these unjust outcomes. This is a shared responsibility of citizens to make these changes. As Young says:

> The social connection model finds that all those who contribute by their actions to structural processes with some unjust outcomes share responsibility for the injustice.... Being responsible in relation to structural injustice means that one has an obligation to join with others who share that responsibility in order to transform the structural processes to make their outcomes less unjust. (Young 2010, p. 96)

This sense of responsibility doesn't replace the liability model but is in addition to it. Living in a political society in which injustices occur because of social processes of society, whether they result in rules or practices or even norms, means that we are collectively responsible for those harms. Collectively through our institutions we maintain these processes, and we can change those that are contributing to inequalities.

Solving the problems of injustices inherent in the food system requires that we change the background conditions that structure the relationships in society and not focus merely on individual bad actors. Again, quoting Young: "promoting justice in social structure and their consequences implies restructuring institutions and relationships to *prevent* these threats to people's basic well-being" (Young 2010, p. 34). With structural injustices the bad outcomes are a result of many social structures that function to oppress certain groups of people. In Dolores's case she finds herself caught in a network of social structures that grossly disadvantage her; they leave her without basic opportunities that others in society have: they result in her being oppressed by the social structure. If we acknowledge that those social structures oppress some groups in society, and if we are committed to a political theory that requires that everyone have the social conditions of freedom in terms of basic capabilities for well-being (Anderson 1999, p. 316) then we are collectively responsible to change those social structures that result in some people not having those social conditions for freedom. This is true whether we are personally benefiting from the injustices suffered by some groups. Society may not have to guarantee equality of resources, according to egalitarian justice, but society is obligated to ensure that people's basic capacities are roughly the same (at least for those capacities necessary for human well-being). There is a particular responsibility for redress if there are limitations on freedom that are a result of social arrangements created and sustained by the political system.

The social system can be changed; as John Rawls noted "The social system is not unchangeable order beyond human control but a pattern of human action" (Rawls 1999, p. 88). Through structural reform we can change institutional rules, social practices, structural relationships, social background conditions that lead to limited opportunity sets, such as those we see in the food system. We are responsible for preventing those injustices that are a product of our social structures even if we do not intend those oppressive outcomes. Changing the social structure so it does not produce unfair outcomes in one domain will have effects in others. For example, expanding capacities to participate in processes where decisions are made, having access to political power, education, and other opportunities that lead to wealth, will change the distributional outcomes, and provide agency to those with the expanded capacities. Changing the policies and incentives around where grocery stores are located, constructing favorable zoning and taxation (Noll 2020; Dieterle 2015, p. 50), changing the government's policies about what foods it subsidizes, what chemicals can be used in agriculture, what foods it requires in school lunch programs, changing the rules around marketing unhealthy foods, particularly to children, are some of the changes to the social structure particularly in regard to the government's role that would make significant changes to individuals' lives. There are formal and informal social rules around food that may be more difficult to change. Beliefs about what foods are healthy and tasty, for example, are difficult to change. Nevertheless, there was successful change in the social rules around tobacco use, so there is precedent that indicates that positive change could be realized. Larger societal changes around alleviating gross income inequality, lack of affordable housing and childcare, and so on would also greatly impact the food choices of those with low income and minorities.

6 Summary and Conclusion

Acknowledging that harms perpetrated by the background social structure within which individuals act in relation to the food system are wrongful matters of justice is to identify them as violations against what people are owed, what they deserve. People deserve equality, meaning, among other things, that they deserve equal opportunities for developing their capabilities to live good lives. Egalitarian justice of this sort is not so concerned about equality of resources. Rather the questions are whether individuals have the capabilities to live meaningful lives, and whether their opportunities are constrained by our collective human arrangements. I have focused to a large extent on the background conditions which limit people's opportunities and abilities, which result in these wrongful differential impacts. Importantly, I pointed out that these harms are not all the result of bad actors, racists trying to perpetrate harm on certain populations, for example. They are wrongs without wrongdoers. Rather, many, maybe most, are products of agents within the processes of the social structure advancing their own interests. Indeed, some of those unwittingly perpetrating harms are acting within systems which are products of historical structural injustices in society that cause populations to be vulnerable to these abuses. Again, the actors themselves did not create those injustices. These injustices result from the social structures within which actors act. Individuals who find themselves with these unequal capacities, vis-à-vis other actors in society, are oppressed by these circumstances. These circumstances affect their agency, which in turn affects their moral standing in society; they cannot stand as equal citizens to others. Their children eat unhealthy diets, which results in bad health outcomes well into the future. Those diets also affect their children's academic abilities, in turn resulting in long-term diminished abilities for them. All these effects result in dignity harm to the victims. Egalitarian theories of justice are concerned with ensuring that individuals can stand up as equals with one another. These limitations on individuals' capacities make that difficult or impossible.

Claims of injustice are linked with calls for responsibility, who owes the debt or treatment to another. If we acknowledge that the current patterns of distribution of burdens, opportunities, and powers are unfair, who is responsible for ensuring that the wrongful harms are not perpetrated going forward? Because so much of the structural injustices are not products of individual action, attributions of responsibility are resisted. There is not necessarily someone or some government policy at fault for the unfair treatment of the poor and minorities. Traditionally, theories of responsibility have focused on the guilty party who caused the harm or is liable for harm. Accounts of responsibility are often backward-looking, assigning blame based on fault or liability to harm. Here I argued for a notion of collective responsibility for "taking responsibility" to prevent injustices going forward. This account of responsibility is to collectively assume responsibility for changing the social structures that produce and reproduce these unjust outcomes. This is a shared responsibility of citizens to make these changes. As a start on those changes, we should recognize that (healthy) food and a decent environment are not the same types of goods as other goods. They are not commodities that we might or might not have, nor are they fungible goods that could be traded off for other goods. They are preconditions to the exercise of other capacities, such as health, political participation, or education. Not having access to decent food or living in an unhealthy environment undermines the exercise of these other capacities. Hence, healthy food and a decent environment are necessary conditions for exercising the capacities to live any life. Conceiving of healthy food and a healthy environment as basic human rights acknowledges that people cannot do or be anything without adequate (and healthy[5]) food and a decent environment.

References

ACLU (2010) Unshared bounty: how structural racism contributes to the creation and persistence of food deserts. https://digitalcommons.nyls.edu/cgi/viewcontent.cgi?article=1002&context=racial_justice_project

Aldon A, Agyeman J (2011) Cultivating food justice. The MIT Press, Cambridge

Alkon A, Mare TM (2012) Food sovereignty in US food movements: radical visions and neoliberal constraints. Agric Hum Values 29:347–359

Almarshad MI, Algonaiman R, Alharbi HF, Almujaydil MS, Barakat H (2022) Relationship between ultra-processed food consumption and risk of diabetes mellitus: a mini-review. Nutrients 14(12):2366. https://doi.org/10.3390/nu14122366. PMID: 35745095; PMCID: PMC9228591

Anderson E (1999) What's the point of equality? Ethics 109(2):287–337

Bjornstad P, Drews KL, Caprio S, Gubitosi-Klug R, Nathan DM, Tesfaldet B, Tryggestad J, White NH, Zeitler P (2021) Long-term complications in youth-onset Type 2 Diabetes. N Engl J Med 385:416–426

Bower KM, Thorpe RJ Jr, Rohde C, Gaskin DJ (2014) The intersection of neighborhood racial segregation, poverty, and urbanicity and its impact on food store availability in the United States. Prev Med 58:33–39

Brownell K, Warner K (2009) The perils of ignoring history: big tobacco played dirty and millions died. How similar is big food? The Millbank Quarterly

[5] There is limited space to argue for the claim that the right to food is a right to "healthy food" (and culturally appropriate) and not just any food. If the current food injustices show us anything, it is that unhealthy calories are detrimental to the capability to live a flourishing life. See: Gonzales (2012); Raponi (2017).

Chung C, Meyer S (1999) Do the poor pay more for food? An analysis of grocery store availability and food price disparities. J Consumer Aff 33(2):276–296
Dieterle JM (2015) Food deserts and Lockean property. In: Dieterle JM (ed) Just food. Rowman & Littlefield, London
Dworkin R (1981) What is equality? II. Equality of resources. Philos Public Aff 30(10):283–345
Fields S (2004) The fat of the land: do agricultural subsidies foster poor health? Environ Health Perspect 112(14):A820–A823. https://doi.org/10.1289/ehp.112-a820
Franck C, Grandi SM, Eisenberg MJ (2013) Agricultural subsidies and the American obesity epidemic. Am J Prev Med 45:327–333
Freeman A (2007) Fast food oppression. Calif Law Rev 95. No 2221
Gilson E (2014) Vote with your fork? Responsibility for food justice. Soc Philos Today 30
Gonzales C (2012) The global food system, human right, and the environment. Nat Resour Environ 26
Guthman J (2008) "If They Only Knew": color blindness and universalism in California Alternative Food Institutions. Prof Geogr 60(3):387–397
Guthman J (2011) Weighing in obesity, food justice, and the limits of capitalism. UC Press
Hall KD et al (2019) Ultra-processed diets cause excess calorie intake and weight gain: an inpatient randomized controlled trial of Ad Libitum food intake. Cell Metab 30(1):67–77. e3
Harmon K (2010) Addicted to fat: overeating may alter the brain as much as hard drugs. https://www.scientificamerican.com/article/addicted-to-fat-eating/
Haslanger S (2012) Resisting reality: social construction and social critique. Oxford University Press
Ip SS, Arcury TA, Grzywacz JG, Trejo G, Quandt SA (2015) Profiles of food security for US farmworker households and factors related to dynamic of change. Am J Public Health 105(10):e42–e47
Jones A, Silverstone T, Duncan M, Gormley J, Michael C (2019) The food deserts of Memphis: inside America's hunger capital | Divided Cities. The Guardian, Nov. 20. https://www.theguardian.com/cities/video/2019/nov/20/theres-food-its-just-not-real-food-inside-americas-hunger-capital-video
Karpyn AE, Riser D, Tracy T, Wang R, Shen YE (2019) The changing landscape of food deserts. UNSCN Nutr 44:46–53. PMID: 32550654; PMCID: PMC7299236
Khazan OK (2014) Fast-food chains disproportionately target black children. The Atlantic
Kitch S, Joan MG, Mauricio Mejía G, El-Sayed S, Spackman C, Vitullo J (2021) Gendered and racial injustices in American food systems and cultures. Humanities. https://www.mdpi.com/journal/humanities
Moellendorf D (2014) The moral challenge of dangerous climate change. Cambridge University Press, Cambridge
Natasha G (2012) One-third of our greenhouse gas emissions come from agriculture. Nature. 10.1038. https://science.sciencemag.org/content/360/6392/987; https://insideclimatenews.org/news/08082019/ipcc-agriculture-report-food-system-overhaul-climate-change-deforestation
Neff RA et al (2009) Food systems and public health disparities. J Hunger Environ Nutr 4,3–4 : 282-314. https://doi.org/10.1080/19320240903337041
Nesheim MC, Oria M, Yih PT (eds) (2015) A framework for assessing effects of the food system. Committee on a Framework for Assessing the Health, Environmental, and Social Effects of the Food System. National Academies Press (US), Washington (DC)
Nestle M (2002) Food politics. UC Press, Berkeley
Nestle M (2018) Unsavory truth. Basic Books, New York
Noll S (2020) Growing resistance to systems of oppression: an exploration of the transformative power of urban agriculture. Open Philos 3(1):56
Nussbaum M (2003) Capabilities as fundamental entitlements: Sen and Social Justice. Fem Econ 9(2–3):33–59
Odoms-Young AM (2018) Examining the impact of structural racism on food insecurity: implications for addressing racial/ethnic disparities. Fam Community Health 41(Suppl 2 FOOD INSECURITY AND OBESITY):S3–S6

Penniman L (2018) Farming While Black: soul fire farm's practical guide to liberation on the land. Chelsea Green Publishing
Petersen R, Pan L, Blanck HM (2019) Racial and ethnic disparities in adult obesity in the United States: CDC's tracking to inform state and local action. Prev Chronic Dis 16:180579
Pew Research Center (2015) The American Middle Class is Losing Ground. http://www.pewsocialtrends.org/2015/12/09/the-american-middle-class-is-losing-ground/
Pollan M (2009) Food rules. Penguin, New York
Raponi S (2017) A defense of the human right to adequate food. Res Publica 23:102
Rawls J (1999) A theory of justice, Revised ed. Harvard University Press, Cambridge
Rothstein R (2017) The color of law. Norton and Company, New York
Schieder J, Gould E (2016) "Women's work" and the gender pay gap: how discrimination, societal norms, and other forces affect women's occupational choices—and their pay. Economic Policy Institute. https://www.epi.org/publication/womens-work-and-the-gender-pay-gap-how-discrimination-societal-norms-and-other-forces-affect-womens-occupational-choices-and-their-pay/
Schmitz D (1998) Taking responsibility. In: Schmitz D, Godin R (eds) Social welfare and individual responsibility. Cambridge University Press, Cambridge
Sen A (1992) Inequality reexamined. Harvard University Press, Cambridge
Strings S (2019) Fearing the black body the racial origins of fat phobia. NYU Press, New York
Szende J (2015) Food deserts, justice and the distributive paradigm. In: Dieterle JL (ed) Just food. Rowman & Littlefield, London
Thomson P (2015) From field to fork. Oxford University Press, New York
Unshared Bounty: How structural racism contributes to the creation and persistence of food deserts (with American Civil Liberties Union). https://digitalcommons.nyls.edu/racial_justice_project/3/
USDA (n.d.). https://www.ers.usda.gov/data-products/food-access-research-atlas/go-to-the-atlas/
Veerman J, Lennert EF, Beeck V, Jan J, Barendregt JP, Mackenbach J (2009) By how much would limiting TV food advertising reduce childhood obesity? Eur J Public Health 19(4):365–369
Véliz C et al (2019) Sugar, taxes, & choice. Hastings Center Rep 49(6):22–31
Werkheiser I, Noll S (2014) From food justice to a tool of the status quo: three sub-movements within local food. J Agric Environ Ethics 27:201–210
Young IM (2010) Responsibility for justice. Oxford University Press, Cambridge

Advancing an Unjust Neutrality: Christian Nationalism as a Majority Right

Emily R. Gill

Abstract Christian nationalism provides a good example of a movement that purports to represent a vulnerable majority and also of the dangers of such a movement to liberal democracy. First, it does not represent a majority. On several measures Christian nationalism and personal religiosity correlate inversely rather than directly. Second, self-identified Christian conservative Paul Miller incisively critiques Christian nationalism as an effort to protect the majority cultural identity as a way of maintaining cultural power. Finally, although Miller advocates for cultural neutrality, I question his interpretation of it because it too easily elides into a type of majority rights.

1 Introduction

The last two decades of the twentieth century witnessed new attention to the rights of minorities or minority cultures as a central component of political justice. Will Kymlicka, for example, has advocated extensively for the recognition of cultural diversity. National minorities, whether Canada's indigenous people or the Québécois, are territorially concentrated cultures now incorporated into a large, multination state. Self-government or group-differentiated rights, he argued, should protect the cultural autonomy of the particular societal culture, which provides a context of choice, including both "a range of meaningful options" and "a secure sense of identity and belonging" (Kymlicka 1995, pp. 83, 105; see also pp. 10–11, 14–15, 26–33, 45–48, 58–59). The existence of ethnic groups within a national community, on the other hand, results from immigration, which we typically regard as a matter of choice as opposed to involuntary subsumption under a broader national authority, although these individuals or groups may still claim various rights and exemptions

E. R. Gill (✉)
Bradley University, Peoria, IL, USA
e-mail: gill@fsmail.bradley.edu

G. A. Babst, W.-c. Lee (eds.), *Contemporary Facets of Injustice*, AMINTAPHIL: The Philosophical Foundations of Law and Justice 13,
https://doi.org/10.1007/978-3-031-93783-5_6

that facilitate the expression of particularity within the dominant culture (pp. 62, 66–69, 78, 95–101, 177–178). Kymlicka's general point is that whereas immigrants or ethnic groups may sometimes accuse the larger community of forced *exclusion*, they cannot charge the larger community with forced *inclusion*.

The ground has now shifted to a debate about the need for majority rights. Some argue that in many cases, numerical majority preferences are not reflected in policy decisions concerning immigration and cultural issues. This is partly because elites are often perceived to subscribe to a cosmopolitan ethos differing from that of ordinary citizens, and partly because legal developments protecting minority rights such as court decisions block particular majority demands. In fact, even political advocacy in terms of majority ethnicity is frowned upon (Koopmans and Orgad 2023, pp. 6–9; see also Kaufmann 2023, pp. 77–79).[1] Meanwhile, majorities feel vulnerable to demands that they adapt to minority rights and interests. Koopmans and Orgad note that while minority religious groups may practice their religion as part of their group identity, majority members exercise their right to religious expression and practice only as individuals rather than as a group, because their public identity is required to be neutral. "Yet, if minorities have a right to preserve their religious identities, why should majorities, on equal conditions, not have such a right?" (Koopmans and Orgad 2023, p. 23; see also pp. 15, 22–28).

More specifically, majority-rights advocates dislike the fact that although they can freely exercise their right to religious expression and practice, it is within the context of a public sphere that in a liberal democracy is supposed to be neutral toward all manifestations of religion as well as nonreligion. That is, although they share a religious identity, they lack the type of recognition that is accorded to minority religions or cultures. Jehovah's Witness children, for example, need not salute the flag in school (*West Virginia Board of Education v. Barnette* (319 U.S. 624 [1943]), Seventh-Day Adventists need not forego unemployment compensation by refusing to work on their Sabbath of Saturday (*Sherbert v. Verner*, 374 U.S. 398 [1963]), and the children of Old Order Amish may terminate their schooling short of the state-mandated requirement (*Wisconsin v. Yoder* (406 U.S. 205 [1972]). A majority that feels threatened, however, cannot as a group protect itself against what it views as the incursions of the larger society that threaten the maintenance of its own identity or solidarity. The rights of minority groups secure their protection, but the rights of a majority to secure legislation that allows its members in accordance with their religious beliefs to discriminate against Muslims or sexual minorities, for example, go unrecognized.

The majority-rights initiative emerges in part from a slide from thin multiculturalism, in which different cultural groups all endorse basic liberal principles, to thick multiculturalism, which recognizes both liberal and illiberal cultures. Although both types may involve external protections against forced assimilation into the national culture, on Kymlicka's view the state should not allow a culture to enforce

---

[1] Orgad and Koopman's anthology is a fine compendium of chapter that gave rise to the idea that Christian nationalism is species of claims to majority rights.

against its members the preservation of any particular cultural character. This would reflect the ideal of thin multiculturalism. Thick multiculturalism, however, would argue that organizations or groups "must *to some extent* be impervious to the values of the wider liberal society" if they are to maintain their integrity (Kukathas 1992a, p. 680, emphasis original; see also Kukathas 1992b; Kymlicka 1992, p. 142; Kymlicka 1995, pp. 104, 113). Although this debate is beyond the scope of this essay, it resonates with the point that "The rebellion against minority rights emerged due to a growing suspicion that such rights could be used to enhance a cultural and religious takeover" (Tamir 2023, p. 195; see pp. 189–198).

Christians are a religious majority in many nations such as the United States, yet some Christians, particularly conservative Christians, feel threatened by a combination of the increasing secularity of the culture and the perception that their concerns are not taken seriously, unlike those of other groups. These Christians want to protect the traditional values that they espouse and that they understand to be central to the nation's identity. That is, they may constitute a religious majority, but they do not experience their identity as that of a cultural majority. As a result, they do not think that the government is truly neutral when the values of other groups protected but their own are not.

It is crucial that groups such as Jehovah's Witnesses, Seventh-Day Adventists, and Old Order Amish sought exemptions solely for their own religious practices within their groups, not for practices that would impinge upon the lives of people who do not share their beliefs. The Supreme Court has made a number of decisions protecting religious liberty that were not exemptions. Rather, the rationale was embedded in the protection of additional rights that were not necessarily religious in nature. In *Meyer v. Nebraska* (262 U.S. 390 [1923]), the court upheld the right of a Lutheran school to teach children in German, invalidating a state law that had prohibited this practice until eighth grade. In *Pierce v. Society of Sisters* (268 U.S. 510[1925]), the court struck down an Oregon law that required children to attend public schools rather than private ones, religious or not. These are "lynchpins of constitutional law—not as decisions about religious exemptions from otherwise acceptable norms, but rather as decisions about protecting the rights of parents to direct their children's education" (Lupu and Tuttle 2014, p. 184; see 183–184). This protection aimed to protect good public policy.

Other jurisprudence has protected religious liberty as part of a broad right to expressive liberty, freedom of association, and equality. In *Cantwell v. Connecticut* (310 U.S. 296 [1940]), for example, the court protected street proselytization by Jehovah's Witnesses, but clarified in subsequent decisions that this right was not limited to religious persuasion (Lupu and Tuttle 2014, p. 185). In *West Virginia Board of Education v. Barnette* (319 U.S. 624 [1943]), the court could have granted a religious exemption to Jehovah's Witnesses protecting schoolchildren from being forced to support the American flag while reciting the Pledge of Allegiance. Instead, however, the court simply barred the enforcement of the flag salute, meaning that "all students have a right to refuse a state-compelled affirmation of political loyalty," whether for religious or other reasons (Lupu and Tuttle 2014, p. 187; see 183–190). Secular claims may have moral force equal to religious ones. They may sometimes exert greater moral force when they reflect our national commitment to free and equal citizenship. All of these decisions expand the application of the core commitments of a liberal polity, rather than augmenting them for some people at the expense of others. Majority-rights advocates, however, in Kymlicka's terms advocate for thick multiculturalism, which would allow a majority to operate in some ways that are impervious to wider liberal values. Broad rights to expressive liberty and equality that protect cultural or religious minorities are not "special rights," as some formerly termed LGBT antidiscrimination laws. They pertain to everyone. Rather, the rights desired by some majority-rights advocates could themselves be termed "special rights" when they would permit the enforcement of religious and cultural norms upon those who do not share them.

Christian nationalism provides a good example of a movement that purports to represent a vulnerable majority in need of protection and also of the dangers of such a movement to liberal democracy. First, I shall sketch the contours of the Christian nationalist movement. Although many conservative Christians purport to be vulnerable despite Christianity's majority status in the United States, Christian nationalists do not even represent a thwarted majority of Christian religionists. Their seeking after political power and influence is less an effort to preserve a threatened identity as Christians than a desire to impose their particular interpretation of American culture on all. Second, I shall summarize an incisive critique of Christian nationalism by self-identified Christian conservative Paul Miller. For him, the problem with Christian nationalism is the belief that government should protect and promote the nation's majority cultural identity. The Christian right "shows more nationalism and less republicanism, more concern for restoring Christian power than for shoring up the institutions and norms of republican governance" (Miller 2022, p. 165). He is correct in much of this critique. Finally, however, I shall question Miller's contention that we can embrace cultural neutrality while eschewing moral neutrality. He implies that recent public policies protecting the free exercise of religion are culturally neutral in their protection of liberty, resulting in both legal and cultural disestablishment and strengthening neutrality. I suggest that what he terms cultural neutrality in religion is a type of majority rights.

2 Conservative Christianity and Christian Nationalism

"The notion of cultural majority rights is empirically implausible, conceptually incoherent, and normatively indefensible on liberal and democratic grounds" (Bauböck 2023, p. 36; see pp. 36–45; see also Goodhart 2023, pp. 281–282; Ziblatt 2023, pp. 304–305). Empirically, majorities are divided enough that no segment is truly a majority. Conceptually, majorities may vote to protect specific facets of a public culture, but they change through the formation of ever-shifting coalitions. Normatively, possible definitions of majorities that might ground majority rights are insufficiently firm. Advocates "must argue instead that groups that used to belong to historically dominant majorities have become minorities and this is what justifies their claims to cultural protection and rights" (Bauböck 2023, p. 56; see pp. 45–56). Ranier Bauböck prefers cultural freedom for all in an inclusive and pluralistic public culture. It is one thing for a culture to be shaped through democratic self-government, including contributions by immigrants through their individual rights and citizenship. It is quite another for this shaping to take place through special rights for a particular cultural majority. This state of affairs represents anything but neutrality.

Many conservatives in the United States reject strict separation between church and state, arguing that the government is not neutral toward religion when it accords benefits to secular organizations while withholding them from religious ones. Some who claim that government financial support for religious schools instantiates neutrality, however, are not neutral *among* religions. States have resisted voucher programs on realizing that Muslim schools as well as Christian ones would be eligible. Louisiana adopted such a program only when a Muslim school withdrew a prior request to participate. One state representative there said, "I actually support funding for teaching the fundamentals of America's Founding Fathers' religion, which is Christianity, in public schools or private schools [but] we need to insure [*sic*] that it does not open the door to fund radical Islam schools" (Wexler 2019, pp. 110–111; see also Gill 2019, p. 76; Stewart 2019, p. 204). Some Christians will forego money rather than award it to minority religions (Wexler 2019, p. 121). They do so to protect what they view as the Christian majority.

This example provides a useful segue to the point that much current jurisprudence serendipitously supports the desires of Christian nationalists for political supremacy. Powerful segments of the conservative religious community promote not pluralism, but rather a particular interpretation of Christianity rooted in a biblical worldview. This construction "purports to derive its legitimacy from its claim to represent a specific identity unique to and representative of the American nation" (Stewart 2019, p. 5; see pp. 3–11). Christian nationalism is a political movement as well as a social and cultural one. It treats Bible study as political advocacy, arguing that the Bible mandates adherence to right-wing policy positions on deregulation (pp. 48–51). It treats history not as something to be studied, but instead to be mined and interpreted as a means to its own ends (p. 139). It identifies pastors and congregants who will vote on the basis of biblical values to the extent that it is political beliefs, not religious ones, that signify belonging. To put this differently, it elevates culture and power over principle.

Although Christians are a majority of religionists in the United States, they are not of one mind. Sociologists Andrew Whitehead and Samuel Perry demonstrate that the strongest predictor of Christian nationalism among Christians is political conservatism (Whitehead and Perry 2020, p. 13). However, "religious commitment and Christian nationalism appear to foster distinct moral worldviews that differ in critical ways" (Whitehead and Perry 2020, p. 13). Christian nationalism and white evangelicalism overlap, but many white evangelicals reject it (pp. x, 20). Some have argued not only that white evangelicals are a diverse group, but also that most seek to mobilize religious action rather than political action (Smith 2000). Whitehead and Perry note, however, that just as not all evangelicals are Christian nationalists, not all Christian nationalists are evangelicals. All Christian nationalists, though, want to protect their cultural and political interests (pp. 57–59, 87, 153–154). They explain the 2016 "religious vote" for Donald Trump and their continuing support through the cultural framework of Christian nationalism rather than as a defense of Christian morality (pp. 59–84).

Sociologists Philip Gorski and Samuel Perry identify a number of indicators on which the higher the agreement score, the greater the likelihood that an individual is a Christian nationalist. These statements include: the founding documents are divinely inspired, the success of the U.S. is part of God's plan, the federal government should declare the nation a Christian nation, the federal government should advocate Christian values, the federal government should allow Christian symbols to be displayed in public places, and the federal government should allow prayer in public schools. For one indicator, that the government should strictly separate church and state, a low score is of course a greater measure of Christian nationalism (Gorski and Perry 2022, pp. 15–16). These measures help one resist the impulse to think of all Christian patriots as Christian nationalists. As David French points out, political values and activism may legitimately be shaped by faith, as in the civil rights movement. "The problem with Christian nationalism isn't with Christian participation in politics but rather the belief that there should be Christian *primacy* in politics and law" (French 2024, emphasis original; see also Darling 2024).

For Whitehead and Perry, Christian nationalism is a cultural framework that combines conservative ideology, a literal interpretation of the Bible, an apocalyptic view of social decline, and the centrality of national military power. It identifies American identity with Christian identity. Religious commitment is unsurprisingly associated with Christian nationalism (Whitehead and Perry 2020, p. 13). Whitehead and Perry show, however, that although Christian nationalism correlates with personal religiosity, these characteristics influence Americans' views on many political issues in opposite directions. As Americans become more personally religious or devout in church attendance, Bible reading, and prayer, they are less likely, for example, to say that Middle Eastern refugees are a terrorist threat, less likely to think that citizens must be forced to show respect for American traditions, and more likely to believe that the federal government should have stricter gun laws. Americans in greater agreement with Christian nationalism, however, go the opposite way in their views on all of these issues. "Appeals to someone's religion, in this case Christianity, *may* involve a plea to live out transcendent Christian values of love, mercy, or justice. Appeals to Christian nationalism, by contrast, involve either a proprietary claim or a call to arms, always in response to a perceived threat. In short, Christian nationalism is all about power" (Whitehead and Perry 2020, p. 86, italics original; see pp. 82–87; 14–15). Personal religiosity and Christian nationalism, however, both track in a conservative direction regarding family values. Threats to the traditional family appear not only as symptoms of sin, "but as threats to the very fabric of American society" (p. 148; see pp. 121–149). Therefore, Christian nationalists desire public policy that reflects these values, including liberty to discriminate against those who represent a threat to them. Without such protection, in

Koopmans and Orgad's terms they feel pressured to adapt to the demands of a minority's rights and interests.

Christian nationalists support boundaries, both physical and cultural, holding that "*real* Americans are native-born white Protestants" (Whitehead and Perry 2020, p. 91, emphasis original). They are suspicious even of Christian immigrants such as Mexicans, out-groups such as overwhelmingly-Christian blacks, and those of other religions or no religion (pp. 90–114). Much of their animosity, Whitehead and Perry suggest, embodies the idea that "Christian nationalism is fundamentally about *preserving or returning* to a mythic society in which traditional hierarchical relationships ... are upheld, and authority structures are biblical and just" (Whitehead and Perry 2020, p. 105, emphasis original; see pp. 90–119). Christian nationalists in this way exemplify Bauböck's point about historically dominant groups that have become minorities but believe that their former dominance entitles them to cultural protection.

Whitehead and Perry argue that the existence of Christian nationalism influences the lives of all Americans because all must interpret it, whether by embracing, accommodating, resisting, or rejecting it. This imperative cannot help but show up politically in election outcomes. Moreover, those who embrace or resist it are more alike across religious traditions than are those who, for example, embrace and resist it within the same tradition. By portraying specific aims in religious garb, it "serves to legitimate the demands, wants, and desires of those embracing Christian nationalism in the transcendent. If God says the United States should take a particular stance, or pass a specific law, who are we to argue?" (Whitehead and Perry 2020, p. 153; see pp. 152–161). Those who are non-Christian ostensibly have the right to adhere to their beliefs and to advocate for them, but implicitly they should avoid drawing attention to themselves—on my view a form of closeting. In sum, "Christian nationalist ideology is fundamentally focused on gaining and maintaining access to power. It seeks to ensure that one particular group, with a specific vision for the country, enjoys privileged access to the halls of power and has the ability to make the culture in its own image" (p. 161).

3 Christian Nationalism as Culturalist

As described by Paul Miller, nationalists in general believe that nations comprise "internally coherent cultural units," that each nation should constitute its own state both culturally and politically, and that each government must preserve its nation's cultural inheritance. Governments exist in part to preserve an intrinsically valuable national identity, human beings require this cohesiveness if they are to flourish, and nations themselves depend upon a strong predominant culture if they are to survive. Christian nationalists add to this formulation the fact that the United States is dominated by Anglo-Protestant or European Christian culture. This culture was an essential precondition for its formation and a necessary condition for its continuing sustenance (Miller 2022, p. 59; see also pp. 30–37). For Miller, Anglo-Protestant nationalists hold that people of any ethnicity or race can assimilate to the national culture. But they also "believe that Christianity should keep its historic place as the unquestioned and dominant cultural framework in the United States, and that the government should actively construct and defend that cultural framework" (p. 60; see also pp. 59, 84, 145).

Miller points out that because cultures overlap and change over time, they cannot be considered distinct or internally coherent. Moreover, how does a nation identify one shared or unifying trait, such as language or religion, as indispensable, and who gets to decide? The United States, like many other nations, comprises many religions, as well as a number of versions of some of them. And people of these religions also exist within other nations (Miller 2022, pp. 63–71). National boundaries arguably have a practical value, but nations themselves are constructions of the imagination. "Nationalism amounts to Jim Crow on a global scale, an insistence that cultural majorities have a presumptive right to defend their culture with the power of the state" (p. 75; see pp. 71–77). Although individual rights and modern democracy—pagan Greeks invented electoral democracy—originated within an Anglo-Protestant context, these features can and do exist independently of it. "There is nothing uniquely Western about not wanting to be oppressed" (p. 83; see pp. 84–86). Yet Christian nationalists believe that without our historic Protestant public culture, support for the ideals of the Constitution and Declaration of Independence would disappear.

Some people are led astray by seeing the United States as a chosen people and thinking that it, like ancient Israel, is the ideal, the city on the hill, and a template for nation formation that we embody and should induce all other nations to emulate. They get this about as wrong as possible, argues Miller. "To the extent that the Bible presents Israel as a light for the nations, it is because Israel was meant to be an example of righteousness and obedience (Isaiah 42:6), a unique display of God's mercy, glory, beauty, and power (Isaiah 60), and because Israel was the vehicle for the Messiah who would accomplish salvation for all nations (Isaiah 49: 6)—not because of Israel's model of political organization, its tribal confederacy, or its cultural distinctiveness from other people" (Miller 2022, pp. 119–120; see pp. 112–142). Love of country when rightly ordered is good, but nationalism is self-love and a form of idolatry (pp. 138, 142).

Civic republicanism with its emphasis on individual civic virtue as the sustenance of political liberty is healthy, notes Miller. But the Christian Right holds that only Christian values can sustain civic virtue. Because it tends to prioritize Christianity and its power, it elides into Christian nationalism at the expense of Christian republicanism (Miller 2022, p. 160; see pp. 143–145, 151–160). In fact, "For most of American history, the ideology of Christian republicanism was little more than the moral fig leaf that White supremacy wore" (p. 161; see also p. 170). That is, the history of nationalism in the United States has manifested both racism and sectarianism. What Miller terms Jacksonian Christianity expresses a conformity to social and cultural values, or a tribal evangelicalism that may or may not extend to churchgoing or religious evangelicalism. Although Jacksonian nationalism has expanded to include both ethnic and religious minorities of which it approves, "Jacksonian tribalism is *culturalist*: they discriminate, fundamentally, on the basis of culture" (p. 170, emphasis original; see pp. 167–172; 180). By viewing themselves as the "real" Americans, they reject the true equality of all Americans.

In Miller's view (and in mine), many white evangelicals appear not to recognize the reality of intergenerational racial inequality or of systemic racism. With the diminution of legal discrimination, they view racism as primarily a matter of individual animus rather than as possessing corporate or institutional components (Miller 2022, pp. 181–194). This point is reflected by other commentators (Jones 2020, pp. 93–101; Butler 2021, pp. 86–88). Moreover, critics of government entitlements and or aid to the poor can "make racist arguments without using racist language" (Miller 2022, pp. 123–124). As diversity has led to a decline in conservative white Christian power, these Christians have become convinced that restoring this power is a precondition of the future of the United States. "Nationalism is an invitation to take one's group identity and make it an official state creed … the effort by social movements to gain the heft, prestige, and resources of a government, to use that government to solidity its privileges and pursue its goals" (Miller 2022, p. 199; see pp. 198–199).

It is the ideas, not the culture, that should be valorized as constitutive of American identity, concludes Miller. Drawing on Rogers Smith's conception of ethically constitutive stories (Smith 2003), he argues that there are better and worse methods of defining a common identity. Nationalism relies on an enforced cultural unity that the government must replicate and defend, whereas leftist multiculturalism breaks down into a tribalism that seems to reject our cultural heritage altogether. "Relentlessly deconstructing American patriotism is likely to fuel White nationalism on the one side and identity politics for minority groups on the other" (Miller 2022, p. 238; see pp. 231–242).

In fact, nationalism in its variations is for Miller itself a form of identity politics, but for the majority rather than a minority. It is divisive, as attempts at forced assimilation to Anglo-Protestant culture impels those who are not part of that culture to "flock to identity politics and tell us that we should define ourselves by some trait *other* than Anglo-Protestant nationality" (Miller 2022, p. 104, emphasis original; see pp. 104–109). We should honor the positive contributions of the founders and others but simultaneously recognize our failings. The ideals of the Declaration of Independence, the Constitution, and the writings of Abraham Lincoln and Frederick Douglass are universal, and can beckon us beyond both cultural and tribal loyalties to universalism. It is these ideals that should claim the assimilation of immigrants, not Anglo-Protestant culture, as the preeminent basis of the American nation. Dedication to these ideals excludes some, to be sure, but it is the correct basis for exclusion (pp. 242–244).

4 The Impossibility of Neutrality

Miller's trenchant critique of Christian nationalism is on point. He is committed to viewpoint neutrality, or the idea that the government should rarely intervene in or try to police culture. Several areas exist, however, in which he believes the state should not or cannot be neutral. First, although he elevates cultural pluralism over cultural uniformity, he also distinguishes between culture, on the one hand, and universal values or standards of justice, on the other. He argues that the government can promote civic virtue based on natural law but still eschew cultural engineering. "Natural law is the objective and universal moral code inherent in the created order accessible to the rightly formed intellect and applicable across boundaries of time and culture" (p. 89; see pp. 88–90, 93–97). Therefore, a government can embrace cultural neutrality without abandoning moral neutrality. That is, he believes that the government should embrace a "transcultural standard of justice" (p. 93). For him, the standard of natural law is that of human flourishing, or of aspects of life such as "laughter, sex, abstract thought, family, physical health and wholeness" that are intrinsic to a fully realized life (p. 94). Natural law, he asserts, protects democracy, religious freedom, and free culture from the extremes of both relativism and theocracy, and is therefore a key to justice.

Second, for Miller a state cannot be neutral regarding its own theory of justice. The government can promote American ideals without endorsing Anglo-Protestant culture. Third, states cannot be neutral regarding their own history. National symbols, holidays, and the commemoration of historical leaders are educational and they create emotional bonds. But "it is vitally important, in teaching our history, to leave it open to reinterpretation, reappropriation, and remixing with new cultural approaches" (Miller 2022, p. 96). Finally, the state cannot be neutral regarding mutually exclusive beliefs that carry implications for public policy. For example, it cannot be neutral between the conviction that human sexuality is fixed by nature and objective, and the conviction that it is socially constructed and malleable, without repealing all law pertaining to marriage and family. Substantive philosophical commitments in general should include the scope of religious freedom, civil rights, and antidiscrimination policy, as well as the meaning of the First Amendment and, crucially, "the purpose of the state itself" (p. 96; see pp. 95–96).

Justice rooted in natural law as human flourishing, however, does not appear as transcultural as Miller imagines. First, he notes that court battles in recent decades have resulted in large gains for religious freedom. "Though it may surprise many Christians to hear it, we are winning: not at imposing our view of the good on society, but at protecting the principle of liberty of conscience for everyone. And this is the right battle to wage" (Miller 2022, p. 100). Miller's choice of "winning" to describe our current jurisprudence is telling. In most cases, where there are winners there are also losers. With increasing public funds for some aspects of religious education, under equal access policies taxpayers must support religious beliefs with which they disagree. For some conservative Christians, liberty of conscience means the instantiation of public policy that allows employers to withhold from employees health benefits to which they have religious objections. Although Miller holds that "the solution isn't to give up on neutrality; it is to *strengthen* neutrality" (p. 101, emphasis original), the results of some of this strengthening are far from neutral for some.

Second, Miller says that the government cannot be neutral between mutually exclusive beliefs, particularly about family law. But consider marriage equality, for example. Although he does not specifically address this issue, is it not a compromise between confining marriage to traditional couples, on the one hand, and abolishing marriage altogether as a public institution, on the other? The government is neutral between traditional couples and same-sex couples desiring to marry. On the other hand, a substantive philosophical commitment concerning civil rights and nondiscrimination policy *could* exclude LGBT individuals from nondiscrimination policy if this were in accordance with what some would define as their free exercise of religion. But this policy would not be neutral between the interests of LGBT individuals and the interests of those who wish to discriminate because of their religious convictions. If justice requires that we not give up on neutrality but strengthen it instead, how do we decide on which issues we should be neutral? Moreover, majorities are formed from changing coalitions of smaller groups that are divided among themselves (Bauböck 2023, p. 36), as James Madison famously recognized. To put this differently, "All democratic politics is un-pluralistic in the simple sense that all parties and movements want to win, which means imposing their vision and their policy solutions on many people who object to them" (Ziblatt 2023, p. 282). That is, even when national majorities are formed, they are not necessarily democratic ones.

Third, Miller states, "Nationalism is the effort by social movements to gain the heft, prestige, and resources of a government, to use that government to solidify its privileges and pursue its goals" (Miller 2022, p. 199; see pp. 198–199). But if "we are winning," are not many Christian conservatives mounting an effort to gain public resources so that they may solidify their own interpretation of religious freedom as the correct one? Miller as a self-described conservative Christian has mounted an incisive critique of Christian nationalism. If American history should properly be open to reinterpretation and reappropriation as he declares, however, should not interpretation of the dictates of natural law be similarly open? Miller does not elaborate upon his conception of natural law beyond the standard of human flourishing.

Although I am not at all imputing to Miller the view about marriage of those termed the new natural lawyers, these advocates believe that secular, biologically based arguments should ground traditional marriage to the exclusion of other arrangements. Robert George, for example, has argued that marriage "is consummated and actualized by acts that are procreative in type, whether or not they are procreative in effect" (George 2003, p. 120). No other relationship can actualize this unity. For the new natural lawyers, pleasure, including masturbation and sexual activity that does not lead to vaginal intercourse even by a married couple, cannot properly ground sexual activity, because it is merely an instrument to achieve a good; it is not an intrinsic value such as that of marriage (Bamforth and Richards 2008, pp. 96–101). It is only a simulacrum, a futile attempt to reproduce, as it were, a good that is incapable of reproduction outside the norm.

I use this example because the new natural law theorists have grounded their arguments that particular goods, such as marriage, exert exclusive moral claims on individuals as they strive to realize the kind of life best suited to human nature and necessary to human flourishing. Although Miller opposes the tyranny of an enforced cultural unity, he appears to condone the longstanding tyranny of heteronormativity, or the idea that heterosexuality—and for that matter cisgender identity—is the norm in American culture. As put by Gordon Babst, heteronormativity instantiates monism, or the idea that one way of being is "normal" and that alternatives are deviations. Human sexual pluralism, on the other hand, is premised on the assumption "that human beings are sexual beings, not types of sexual beings" (Babst 2009, p. 185). Heteronormativity is akin to an establishment of religion: one kind of sexuality or of religion is the norm, and it is superior to all others. By contrast, in liberal democratic societies different people hold different ideas about what human flourishing means to them. As long as the pursuit of one's own vision of human flourishing does not harm others, advocates of natural law based on human flourishing should not be opposing it.

Miller rightly criticizes constitutional lawyer Adrian Vermeule's conviction that the government should direct people toward a correct version of the good in what Vermeule terms common-good constitutionalism. This type of constitutionalism opposes both viewpoint neutrality and cultural pluralism. Liberalism to Vermeule is not neutral, and therefore conservatives need to fight back (Miller 2022, p. 91). Miller, however, thinks that neutrality should be strengthened rather than abandoned. A good example is his assertion that viewpoint neutrality allows both drag queens and fundamentalist Christians to use public libraries and host events there. Libraries can regulate conduct, but not belief or identity (pp. 99–100). I question, however, the neutrality of some of his other views.

If conservatives are worried about the future of Western civilization, Miller argues, Western ideas should be revived not on the national level but locally—"in the home, the pews, the classroom, the school board, and the city council: localism is far more accountable and carries fewer dangers than nationalism" (Miller 2022, p. 110; see pp. 110–111). He champions federalism as a means for people of diverse views of justice to live in peace, since each is a local majority. What if San Francisco wants to defund the police and become "a green, eco-communist, pot-smoking, drag-queen-dancing hippie utopia," or what if Texas wants to abolish regulations and taxes and become "the world's most well-armed anarcho-libertarian paradise? Why should I care, and why should I stop them? More to the point, why should Washington, DC [*sic*], stop them?" This approach, however, merely shifts the geography of the majority-minorities issue without granting either side the relief it might crave.

For Miller, then, pluralism means openness to "a diversity of *ways of living*, a diversity of communities, subcultures, and ideas for how to govern" (p. 260, italics original). As we have seen, one of the areas where the government cannot be neutral is concerning its own theory of justice. Miller's preferred theory is locally based. But if nationalism is Jim Crow on a global scale that favors cultural majorities, his version of localism is Jim Crow a local scale. The proponents in each case insist "that cultural majorities have a presumptive right to defend their culture with the power of the state" (p. 75). The problem is not that a case cannot be made for his theory. The problem instead is that he presents his theory as augmenting neutrality.

5 The Lure of Majority Culture

Some current advocates for majority rights point to the extent to which national majorities may be vulnerable to the cultural and economic forces of globalization. Although international law has mandated the protection of minority interests from majority nationalism, nations may adopt policies to protect their domestic languages and cultures internationally. This point suggests through a "parity of reasoning argument" that both minority and majority rights require protection but in different forums (Da Silva and Weinstock 2023, pp. 132–145). Kymlicka agrees that majorities can be vulnerable in this way, but he also points out that our concern should be "not just about having a commitment to liberal democracy, but also about having a moral commitment to enacting liberal democracy within a particular unit—that is, among a particular group of people on a particular territory" (Kymlicka 2023, p. 89). He would undoubtedly agree with Miller that nations should beware of an overriding dedication to preserving the majority national culture. A story of peoplehood perpetuated in any nation "will inevitably give centrality to the history, language, and culture of the historic founding majority, while viewing the history, language, and culture of minorities as at best abnormal, and at worst, as a threat to the cohesion or survival of the people" (p. 97; see also p. 102; Sandelind 2023, pp. 159–160). This description is congruent with many facets of Christian nationalism. It also resonates with the furious reaction of many political conservatives to the *New York Times*'s 2019 Project, which highlights the introduction of slavery into the American colonies.

Although Michael Da Silva and Daniel Weinstock argue that both majority and minority cultures may require protections under particular circumstances, they also make the crucial point that a majority's *perception* of vulnerability does not necessarily align with the *reality* of vulnerability. A national majority may feel a sense of loss on giving up an earlier unjust position of superiority, one that evolved that way, became assumed as the norm, and was resistant to challenge and hence achieved political consolidation. It did not form and grow in the light of our political principles, though it was always presented that way. Additionally, political movements and the media may contribute to or even induce perceptions of vulnerability (Da Silva and Weinstock 2023, pp. 146–147; see also Ziblatt 2023, pp. 294–295, on the rise of populism). Both of these points fit well with the rise of Christian nationalism. The growing diversity of religions in the U.S. and the recognition of LGBT rights have translated as a perceived threat in the eyes of many conservative Christians. These developments have also fed the perception that simply by having to recognize the rights of groups that formerly did not enjoy them, they are stripped of the enjoyment of their own rights as they interpret them. Therefore, they desire legal protection of the formerly dominant consensus.

Finally, the valorization of shared commitment to the universal ideals of our founding documents by those such as Miller still cannot guarantee cultural neutrality. This commitment is what Jared Goldstein terms constitutional nationalism, in contrast to ethnonationalism or religious nationalism, which focus upon race, ethnicity, or religion. The problem is that all adherents harbor different and conflicting national visions that they claim are grounded in constitutional devotion. "The Constitution has served as a magic mirror onto which Americans have gazed and found projections of themselves and their dreams for the nation" (Goldstein 2022, p. 6; see pp. 5–10). Goldstein's chapters each address a different tradition or identity that a particular group views as inscribed into the Constitution, such as white, Christian, nativist—and even violent.

The difficulty of identifying universal ideals is also born out in the work of Kermit Roosevelt III, who argues that we should not be looking to the Declaration of Independence or the Constitution at all for inspiration today. The Declaration was a justification for revolution and for the natural equality of the white men who mounted it, which is why the Confederates claimed that it justified their separation from an unjust government. Reconstruction, though short-lived, destroyed founding America. We should look instead to the "new birth of freedom" enshrined in the Gettysburg Address and to the Civil War amendments, the aim of which was not unity but justice (Roosevelt 2022)—which itself is of course subject to multiple interpretations.

6 Conclusion

Much of liberal theory rests on the claim that the state should be neutral among rival conceptions of the good. But neutrality is never possible across the board. Commitment to the complete range of possibilities for diversity is unachievable, as is the realization of a thoroughgoing neutrality. A liberal democratic polity must be grounded in the particular range of values or preferences that a given interpretation of liberal democracy puts forward (Gill 2012, pp. 34–39). At their best, our own commitments are to a pluralism that valorizes individual rights. Christian nationalists, however, appear to view Anglo-Protestant culture as the norm, and as therefore neutral in some sense. This is why some maintain that they are disadvantaged by having to engage in religious practice "merely" as individuals, whereas the practice of minority religious groups is part of their group identity. Those who deviate from it threaten it. But a norm is not automatically neutral; it is merely the standard against which deviations are measured. As put by Clara Sandelind, "It may be that it is precisely because nationalism goes unnoticed that stories of nationhood that contain the violent [or nonviolent] oppression of minorities can be reproduced relatively uncontested, as the 'natural order of things'" (Sandelind 2023, p. 162). What Babst terms the "shadow establishment" exemplifies this point: Sunday closing laws, for instance, were based on a hidden and sometimes unnoticed sectarian rationale disguised as the secular purpose of providing a family day of rest (Babst 2002, pp. 57–58, 72–78).

Before recent advances in LGBT rights, many people implied that only gay, lesbian, or bisexual statuses were sexual orientations. They did not see straightness as a sexual orientation. When the Black Lives Matter movement arose, many people wanted to replace the slogan with "All Lives Matter." This alteration supposedly connoted neutrality, or equal concern and respect for all lives. When the well-being of the members of some groups is demonstrably of less concern than that of others, however, equity requires a different approach. The public identity of a Christianity-dominated culture appears as neutral to Christian nationalists. But to those who dissent, it is anything but neutral.

References

Babst GA (2002) Liberal constitutionalism, marriage, and sexual orientation: a contemporary case for dis-establishment. Peter Lang, New York

Babst GA (2009) Consuming its own? Heteronormativity *contra* human plurality. In: Babst GA, Gill ER, Pierceson J (eds) Moral argument, religion, and same-sex marriage: advancing the public good. Lexington Books, Lanham, pp 183–203

Bamforth N, Richards DAJ (2008) Patriarchal religion, sexuality, and gender: a critique of new natural law. Cambridge University Press, New York

Bauböck R (2023) Are there any cultural majority rights? In: Orgad L, Koopmans R (eds) Majorities, minorities, and the future of nationhood. Cambridge University Press, Cambridge, pp 35–61

Butler A (2021) White evangelical racism: the politics of morality in America. University of North Carolina Press, Chapel Hill

Cantwell v. Connecticut, 310 U.S. 296 (1940)

Da Silva M, Weinstock DM (2023) Reconciling the cultural claims of majorities and minorities. In: Orgad L, Koopmans R (eds) Majorities, minorities, and the future of nationhood. Cambridge University Press, Cambridge, pp 129–150

Darling D (2024) Christian nationalism is more nuanced than you might think. USA Today: February 19

French D (2024) What is Christian nationalism, exactly? New York Times: February 26

George R (2003) Neutrality, equality, and same-sex marriage. In: Wardle LD, Strasser M, Duncan WD, Coolidge DO (eds) Marriage and same-sex unions: a debate. Praeger, Westport, pp 119–132

Gill ER (2012) An argument for same-sex marriage: religious freedom, sexual freedom, and public expressions of civic equality. Georgetown University Press, Washington, D.C.

Gill ER (2019) Free exercise of religion in the liberal polity: conflicting interpretations. Palgrave Macmillan, Cham, Switzerland

Goldstein J (2022) Real Americans: national identity, violence, and the Constitution. University Press of Kansas, Lawrence

Goodhart D (2023) Legitimate populism and liberal overreach. In: Orgad L, Koopmans R (eds) Majorities, minorities, and the future of nationhood. Cambridge University Press, Cambridge, pp 280–293

Gorski PS, Perry SL (2022) The flag and the cross: white Christian nationalism and the threat to American democracy. Oxford University Press, New York

Jones RP (2020) White too long: the legacy of white supremacy in American Christianity. Simon & Schuster, New York
Kaufmann E (2023) Identity not culture: where ethnic majorities are disadvantaged. In: Orgad L, Koopmans R (eds) Majorities, minorities, and the future of nationhood. Cambridge University Press, Cambridge, pp 62–86
Koopmans R, Orgad L (2023) Majority-minority constellations: toward a group-differentiated approach. In: Orgad L, Koopmans R (eds) Majorities, minorities, and the future of nationhood. Cambridge University Press, UK, pp 1–34
Kukathas C (1992a) Are there any cultural rights? Polit Theory 20(February):105–140
Kukathas C (1992b) Cultural rights again: a rejoinder to Kymlicka. Polit Theory 20(November):674–680
Kymlicka W (1992) The rights of minority cultures: reply to Kukathas. Polit Theory 20(February):140–146
Kymlicka W (1995) Multicultural citizenship: a liberal theory of minority rights. Clarendon Press, Oxford
Kymlicka W (2023) Nationhood, multiculturalism, and the ethics of membership. In: Orgad L, Koopmans R (eds) Majorities, minorities, and the future of Nationhood. Cambridge University Press, Cambridge, pp 87–128
Lupu I, Tuttle RW (2014) Secular government, religious people. William B. Eerdmans, Grand Rapids
Meyer v. Nebraska, 262 U.S. 390 (1923)
Miller PD (2022) The religion of American greatness: what's wrong with Christian nationalism. InterVarsity Press, Downers Grove
Pierce v. Society of Sisters, 268 U.S. 510 (1925)
Roosevelt K III (2022) The nation that never was: reconstructing America's story. University of Chicago Press, Chicago
Sandelind C (2023) Linking minority rights and majority attitudes: multicultural patriotism. In: Orgad L, Koopmans R (eds) Majorities, minorities, and the future of nationhood. Cambridge University Press, Cambridge, pp 151–175
Sherbert v. Verner, 374 U.S. 398 (1963)
Smith C (2000) Christian America: what evangelicals really want. University of California Press, Berkeley
Smith RM (2003) Stories of peoplehood: the politics and morals of political membership. Cambridge University Press, Cambridge
Stewart K (2019) The power worshippers: inside the dangerous rise of religious nationalism. Bloomsbury Publishing, New York
Tamir Y (2023) The liberalism of fear: the second coming. In: Orgad L, Koopmans R (eds) Majorities, minorities, and the future of nationhood. Cambridge University Press, Cambridge, pp 176–200
West Virginia Board of Education v. Barnette, 319 U.S. 624 (1943)
Wexler J (2019) Our non-Christian nation: how atheists, paganists, and others are demanding their rightful place in public life. Redwood Press of Stanford University Press, Stanford
Whitehead AL, Perry SL (2020) Taking America back for God: Christian nationalism in the United States. Oxford University Press, New York
Wisconsin v. Yoder, 406 U.S. 205 (1972)
Ziblatt D (2023) The causes of populism and the problem of cultural majority rights. In: Orgad L, Koopmans R (eds) Majorities, minorities, and the future of nationhood. Cambridge University Press, Cambridge, UK, pp 294–306

The Democratic Principle and the Tyranny of the Majority

Imer B. Flores

Abstract In this chapter, the author examines the relationship between the democratic principle, *i.e.*, the principle of self-determination, self-government, or democratic rule, and the dangers of degenerating into a facet of injustice, *i.e.*, the tyranny of the majority. In that sense, reviews the literature on the tension between the legitimacy of both the majority rule and the protection of the minorities and confronts two different conceptions of democracy. He advocates for a partnership conception of democracy as the government of all, both many and few, *i.e.*, the consenting majority and the dissenting minority; and reinforces that it is necessary not only to defend the society against the domination of its rulers but also to guard the minority from the persecution of the majority.

1 Introduction

Constituting—and reconstituting—principles to the core not only of legal standards and tests but also of legal analysis and reasoning has been one of the major developments in contemporary jurisprudence for at least the past fifty years. This development coincides with the passing away of Hans Kelsen (1881–1973) and can be traced mainly to Ronald Dworkin's[1] early critique of H.L.A. Hart's[2] legal positivism as a model of rules, which he confronted with a model of principles, and debunked

[1] See Dworkin (1967, 1972); both reprinted in Dworkin (1977).

[2] See Hart (1961).

I. B. Flores (✉)
Law School and Legal Research Institute, UNAM (National Autonomous University of Mexico), Mexico City, Mexico
e-mail: imer@unam.mx

G. A. Babst, W.-c. Lee (eds.), *Contemporary Facets of Injustice*, AMINTAPHIL: The Philosophical Foundations of Law and Justice 13,
https://doi.org/10.1007/978-3-031-93783-5_7

it as the ruling theory throughout his later works with his constructive interpretation *aka* interpretivism and the unity of value.[3]

Moreover, in what follows I aim to focus on Kelsen's contribution and some of his contemporaries to the discussion. As it is well known, in 1960, on the one hand, Kelsen published the second (revised and enlarged) edition of his *Reine Rechtslehre* with the ambition "to free the science of law from alien elements";[4] and, on the other hand, a disciple of his fellow Austrian colleague and friend Ludwig von Mises (1881–1973), *i.e.*, Friedrich August von Hayek (1899–1992) published *The Constitution of Liberty* with the aspiration to interweave "the philosophy, jurisprudence, and economics of freedom".[5]

Let me clarify, the despite the contradictory aims: on one side, the great Austrian jurist and author of the draft of Austria's constitution, which was enacted on October 1, 1920, had empowered a constitutional court to guard the constitutional principles embedded in it and did not deny the existence of principles of law throughout his work, including the first edition of his *Reine Rechtslehre*.[6] What's more, in his *General Theory of Law and the State* he did recognize not only the existence of "the principle of self-determination" and of "the principle of majority" but also suggested that "If the principle of self-determination is to be made the basis of a social organization, it must be somewhat restricted."[7]

Furthermore, he added:[8]

> The principle of the majority is by no means identical with absolute dominion of the majority, the dictatorship of majority over minority. The majority presupposes by its very definition the existence of a minority; and the right of the majority thus implies the right of existence of the minority. The principle of majority in a democracy is observed only if all citizens are permitted to participate in the creation of the legal order, although its contents are determined by the will of the majority. It is not democratic, because [it is] against the principle of majority, to exclude any minority from the creation of the legal order, even if the exclusion should be decided upon by a majority.
>
> If the minority is not eliminated from the procedure in which the social order is created, there is always a possibility for the minority of influencing the will of the majority. Thus it is possible to prevent, to a certain extent, the contents of the social order determined by the majority from coming into absolute opposition to the interests of the minority. This is a characteristic element of democracy.

The problem is that—for Kelsen—principles, and values are not strictly speaking part of legal science, but legal policy, and a such relative and subjective: "Justification means evaluation, which is always subjective and therefore a matter of ethics and

---

[3] See Dworkin (1985, 1986, 1996, 2006a, b, 2011). See also Flores (2015), pp. 157–192; Flores (2018), pp. 101–129; and Flores (2022).

[4] Kelsen (1967), p. 1. See Kelsen (1997), p. 7: "[T]he Pure Theory aims to free legal science of all foreign elements."

[5] Hayek (1960), p. 1.

[6] Kelsen (1997), p. 94: "the 'principle of law' (*Rechtsprinzip*)".

[7] Kelsen (1945), pp. 285–286.

[8] Kelsen (1945), p. 287.

politics, not of objective cognition. It is objective cognition alone that legal science, too, must serve, if it aims to be a science and not politics".[9]

On the other, the great Austrian economist, insisted the problem—especially in a democracy—is whether a consenting majority is entitled to enforce its rule on a dissenting minority or whether the majority rule is limited by constitutional principles. According to him:[10]

> The important question that arises here is whether the agreement of a majority on a moral rule is sufficient justification for enforcing it on a dissenting minority or whether this power ought not also to be limited by more general rules—in other words, whether ordinary legislation should be limited by general principles just as the moral rules of individual conduct preclude certain kinds of action, however good may be their purpose. There is as much need of moral rules in political as in individual action, and the consequences of successive collective decisions as well as those of individual decisions will be beneficial only if they are all in conformity with common principles.

Hence, in this chapter, I intend to recall the constitution of principles, in general, and of "democratic principle", *i.e.*, the principle of self-determination, self-government, or democratic rule. Additionally, we will remember the existing tensions between constitutional principles, such as the two concepts of liberty, *i.e.*, "negative" and "positive", by analyzing the relationship between individual liberty and the democratic principle, not only to reinforce the priority of the former over the latter, but also to review whether the so-called "majority principle" is really a principle and can be identified with the "democratic principle" or not. In my opinion, even if the "majority rule" is a principle and compatible with the "democratic principle", it is a mistake to equate—or even reduce—the "democratic principle" to the "majority rule", *i.e.*, to whatever pleases the majority. In that sense, I would like to confront two competing conceptions of democracy, in the quest for an authentic, pure, or true "democracy". For that purpose, after remembering its etymology as "government of the people" neither of the many nor of the few, but of the people, not some but all, we will contrast two conceptions: on the one hand, the *majoritarian conception* as the government of the many—and even of the few on behalf of the many, *i.e.*, the consenting majority; and, on the other hand, the *partnership conception* as the government of all, both many and few, *i.e.*, the consenting majority and the dissenting minority. The distinction between the two conceptions can be traced all the way down to John Stuart Mill's *Considerations on Representative Government*[11] and was reintroduced in Ronald Dworkin's *Is Democracy Possible Here? Principles for a New Political Debate*,[12] who by embracing the partnership conception has become the champion of democracy and of the "democratic principle", and the main critic of the "majority rule".

---

[9] Kelsen (1997), p. 106. See Kelsen (1957).

[10] Hayek (1960), pp. 67–68.

[11] See Mill (1958).

[12] See Dworkin (2006b). See also Flores (2021).

2 The Constitution of Principle and of Democratic Principle

In this part, we pretend to recall the constitution of principle, in general, and of "democratic principle", *i.e.*, the principle of self-determination, self-government, or democratic rule, and for that purpose we start by recalling the existing tensions not only between liberty and other values but also between the two concepts of liberty, *i.e.*, "negative" and "positive". In addition, we will reinforce the priority of the former over the latter, by analyzing the relationship between individual liberty and "democratic principle", and by critically assessing the problem of the limits of the "majority rule".

To get started, let me quote the "Introductory Chapter I" of John Stuart Mill's *On Liberty*:[13]

> The aim, therefore, of patriots was to set limits to the power which the ruler should be suffered to exercise over the community; and this limitation was what they meant by liberty. It was attempted in two ways. First, by obtaining a recognition of certain immunities, called political liberties or rights, which it was to be regarded as a breach of duty in the ruler to infringe, and which, if he did infringe, specific resistance, or general rebellion, was held to be justifiable. A second, and generally a later expedient, was the establishment of constitutional checks, by which the consent of the community, or of a body of some sort, supposed to represent its interests, was made a necessary condition to some of the important acts of the governing power.

Later on, in due time, the rulers became identified with the ruled, by assuming that they were elected by them as their representatives: "What was now wanted was, that the rulers should be identified with the people; that their interest and will should be the interest and will of the nation."[14] To the extent that, apparently, there can be no deviation and much less tension between the ruler and the ruled giving rise to the ideals of "self-determination", "self-government" and of "the power of the people over themselves". However, as Mill recognized:[15]

> The 'people' who exercise the power are not always the same people with those over whom it is exercised; and the 'self government' spoken of is not the government of each by himself, but of each by all the rest. The will of the people, moreover, practically means the will of the most numerous or the most active *part* of the people; the majority, or those who succeed in making themselves accepted as the majority; the people, consequently, *may* desire to oppress a part of their number; and precautions are as much needed against this as against any other abuse of power.

The "tyranny of the majority"—as any other tyrannical form—operates mainly through the actions and laws of the public authorities, but it may be the case that one part of the society oppresses the other. In Mill's voice:[16]

---

[13] Mill (1989), p. 6.

[14] Mill (1989), p. 7. *Cfr*. Kelsen (1955), p. 2: "the essence of the political phenomenon designated by the term [*i.e.*, democracy] was the participation of the governed in the government".

[15] Mill (1989), pp. 7–8.

[16] Mill (1989), pp. 8–9.

> Protection, therefore, against the tyranny of the magistrate is not enough: there needs protection also against the tyranny of the prevailing opinion and feeling; against the tendency of society to impose, by other means than civil penalties, its own ideas and practices as rules of conduct on those who dissent from them; to fetter the development, and, if possible, prevent the formation, of any individuality not in harmony with its ways, and compel all characters to fashion themselves upon the model of its own. There is a limit to the legitimate interference of collective opinion with individual independence: and to find that limit, and maintain it against encroachment, is as indispensable to a good condition of human affairs, as protection against political despotism.

For this reason, it is necessary to check the power not only of formal institutions but also of informal instruments which facilitate the imposition of one conception over the others, by legal and moral means. The majority cannot cancel the possibility of some individuals—a significant minority and even a numerical majority of the society—of freely conceiving and responsibly fulfilling their own plan of life. As Mill clarifies:[17]

> The object of this Essay is to assert one very simple principle, as entitled to govern absolutely the dealings of society with the individual in the way of compulsion and control, whether the means used be physical force in the form of legal penalties, or the moral coercion of public opinion. That principle is, that the sole end for which mankind are warranted, individually or collectively, in interfering with the liberty of action of any of their number, is self-protection. That the only purpose for which power can be rightfully exercised over any member of a civilised community, against his will, is to prevent harm to others.

In consequence the only time in which it is possible to interfere with the realization of someone's plan is to avoid harm to others. The so-called "harm principle" of Mill constitutes a clear limit to the exercise of liberty since it must always de exercise with responsibility in order not to harm others and less impede someone else from achieving their own ends in life. In Mill's own words:[18]

> No society in which these liberties are not, on the whole, respected, is free, whatever may be its form of government; and none is completely free in which they do not exist absolute and unqualified. The only freedom which deserves the name, is that of pursuing our own good in our own way, so long as we do not attempt to deprive others of theirs, or impede their efforts to obtain it.

At the heart of Mill's doctrine on liberty there is the pursuit of our own plan of life if it does not harm others. Moreover, in a lengthy paragraph, he acknowledges the appropriate region of human liberty and recognizes:[19]

> It comprises, first, the inward domain of consciousness; demanding liberty of conscience, in the most comprehensive sense; liberty of thought and feeling; absolute freedom of opinion and sentiment on all subjects, practical or speculative, scientific, moral, or theological. The liberty of expressing and publishing opinions may seem to fall under a different principle, since it belongs to that part of the conduct of an individual which concerns other people; but, being almost of as much importance as the liberty of thought itself, and resting I great part on the same reasons, is practically inseparable from it. Secondly, the principle

[17] Mill (1989), p. 13.

[18] Mill (1989), p. 16.

[19] Mill (1989), pp. 15–16.

> requires liberty of tastes and pursuits; of framing the plan of our life to suit our own character; of doing as we like, subject to such consequences as may follow: without impediment from our fellow-creatures, so long as what we do does not harm them, even though they should think our conduct foolish, perverse, or wrong. Thirdly, from this liberty of each individual, follows the liberty, within the same limits of combination among individuals; freedom to unite for any purpose not involving harm to others: the persons combining being supposed to be of full age, and not forced or deceived.

In this paragraph Mill not only establishes the "harm principle" as a limit to both individual and collective liberty, but also stipulates two priorities: (1) liberty—and its different kinds—over other ends of life; and (2) individual liberty over collective liberty. To reinforce these priorities, let me bring to attention that it was Henri Benjamin Constant de Rebeque's distinction amid "liberty of the ancients" and "liberty of the moderns",[20] which captured, first, the conflict that Isaiah Berlin, the champion of pluralism, later, popularized among the "two concepts of liberty", *i.e.*, between "negative" and "positive" liberties.[21]

The former is a liberty "from" and entails "absence of interference"; whilst the latter is a liberty "to" and involves "presence in self-government". As a result, there are two competing concepts of liberty: one of the ancients or republican, identified with a liberty to participate in democratic rule, where the collective or political liberty is accentuated and so community and equality are emphasized; and, other of the moderns or liberal, identified with a liberty from interference, where the individual or civil liberty is highlighted and so individuality and liberty are stressed.

Although the two concepts are in competition nothing precludes the possibility of their collaboration. As Berlin acknowledges "Self-government may, on the whole, provide a better guarantee of the preservation of civil liberties than other régimes, and has been defended as such by libertarians. But there is no necessary connection between individual liberty and democratic rule."[22] Actually, if democratic rule can suppress individual liberty, as Berlin points out, for a society to be truly free it is necessary to be governed by two interrelated principles:[23]

> [F]irst, that no power, but only rights, can be regarded as absolute, so that all men, whatever power governs them, have an absolute right to refuse to behave inhumanly; and, second, that there are frontiers, not artificially drawn, within which men should be inviolable, these frontiers being defined in terms of rules so long and widely accepted that their observance has entered into the very conception of what it is to be a normal human being, and, therefore, also of what it is to act inhumanly or insanely; rules of which it would be absurd to say, for example, that they could be abrogated by some formal procedure on the part of some court or sovereign body.

Both principles reinforce the primacy of a right—negative liberty—over a power—positive liberty—not only to the degree that certain rules cannot be abrogated by

---

[20] See Constant (1820).

[21] See Berlin (1969), pp. 118–172.

[22] Berlin (1969), p. 130.

[23] Berlin (1969), p. 165.

formal procedures but also to the extent that certain minimum area of individual liberty must not be violated by democratic rule:[24]

> Consequently, it is assumed... that the area of men's free action must be limited by law. But equally it is assumed... that there ought to exist a certain minimum area of personal freedom which must on no account be violated; for it is over-stepped, the individual will find himself in an area too narrow for even the minimum development of his natural faculties which alone makes it possible to pursue, and even to conceive, the various ends which men hold good or right or sacred. It follows that a frontier must be drawn between the area of private life and that of public authority.

Additionally, Berlin's suggestion is summarized in a well-known paragraph:[25]

> Pluralism, with the measure of 'negative' liberty that it entails seems to me a truer and more humane ideal than the goals of those who seek in the great disciplined, authoritarian structures the ideal of 'positive' self-mastery by classes, or peoples, or the whole of mankind. It is truer, because it does, at least recognize the fact that human goals are many, not all of them commensurable, and in perpetual rivalry with one another.

Thus, to reinforce the priority of the negative over the positive liberty, in the remainder of this part we will revisit the relationship between individual liberty and democratic principle, by critically assessing the problem of "majority rule". Before proceeding we must recall, following Kelsen, that it was Jean-Jacques Rousseau who did formulate "the question to which democracy is the answer", namely: "How is it possible to be subject to a social order and still be free?"[26] In the voice of the Geneva's contractarian:[27]

> "Find a form of association which defends and protects with all common forces the person and goods of each associate, and by means of which each one, while uniting with all, nevertheless obeys only himself and remains as free as before?" This is the fundamental problem for which the social contract provides the solution.

In the words of the Vienna's jurist: "A subject is politically free insofar as his individual will is in harmony with the "collective" (or "general") will expressed in the social order. Such harmony of the "collective" and the individual will is guaranteed only if the social order is created by the individuals whose behavior it regulates."[28] Likewise, according to him:[29]

> The ideal of self-determination requires that the social order shall be created by the unanimous decision of all its subjects and that it shall remain in force only as long as it enjoys the approval of all. The collective will (the *volonté general*) must constantly agree with the will of the subjects (the *volonté de tous*). The social order can be changed only with the approval of all subjects; and each subject is bound by the order only as long as he consents thereto.

---

[24] Berlin (1969), p. 124.

[25] Berlin (1969), p. 171.

[26] Kelsen (1945), p. 285.

[27] Rousseau (1987), p. 148.

[28] Kelsen (1945), p. 285.

[29] *Id.*

Since the "unanimity" is virtually impossible, the "majority principle" has been adopted as a device that enables the government to rule by facilitating, on one side, the election of our representatives and so the configuration of (national) representation, and, on the other, the decision-making process and thus the conformation of government. However, the "majority principle" does not imply that any election or decision is justified *per se*. As we have already pointed out, by quoting Kelsen, it is not enough to comply with adjective-formal procedures but to abide by substantive-material principles as well:[30]

(1) "The principle of the majority is by no means identical with absolute dominion of the majority, the dictatorship of majority over minority."
(2) "The majority presupposes by its very definition the existence of a minority; and the right of the majority thus implies the right of existence of the minority."
(3) "It is not democratic, because [it is] against the principle of majority, to exclude any minority from the creation of the legal order, even if the exclusion should be decided upon by a majority."
(4) "If the minority is not eliminated from the procedure in which the social order is created, there is always a possibility for the minority of influencing the will of the majority."

Additionally, as Kelsen emphasizes:[31]

> The will of the community, in a democracy, is always created through a running discussion between majority and minority, through free consideration of arguments for and against a certain regulation of a subject matter. This discussion takes place not only in parliament, but also, and, foremost, at political meetings, in newspapers, books, and other vehicles of public opinion. A democracy without public opinion is a contradiction in terms…

In that sense, "insofar as public opinion can arise only where intellectual freedom, freedom of speech and press and religion, are guaranteed",[32] democracy, *i.e.*, the "democratic principle", coincides with individual liberty, and with the "majority principle", but not with a "majority rule". Furthermore, as Kelsen acknowledges:[33]

> Free discussion between majority and minority is essential to democracy because this is the way to create an atmosphere favorable to a compromise between majority and minority; and compromise is part of democracy's very nature. Compromise means the solution of a conflict by a norm that neither entirely conforms with the interests of one party, nor entirely contradicts the interests of the other… It is precisely because of this tendency towards compromise that democracy is an approximation to the ideal of complete self-determination.

All in all, the problem is that, even if the "majority principle" is compatible with the "democratic principle", the "majority rule" is not identical to a "democratic rule". In a democracy it does not suffice to be concerned with the legitimate interests of

[30] Kelsen (1945), p. 287.
[31] Kelsen (1945), pp. 287–288.
[32] Kelsen (1945), p. 288.
[33] *Id.*

the majorities since the minorities must also be respected for the legislative decisions to represent the common general interest and be truly general in both their creation and application.

Even though it is true that the majority is legitimated to rule it is also true that it represents—and must represent—the minorities, by respecting their legitimate interests. The problem is that the majority principle tends to degenerate into majority rule by creating winners that take it all without sharing the corresponding part with the losers that end up with nothing at all. In a nutshell, the majority rule, in which the winner takes it all, makes politics a zero-sum game of win-lose (them or us), instead of a win-win situation for all (them and us).

The justification of the majority principle relies on the notion of "virtual representation", *i.e.*, the winners represent all, both those who voted for and against them, and two principles of reciprocity: (1) the majorities are fluid and not fixed beforehand; and (2) the minorities can become part of the governing coalition or majority in the future. Moreover, when the majority consistently and constantly excludes the minority and/or systematically and thoroughly rejects its demands, to the extent not only of ignoring their legitimate interests but also of destroying the virtual representation and the principles of reciprocity, by transforming the legitimate "majority principle" into is antithesis: "majority rule"—also known as the "tyranny of the majority".[34] In Mill's words: "in political speculations 'the tyranny of the majority' is now generally included among the evils against which society requires to be in guard."[35] In addition, a couple of years later, he added in his *Considerations on Representative Government* (1861):[36]

> The injustice and violation of principle are not less flagrant because those who suffer by them are a minority; for there is not equal suffrage where every single individual does not count for as much as any other single individual in the community. But it is not only a minority who suffer. Democracy, thus constituted, does not even attain its ostensible object, that of giving the powers of government in all cases to the numerical majority. It does something very different: it gives them to a majority of the majority, who may be, and often are, but a minority of the whole.

The problem is that, despite the virtual representation and the principles of reciprocity, the majority neither recognizes nor represents the interests of the minority, as Alexis de Tocqueville emphasized: "The majority, being in absolute command both of lawmaking and of the execution of the laws, and equally controlling both rulers and ruled, regards public functionaries as its passive agents and is glad to leave them the trouble of carrying out its plans."[37]

Notwithstanding, when the majority possess all the power and exercises it beyond any proportion it may lose all its legitimacy, as James Madison pointed out one of the objectives of establishing a government is to avoid the dominance of any group

---

[34] Guinier (1994), pp. 102–105.

[35] Mill (1989), p. 8.

[36] Mill (1958), p. 104.

[37] Tocqueville (1969), pp. 253–254.

with particular interests by recognizing: "It is of great importance in a republic not only to guard the society against the oppression of its rulers but to guard one part of the society against the injustice of the other part."[38] And, reiterating: "In a society under the forms of which the stronger faction can readily unite and oppress the weaker, anarchy may as truly be said to reign as in the state of nature, where the weaker individual is not secured against the violence of the stronger…"[39]

Tocqueville insisted that the will of the majority is the essence of the democratic rule:[40]

> The moral authority of the majority is partly based on the notion that there is more enlightenment and wisdom in a numerous assembly than in a single man, and the number of the legislators is more important than how they are chosen…
>
> The moral authority of the majority is also founded on the principle that the interest of the greater number should be preferred to that of those who are the fewer.

However, he warns that the germ of the tyranny is found precisely in the "omnipotence of the majority". On this regard, he affirms: "I will never grant to several that power to do everything which I refuse to a single man."[41] The majority will must be moderated to control the possibilities of becoming a tyranny. Moreover, the use of power is not necessarily good: "This irresistible power is a continuous fact and its good use only an accident."[42]

In a democracy, the "majority principle" is justified *prima facie* if the majority does not exercise all the power and oppress the minority, by not protecting their interests. It is incontestable that the majority is entitled to a majority of seats but not all since some of them belong to the minority and much less to be unconstrained. The legislative body ought to be a micro-cosmos of the constituency, where both majorities and minorities are represented according to their true representativeness without either adulterations or dilutions of any type. The majority principle means that it is not sufficient to represent the majority but all the people, including the minority.

Likewise, Alexander Hamilton warned: "Give all the power to the many, they will oppress the few. Give all the power to the few they will oppress the many. Both therefore ought to have power, that each may defend itself against the other."[43] In other words, democracy is more than the government of the majority. In a pure or true democracy, the power is neither in the majority nor in the minority but in all the people. As Mill emphasized:[44]

---

[38] Madison (1961), p. 323.

[39] *Id.*

[40] Tocqueville (1969), p. 247.

[41] Tocqueville (1969), p. 251.

[42] Tocqueville (1969), p. 256.

[43] Hamilton (1985), p. 101.

[44] Mill (1958), pp. 102–103.

> The pure idea of democracy, according to its definition, is the government of the whole people by the whole people, equally represented. Democracy as commonly conceived and hitherto practice is the government of the whole people by a mere majority of the people, exclusively represented. The former synonymous with the equality of all citizens; the latter, strangely confounded with it, is a government of privilege, in favor of the numerical majority, who alone posses practically any voice in the State. This is the inevitable consequence of the manner in which the votes are now taken, to the complete disfranchisement of minorities.

3 The Democratic Principle and the Majority Rule

In this part, since we have been critical of the tendency to reduce the "democratic principle" to the "majority rule", *i.e.*, to whatever pleases the majority, we would like to confront two competing conceptions of democracy. For that purpose, after remembering its etymology as "government of the people"—neither of the many nor of the few, but of the people, not some but all—we will contrast two conceptions: on the one hand, the *majoritarian conception* as the government of the many—and even of the few on behalf of the many, *i.e.* the consenting majority; and, on the other hand, the *partnership conception* as the government of all, both many and few, *i.e.* the consenting majority and the dissenting minority.

According to its etymology—*demos* (people) and *kratos* (government, power or rule)—"democracy" means "government, power or rule of the people". It is *prima facie* a form of government in contraposition to other forms of government. The classical typology includes not only three "pure" forms: (1) "autocracy" (better known as "monarchy") as government of *one*—*i.e.*, the monarch; (2) "aristocracy" as government of *few*—*i.e.*, the better ones; and (3) "democracy" as government of *all*—*i.e.*, the people.[45] But also three "impure" or "corrupt" forms: (1) "tyranny" as government of *one*—*i.e.*, the tyrant; (2) "oligarchy" as government of *few*—*i.e.*, the rich; and (3) "demagogy" as government of *many* (on behalf of all)—*i.e.*, the poor (or the mob).

It is worth to mention that Aristotle considered "democracy" pejoratively, an equivalent to the term "demagogy", as one vicious extreme in contraposition to

---

[45] Hans Kelsen not only did criticize the traditional classification and its trichotomy but also distinguished between two types of constitutions: (1) democracy and (2) autocracy. See Kelsen (1945), p. 284: "Democracy means that the "will" which is represented in the legal order of the State is identical with the wills of the subjects. Its opposite is the bondage of autocracy. There the subjects are excluded from the creation of the legal order, and harmony between the order and their wills is in no way guaranteed." Additionally, he distinguished between "two types of democracy, a democracy with restricted, and a democracy with unrestricted, power of government" (Kelsen 1955, p. 95). For some who accentuate the principle *of* popular sovereignty "the power of the people is unrestricted". On the contrary, for those who emphasize the principle of political participation *by* the people, following a preestablished procedure, it "means restriction of governmental power, whatever form the government may assume. It means also restriction of democratic power. Hence democracy is essentially a government *by* the people" (Kelsen 1955, pp. 3–4).

"oligarchy" as the other vicious extreme, whereas his *politeia* was the virtuous middle term by comprising the government of the middle class and as such of both the poor and the rich, *i.e.* of both the many and the few.[46] Let me explain that dislike him I will reserve "demagogy" for the "impure" or "corrupt" form and "democracy" for the "pure" or "true" one. But I will assume like him that the latter is the government of *all* the people: not only of both the poor and the rich but also of both the many and the few (or alternatively of both the majority and the minority).

The problem is that for some authors "democracy" seems to be reduced to the government of the *many* or of the *majority* in detriment of the *few* or of the *minority*, a so-called majoritarian or populist democracy. On the contrary, an authentic or true "democracy" and democratic government must be neither of poor or rich, nor of many or few (nor of majority or minority), but of all: both of poor and rich, both of many and few (both of majority and minority).

So far, the notion of "democracy" as a form of government and the typology has served to emphasize the ownership (or partnership) "of" the political or sovereign power, depending on whether it corresponds to one, few, many, or all. Nevertheless, the exercise of this political or sovereign power not only must be done directly and indirectly "by" its owners (or partners) and their—legitimate—representatives, but also must be done "for" them and their benefit, not in their detriment. The three ideas already sketched can be put together into an integral definition, such as the one contained in Abraham Lincoln's Gettysburg address and, curiously, in the Fifth French Republic's "Preamble": "government *of* the people, *by* the people, *for* the people".[47]

Thus, a pure or true "democracy" must be the government of, by and for all the people: not only many and few, majority and minority, but also poor and rich, men and women, heterosexuals and homosexuals, believers and non-believers... and so on. Hence, "democracy" is "government *of* all the people, *by* all the people—directly on their own ("direct democracy") or indirectly through their representatives ("representative democracy")—and *for* all the people".[48] Nevertheless, as Kelsen points out "Again and again, political writers tried to demonstrate that autocracy, be it hereditary monarchy or leader-dictatorship, is a better government for the people than a government by the people, *i.e.*, democracy. That there is something true in this argument and that "government for the people" is not identical with "government by the people" cannot be denied."[49] What's more, he even cautioned: "Since not only democracy but also its very contrary autocracy, may be a government for the people; this quality cannot be an element of the definition of democracy."[50]

---

[46] Aristotle (1988), pp. 97–98.

[47] Lincoln (1990), p. 308 (emphasis added).

[48] See Flores (2010), pp. 65–103; Flores (2013), pp. 77–101; and Flores (2014), pp. 103–117. See also Macedo (2010), pp. 1029–1042; Waldron (2010), pp. 1043–1057.

[49] Kelsen, *The Foundations of Democracy*, p. 2.

[50] *Id.*

However, as stated a couple of paragraphs above, the problem is that there are two competing conceptions of democracy. As far as I know the distinction can be traced all the way back to Mill, who almost one-hundred and fifty years ago, in his *Considerations on Representative Government*, under the epigraph "Of True and False Democracy: Representation of All, and Representation of the Majority Only", indicated that the two different ideas were usually confounded under the name "democracy". On one side, the true idea was the "government of the whole people by the whole people equally represented"; and, on the other, the false with "the government of the whole people by a mere majority of the people, exclusively represented".[51]

Nowadays, as Dworkin pointed out the two competing conceptions of democracy not only coexist but also are still in conflict:[52]

> The two views of democracy that are in contest are these. According to the *majoritarian* view, democracy is government by majority will, that is, in accordance with the will of the greatest number of people, expressed in elections with universal or near universal suffrage. There is no guarantee that a majority will decide fairly; its decisions may be unfair to minorities whose interests the majority systematically ignores. If so, then the democracy is unjust but no less democratic for that reason. According to the rival *partnership* view of democracy, however, democracy means that the people govern themselves each as a full partner in a collective political enterprise so that a majority's decisions are democratic only when certain further conditions are met that protect the status and interests of each citizen as a full partner in that enterprise. On the partnership view, a community that steadily ignores the interests of some minority or other group is just for that reason not democratic even though it elects officials impeccably by majoritarian means. This is only a very sketchy account of the partnership conception, however. If we find the more familiar majoritarian conception unsatisfactory, we shall have to develop the partnership view in more detail.

As he acknowledges, the United States of America is neither a pure example of the majoritarian conception of democracy nor of the non-majoritarian (or partnership) one. Although the bipartisan system and the majority rule reinforced the former, since the founding fathers limited the power of the majorities in various forms, by including anti-majoritarian devices, such as the filibuster and the judicial review (of the constitutionality) of the acts of the (elected) branches of government, it can be said that they also supported the latter.[53] On one side, a minority of either thirty-four or forty-one (out of the one-hundred senators) can block the majority of bringing a decision to a final vote, depending on whether it is a substantive or procedural issue. And, on the other, the power of the political majorities is limited by the recognition of individual constitutional rights that the legislative majorities cannot infringe and much less step over.

---

[51] Mill (1958), pp. 102–103.

[52] Dworkin (2006b), p. 131. See Dworkin (1996), pp. 1–38. See also Waluchow (2007), pp. 106–109; and, Flores (2009), pp. 37–74.

[53] Dworkin (2006b), pp. 137 and 135. In fact, the existence of the Senate was designed to divide the most dangerous branch of government and to give stability to the government by protecting the minorities against a speedy and unreflected legislative majority in the House of Representatives. For an illustration of the filibuster, see Capra (1939).

Aside Dworkin alerts that the degraded state of the public debate endangers the partnership conception of democracy and strengthens the majoritarian one, including viewing the other as an enemy and politics as a war:[54]

> If we aim to be a partnership democracy… the degraded state of our political argument does count as a serious defect in our democracy because mutual attention and respect are the essence of partnership. We do not treat someone with whom we disagree as a partner—we treat him as an enemy or at best as an obstacle—when we make no effort either to understand the force of his contrary views or to develop our own opinions in a way that makes them responsive to his. The partnership model so described seems unattainable now because it is difficult to see how Americans on rival sides of the supposed culture wars could come to treat each other with that mutual respect and attention.

Moreover, as Dworkin has emphasized:[55]

> The majoritarian conception purports to be purely procedural and therefore independent of other dimensions of political morality; it allows us to say, as I indicated, that a decision is democratic even if it is very unjust. But the partnership conception does not make democracy independent of the rest of political morality; on that conception we need a theory of equal partnership to decide what is or is not a democratic decision, and we need to consult ideas about justice, equality, and liberty in order to construct such a theory. So on the partnership conception, democracy is a substantive, not a merely procedural, ideal.

4 Conclusion: Democratic Principle *vis-à-vis* Majority Rule

Finally, let me insist, my main claim has been that the "democratic principle" is compatible with the "majority principle", but that it is a mistake to equate—or even reduce—the "democratic principle" to the "majority rule", *i.e.*, to whatever pleases the majority; and, derive from it some conclusions:

First, although the "democratic principle" and the "majority principle" are legitimated, they are limited and as such must respect the "individual liberty" reinforcing the priority of the "negative liberty" over the "positive liberty";

Second, even though the "majority principle" reinforces the view that the majority is legitimated to rule it cannot exclude or eliminate the minority, because that amounts to transforming itself into its antithesis: the "majority rule"—or the so-called "tyranny of the majority"; and

Third, though the "majoritarian conception" of democracy is still very influential in the design of our electoral systems, due to its intrinsic danger to degenerate into a "majority rule" it is necessary to take seriously the "partnership conception" to guarantee democracy as the government of, by and for both the majority and the minority, not merely of the majority.

---

[54] Dworkin (2006b), pp. 132–133.

[55] Dworkin (2006b), p. 134.

References

Aristotle (1988) The politics. CUP, New York
Berlin I (1969) Two concepts of liberty. In: Four essays on liberty. OUP, Oxford, pp 118–172
Capra F (1939) Mr. Smith goes to Washington
Constant B (1820) De la liberté des anciens comparée àcelle des modernes. In Collection Complète des Ouvrages. Béchet Libraire, Paris
Dworkin R (1967) The model of rules. Univ Chic Law Rev 35:14–46 [reprinted in Dworkin R (1977 and 1978, 14–45)]
Dworkin R (1972) Social rules and legal theory. Yale Law Rev 81:855–890 [reprinted in Dworkin R (1977 and 1978, 46–80)]
Dworkin R (1977) Taking rights seriously. HUP, Cambridge, MA [there is a 2nd ed. "With Reply to Critics", 1978]
Dworkin R (1985) A matter of principle. HUP, Cambridge
Dworkin R (1986) Law's empire. HUP, Cambridge
Dworkin R (1996) Freedom's law. The moral reading of the American constitution. HUP, Cambridge
Dworkin R (2006a) Justice in robes. HUP, Cambridge
Dworkin R (2006b) Is democracy possible here? Principles for a new political debate. PUP, Princeton
Dworkin R (2011) Justice for hedgehogs. HUP, Cambridge
Flores IB (2009) The living tree constitutionalism: Fixity and flexibility. Problema. Anuario de filosofía y teoría del derecho 3:37–74
Flores IB (2010) Ronald Dworkin's *Justice for hedgehogs* and partnership conception of democracy (with a comment to Jeremy Waldron's "A majority in the lifeboat"). Problema. Anuario de filosofía y teoría del derecho 4:65–103
Flores IB (2013) Law, liberty and the rule of law (in a constitutional democracy). In: Flores IB, Himma KE (eds) Law, liberty and the rule of law. Springer, Dordrecht, pp 77–101
Flores IB (2014) The problem of democracy in contexts of polarization. In: Cudd AE, Scholz SJ (eds) Philosophical perspectives on democracy in the 21st century. Springer, Cham, pp 103–117
Flores IB (2015) The legacy of Ronald Dworkin (1931-2013): a legal theory and methodology for hedgehogs, Hercules, and one right answers. Problema. Anuario de filosofía y teoría del derecho 9:157–192
Flores IB (2018) Taking (human) dignity and rights seriously: the integrated legal, moral and political philosophy of Ronald Dworkin. In: Khurshid S, Malik L, Rodriguez-Blanco V (eds) Dignity in the legal and political philosophy of Ronald Dworkin. OUP, New Delhi, pp 101–129
Flores IB (2021) Dworkin, Ronald: partnership conception of democracy. In: Sellers M, Kirste S (eds) Encyclopedia of the philosophy of law and social philosophy. Springer, Dordrecht
Flores IB (2022) Dworkin, Ronald: constructive interpretation *aka* interpretivism. In: Sellers M, Kirste S (eds) Encyclopedia of the philosophy of law and social philosophy. Springer, Dordrecht
Guinier L (1994) The tyranny of the majority. Fundamental fairness in representative democracy. The Free Press, New York
Hamilton A (1985) Speech, June 18, 1787. In Selected writings and speeches of Alexander Hamilton. American Enterprise Institute, Washington, D. C. [original publication: 1787]
Hart HLA (1961) The concept of law. OUP, Oxford [there is a 2nd ed., "With a postscript": 1994]
Hayek FA (1960) The constitution of liberty. UChicP, Chicago
Kelsen H (1945) General theory of law and state, trad. Anders Wedberg. HUP, Cambridge
Kelsen H (1955) Foundations of democracy. Ethics. Int J Soc Polit Leg Philos LXVI:1–101
Kelsen H (1957) What is justice? In What is justice? Justice, law, and politics in the mirror of science. Collected essays by Hans Kelsen. UCalifP, Berkeley, pp 1–24
Kelsen H (1967) Pure theory of law, 2nd edn. (trans: Max Knight). UCalifP, Berkeley (original title and publication: Reine rechstlehre, 2ª ed., 1960]

Kelsen H (1997) Introduction to the problems of legal theory (trans: Bonnie Litschewsi Paulson and Stanley Paulson). OUP, Oxford (original title and publication: *Reine Rechstlehre*, 1934)

Lincoln A (1990) New birth of freedom. The Gettysburg address, November 19, 1863. In: Cuomo MM, Holzer H (eds) Lincoln on Democracy. Harper Collins, New York, pp 307–308 [original publication: 1863]

Macedo S (2010) Against majoritarianism: democratic values and institutional design. In Symposium *Justice for hedgehogs*: a conference on Ronald Dworkin's Forthcoming Book. Boston Univ Law Rev 90(2):1029–1042

Madison J (1961) No. 51. In Rossiter C (ed) The federalist papers. Mentor, New York, pp 320–325 [original publication: 1787]

Mill JS (1958) Considerations on representative government. Liberal Arts Press, Indianapolis [original publication: 1861]

Mill JS (1989) On liberty. In: Collini S (ed) On liberty and other writings. CUP, Cambridge, pp 1–115. [original publication: 1859]

Rousseau JJ (1987) On the social contract. In The basic political writings, trad. Donald A. Cress. Hackett, Indianapolis, pp 139–227 [original title and publication: Du contrat social. Ou principes du droit politique, 1762]

Tocqueville A (1969) Democracy in America. Anchor Books, New York [original publication: De la démocratie en Amérique, 1835 and 1840]

Waldron J (2010) A majority in the lifeboat. In Symposium *Justice for hedgehogs*: a conference on Ronald Dworkin's Forthcoming Book. Boston Univ Law Rev 90(2):1043–1057

Waluchow WJ (2007) A common law theory of judicial review. The living tree. CUP, Cambridge

Religious Liberty, Public Accommodations, and Non-discrimination: A Rapidly Emerging Injustice

Gordon A. Babst

Abstract The decision in *Burwell v. Hobby Lobby Stores, Inc.*, suggested to many that the scope of religious liberty was in a principled, logical way expanded to include free expression rights of corporate entities. It is concerning that many champion the decision as a basis for expanding religious exemptions to non-discrimination law as regards public accommodations, especially since the same reasoning that is being used with respect to the contemporary target of discrimination based in religious belief—American citizens who happen to be in a sexual minority—would apply by analogy, as it once did explicitly, to racial minorities. Unfortunately, given the rancor and the indefatigable ardor with which proponents insist on the rightfulness of their cause, we can lose sight of the trickiness that characterizes actual situations and the hurt experienced by individual persons who understand themselves to be uniquely positioned to be discriminated against when exercising their constitutional rights or engaged in ordinary activities in the public space, on the basis of someone else's private religious beliefs. Looking back, I find the extension of exemptions on the basis of religious belief from neutral laws of general applicability inappropriate and to pose a threat to the equality of citizenship guaranteed by the 14th Amendment.

G. A. Babst (✉)
Department of Political Science, Chapman University, Orange, CA, USA
e-mail: gbabst@chapman.edu

G. A. Babst, W.-c. Lee (eds.), *Contemporary Facets of Injustice*, AMINTAPHIL: The Philosophical Foundations of Law and Justice 13,
https://doi.org/10.1007/978-3-031-93783-5_8

1 Introduction

> I don't believe for a minute that lawmakers intended to create a license to discriminate. This bill is not about discrimination, and if I thought it legalized discrimination in any way in Indiana I would have vetoed it. Indiana Governor Mike Pence[1]

> The Indiana General Assembly should not destroy in less than 36 hours the Religious Freedom Restoration Act that took over 65 days to go through the legislative process earlier this year…. Christian bakers, florists, and photographers would no longer have the benefit of Indiana law to help protect them from being forced by the government to participate in a homosexual wedding.—Statements of Eric Miller of Advance America[2]

Eric Miller must have been very disappointed with the final RFRA bill Governor Pence ended up signing, one that in the eyes of many on-lookers far better realizes his assertion above regarding the original bill, because it does not provide a shield against claims of discrimination based in traditional protected classes and now also sexual orientation or gender identity.[3] Governor Pence came to realize that what some perceive as a shield from claims of discrimination so that they can exercise their faith, others perceive as a 'license to discriminate' in contexts where an identifiable group of people reasonably expects to be discriminated against when engaged in ordinary activities such as those public accommodations facilitate.

It was widely thought that the original version of this bill was in fact intended to protect religious believers from claims of discrimination specifically should they not wish to operate their public accommodations for same-sex weddings, the concern likely animating Miller's frustration with the resultant bill.[4] Micah Clark of the American Family Association was less than subtle in public statements with respect to the prospective revised bill, revealingly commenting that "conservatives should

[1] Pence, then Governor, signed Indiana's Religious Freedom Restoration Act (RFRA) into law in a ceremony closed to the public, from which reporters were asked to leave. See Terkel (2015a).

[2] See Terkel (2015b). A deflated Miller, an original backer of the original RFRA bill, was also one of the few people invited to Governor Pence's private signing ceremony. See Ibid. Also at the signing ceremony were Micah Clark, the Executive Director of the American Family Association of Indiana, and Curt Smith, Director of the Indiana Family Institute, who helped to write the bill. See Ford (2015). Noticeably absent from the signing ceremony were members of the clergy from major denominations such as are found in Indiana, beyond some "Franciscan monks and nuns, orthodox Jews"—perhaps the anti-LGBT activists were viewed as an appropriate substitute. See Cook (2015).

[3] In general, state RFRAs mimic the federal RFRA in requiring the government to show a compelling interest if a law is claimed to burden the exercise of religion. If no compelling interest can be shown, the religious claimant is entitled to an exemption. This expands on the prior First Amendment approach to guaranteeing freedom of religious expression by prescribing a heightened level of review and for allowing the assertion of burden to be that claimed by the religious believer. The federal RFRA received perhaps its most scathing criticism in Hamilton (1998), who also successfully argued the case *Boerne v. Flores* (117 S. Ct.2157 [1997]), which ruled that the federal RFRA does not apply to the states.

[4] "[T]he plight of Christian wedding vendors was raised repeatedly during legislative debate prior to the law's passage," and "[a]sked at the time [by civil liberties groups] to add provisions to make certain that discrimination of all kinds would be strictly prohibited…Indiana lawmakers refused." See Somashekhar (2015).

oppose any effort to clarify that the law does not legalize discrimination. *That could totally destroy this bill*."[5] Clark's comments suggest that "what is often presented as a modest proposal to protect religious liberty reflects in actuality *a larger goal to effectively eviscerate existing sexual orientation nondiscrimination protections*."[6] The events in Indiana triggered a backlash against religious freedom laws for reason of their apparently not-so-subtle prejudicial effect on gay rights beyond the federally protected right to same-sex marriage.[7]

It is important to note the following: all previous statutes and now the federal law that allows for same-sex marriage exempt dissenting clergy and their religious institutions from having to perform same-sex weddings. The offending issue, then, is *not* one of compelling clergy to go against their faith upon demand by a same-sex couple that he or she perform a wedding ceremony for them in his or her church. To my knowledge, no clergy who has religious objections has ever been compelled to perform a same-sex wedding, and no law would support it. The issues in Indiana had to do with sexual orientation in commercial transactions associated with public accommodations, and whether RFRA serves to launder social prejudice under the guise of religious freedom.

The Court's 2014 decision in *Burwell v. Hobby Lobby Stores, Inc.* [573 U.S. ___ (2014)] – hereinafter: *Hobby Lobby*—is a precursor to several well-known cases involving bakers[8], florists[9], wedding photographers[10], and wedding web designers[11], at least that is how I situate that pivotal case. There the Court in dictum limited its ruling to allow for-profit entities discretionary religious exemptions so that it did not apply to racial discrimination, leaving open other forms of discrimination.[12] By late 2014 Indiana was required to allow civil marriage for same-sex couples, then one of 35 states and the District of Columbia that did so whether by court order or legislative action, representing 69.4% of the U.S. population before the Court decided

---

[5] See Ford (2015) (emphasis added).

[6] See Flynn (2010) p. 244 (emphasis added).

[7] See Savage (2015) and Holland (2015) finding "solid opposition to allowing businesses to refuse services or refuse to hire people or groups based on religious beliefs."

[8] See Masterpiece Cakeshop v. Colorado Civil Rights Commission, 584 U.S. 617 (2018).

[9] See State v. Arlene's Fowers, Inc., 441 P.3d1203 (2019), a State of Washington case upholding anti-discrimination laws against claims of religious freedom after being sent back to the state by the Supreme Court.

[10] See the 2013 New Mexico case Elane Photography, LLC v. Vanessa Willock, 309 P.3d 53 (N.M. 2013), upholding that state's human rights act against a religious objection grounded in the photographer's religious beliefs.

[11] See 303 Creative LLC v. Elenis, 600 U.S. 570 (2023), a case the facts of which were fabricated to get the case decided in favor of the web designer on the basis of creative expression, and that grounded in the owner's religious beliefs, and the 2019 case involving custom-designed wedding invitations, Brush & Nib Studio, LC, et al., v. City of Phoenix.

[12] See the discussion in Ball (2017), pp. 245–248. Also see the discussion in Ravitch (2016), pp. 102–111, who predicts a backlash against religious freedom for reason of this decision.

Obergefell v. Hodges, legalizing same-sex marriage nationwide as a constitutionally protected right citizens may exercise.[13]

In addition, the original Indiana law expanded the reach of that state's RFRA to cover non-state agents—including for-profit businesses—and interactions where the state is not a party to the case, and also provided that the plaintiff need only assert her feeling that her freedom of religious expression was burdened as in 'merely burdened' rather than severely burdened or some other showing of intense burdening. For all those reasons many on-lookers as well as amateur, professional, and academic legal experts believed that the original laws were meant to provide a greater shield for religious believers who specifically wished not to participate in commercial activity in conjunction with a same-sex wedding, much as Miller, Clark, Smith and no doubt many others were hoping for. And, it is likely that many also believed that the provision of such a shield in the form of religious freedom would fast-track undesirable discrimination against sexual minorities more generally, beyond refusals to cater to the one-time event of a same-sex wedding.

Finally, the Court's 2014 decision in *Hobby Lobby* is popularly understood to stand for the proposition that corporations have First Amendment Freedom of Religious Expression rights under RFRA.[14] While the Court took pains to indicate the nature of Hobby Lobby, Inc., as a closely held corporation, owned and also run at the executive level by the Green Family, which submitted that it exercised its religious beliefs through this corporate entity such as through religion-infused norms of conducting business, this limiting aspect of the decision may or may not endure when tested in subsequent cases that challenge neutral laws of general applicability that are claimed to burden now a corporate entity's freedom of religious expression.[15] As with any extension of exemptions that turn on people's religious beliefs, "[g]ranting an accommodation may not rise to the level of an independent constitutional violation, yet still be in deep tension with important constitutional

---

[13] See Obergefell v. Hodges, 576 U.S. ___ (2015).

[14] Douglas Laycock is adamant on this point: "…it is at least clear that Congress understood the Religious Freedom Restoration Act to apply to for-profit businesses…. Corporations are clearly persons protected by the statutory text, and Congress understood RFRA to protect persons engaged in for-profit activities." See Laycock (2014), pp. 840, 850 (references omitted). However, whenever Laycock discusses the "turf" that must be protected, the space wherein a group "can live its own values and where its rules control" his example is a church: "Inside a Catholic institution has to be a Catholic space." It is doubtful that he would refer to the space inside a Hobby Lobby arts and crafts store as such a space, despite his insistence that the federal RFRA includes corporations engaged in for-profit activities—perhaps because common sense suggests that arts and crafts stores are not religious spaces in and of themselves, as are churches. See Ibid., p. 876.

[15] The corporate entity Hobby Lobby, Inc., owns and operates both Hobby Lobby Stores and Mardel Bookstores, a chain of Christian bookstores—the former probably not recognizable to its customers as a religious entity. Hobby Lobby, Inc., could also own and operate a chain of donut shops and many another type of business, the corporate form being highly elastic yet always providing a stable veil for its owners, importantly protecting them from certain fiscal and criminal liability as well as, now, public accommodations law.

values…. Such singling out might undermine the forms of respect that guarantees of equal protection promote."[16]

In sum, it was not unexpected that owners of public accommodations would read the *Hobby Lobby* case as permitting them to challenge laws they found objectionable solely on the grounds of their religious beliefs—in particular, non-discrimination statutes and the legalization of same-sex marriage. And, owing to the Court's decision in *Thomas v. Review Board* [450 U.S. 707 (1981)], courts must be solicitous of an individual religious believer's understanding of the faith they uphold, regardless of the idiosyncratic nature of that individual's understanding or its divergence from a denomination's creed and practice.[17]

2 The Basic Clash Between Public Accommodations and Religious Believers

Both sides to the overall debate that is the focus of my attention—the rights of religious believers who propose to object to same-sex marriage if not to incidents of homosexuality or even to gay persons themselves as well, on the one hand, and, on the other hand, the rights of gay persons and also others to be treated as equal citizens as they go about their daily activities in the public space, especially when state or local law provides for protections against discrimination based in sexual orientation—may dig in their heels.[18] Owing to this clash of views the law cannot at the same time fully express the viewpoints of both sides. This is no easy task, but American constitutionalism's surest grounding is in a principle of equal citizenship that stands opposed to the inferiorization of any American citizen through the law. As good a statement as any on this latter point can be found in Kenneth Karst's *Belonging to America*, usefully quoted from at length:

> The principle of equal citizenship…means this: Each individual is presumptively entitled to be treated by the organized society as a respected, responsible, and participating member. Stated negatively, the principle forbids the organized society to treat an individual as a member of an inferior caste or as a nonparticipant…. The most heartrending deprivation of all is the inequality of status that excludes people from full membership in the community, degrading them by labeling them as outsiders, denying them their very selves. The harms of

[16] See NeJaime and Siegel (2015) p. 54.

[17] Legal scholar Eugene Volokh writes" "Courts are forbidden from determining whether a belief is reasonable…. internally consistent, or…the lines that a believer draws make sense." See his essay "Religious exemptions – a guide for the perplexed." This maximally protects each citizen's freedom of religious expression, and rightly so; however, interpersonal, intra-religious situations could present themselves in ways that overwhelm such simplifications, highlighting the fact that "[s]ecular claims may have moral force equal to that presented by religious claims." See Gill (2019), p. 57.

[18] Indicating that there are at least two sides should not suggest that the two are easily identifiable, or that any claim either makes is clear. *That neither point may be true in fact is one point of this paper.* Many Christians are gay-friendly and find discrimination intolerable. So too, many gay persons are Christian, and find intolerance in the name of their religion intolerable.

> exclusion unquestionably happen to people one by one, but those individual harms result from the subordination of groups…. the importance of citizenship, which begins in the formal recognition of membership in the community but does not end there.[19]

Equality was written into the Civil Rights Act of 1964, which established the principle that businesses that serve the public must be open to all—no more signage of the sort "we don't serve your kind here"—thus articulating the basic principle of public accommodation law, that has been extended beyond the original target, racial segregation, to various forms of discrimination within 'the public' with the only exception being limited to *within* religious institutions, though some have argued that even there, there is a concern when one conceives of religious institutions as socially powerful agents of culture with political clout.[20]

Many thinkers outside law professionals accord equality a priority of place even in the face of claims by religious believers. By way of example, the American Political Theorist Rogers Smith expresses concern that the equality of civic standing, the country's bedrock principle, is degraded if not endangered when religious free exercise claims are accorded special privilege for being religious.[21] So too the eminent Philosopher Martha Nussbaum contends that "a key thread holding all the key concepts [of religious liberty and liberty of conscience] is the idea of equality, understood as nondomination or nonsubordination," which she qualifies further: "A major part of not being subordinated will be to have equal standing or status in the public realm. Thus, this conception is highly sensitive to dignitary affronts in the symbolic realm, even when they entail no material disadvantage."[22]

Nonetheless and despite the American political regime's placing great emphasis on equality of civic standing irrespective of religion, there has been great resistance to extending the protections of non-discrimination statutes to cover gay persons, especially and perhaps oddly those who are married couples, resulting in a flurry of events in news cycles around the *Obergefell* case, such as the following involving official acts or proposals grounded in religious belief or sexual orientation, or both:

- A Texas lawmaker proposed the legalization of a 'license to discriminate' against gay persons, whether workers or customers, even if the basis of the right in any given case is scripture alone.[23]
- Kansas Governor Sam Brownback signed an executive order rescinding state LGBT worker protections in place since 2007 via language typical in such actions: through reiterating an honorable principle of non-discrimination, and then proceeding to list the categories of persons to whom it applies, but this time leaving out sexual minorities, just as Indiana's original RFRA had failed to men-

[19] See Karst (1989), pp. 3, 4, 9.

[20] See Rutherford (1996).

[21] See Rogers M. Smith, ""Equal" Treatment?" in Monsma and Christopher Soper (1998), pp. 192–193, 197.

[22] See Nussbaum (2008), p. 21.

[23] See Pyke (2014).

tion. As Governor Brownback's new executive order affected only state workers, it sent a particularly powerful message to citizens in Kansas' LGBT community.[24]

- Chief Justice Roy Moore of the Alabama State Supreme Court, a frequent newsmaker, cited state sovereignty when he ordered probate judges across that state *not* to process any same-sex marriages in defiance of a U.S. District court's ruling that overturned the state's same-sex marriage ban. Judge Moore seems intent on taking over the mantle discarded after the arguably embarrassing tenure of former Alabama Governor George Wallace, a staunch segregationist who championed state's rights.[25]

Courts wrestle with finding sincerity, religiosity, or intensity as applied to religious belief, especially in the context of a RFRA's mandatory heightened judicial review coupled with a claim of a substantial burden that is in the eyes of the RFRA claimant.[26] Courts are appropriately concerned both to ensure the religious freedom of each citizen and at the same time to prevent every duly enacted law or regulation from succumbing to strict scrutiny whenever a claim of burden on religious belief is asserted, and all that in the context of ambiguity regarding what constitutes an 'exercise' of religious expression and lack of clear guidelines as regards the 'substantiality' of a burden thereunto.[27] All these tricky determinations are likely to be just as difficult when assessing a corporation's claims for exemptions on the grounds of First Amendment Freedom of Religious Expression in the wake of the *Hobby Lobby* decision.[28]

Unfortunately, in the rancor surrounding events such as those listed above, and the indefatigable ardor with which proponents insist on the rightfulness of their cause, we can lose sight of the hurt experienced by the parties as individual persons, especially those citizens who understand themselves uniquely positioned to suffer discrimination against them when exercising their rights or engaged in ordinary activities in the public space, on the basis of someone else's private religious beliefs for which there is no accountability despite the third-party effects.

[24] See The Kansas City Star (2015).

[25] See Robertson and Dewa (2015) and Chandler (2015).

[26] See the discussion in Smith (2014), p. 761.

[27] Ibid., p. 749.

[28] Smith offers that "RFRA will have no boundaries," especially not if given a "broad hands-off interpretation" that she believes will not allow accommodation ever constitutionally to be denied. See Smith (2014), p. 731.

3 A Possible Clash between Religious Believers Over Public Accommodations

As luck would have it, I happened to be in the Bloomington Blooms flower shop in Gary, Indiana, around six in the evening and overheard the following conversation between the clerk—Josie—and a customer—Susan—who was picking up a floral arrangement she had apparently pre-ordered from the online catalog.[29] The date was April 27, 2015, the day after Indiana Governor Pence signed that state's original RFRA into law, and before he subsequently requested a revised version to sign into law—which he did six days later to clarify the misunderstanding so that the law "cannot be used to discriminate against anyone."[30] Hence, the original Indiana RFRA, which provides a religious exemption specifically with respect to sexual orientation and same-sex weddings, was in effect when I imagined the following exchange to have taken place.[31] This completely made-up exchange is illustrative because the dialogue form helps to simplify the surprisingly many factors at work in an ordinary setting, with my bracketed reflections on the relevant scholarship and caselaw suggesting the bigger picture.

Josie: "Good Evening – welcome to Bloomington Blooms."

Susan: "Thank you. That's a lovely arrangement in the walk-in over there, but I don't think it's mine."

Josie: "No, that's for Mrs. Osgood. Kinda funny – it's her fourth walk down the aisle – some guy from Chicago's South Side – she's always gotten hitched to Black men so I'd think she'd have learned her lesson by now. But, different strokes for different folks – what do I care – it's her business, not mine – all that matters is that they're happy, no?"

[Josie is distinguishing her personal beliefs—here, about interracial relationships including marriage—from her professional obligations as a floral vendor serving the public at large. Neither the grounds nor the extent of her distaste for interracial relationships can be made out, though they could be based on religious beliefs.]

Susan: "Yes, that's becoming more rare these days. Is that my arrangement to the right?"

Josie: "If you're Susan Jones it is. It's for a rehearsal dinner, right?"

Susan: "Yes. My sister is getting married in our church tomorrow afternoon. Say, haven't we met before?"

[29] "Bloomington Blooms," as I imagine it, is a chain of 12 flower shops throughout Indiana owned by a devout Catholic couple in Bloomington with about 151 employees overall. Gary is not one of the eleven municipalities in Indiana that prohibit discrimination in employment based in sexual orientation, nor is it located in one of the two counties that prohibit the same.

[30] See David and DeMillo (2015).

[31] These are the aspects of the original bill that have been deleted and replaced with language that specifically prohibits business from denying goods or services to LGBT individuals by adding the latter to the list of persons protected by Indiana's public accommodation law. See Terkel (2015).

[We don't know whether Susan is gifting the floral arrangement for the occasion unbeknownst to her sister, or whether she is procuring it on behalf of her sister.]

Josie: "I can't recall."

Susan: "Don't you go to Gary Presbyterian over on Hill Street? That's my church. My family has been going there since we were kids."

Josie: "Mine too, but I have to admit I only go on the big holidays. But I sure do like Pastor Franck."

Susan: "Me too – we're cousins, in fact. He's officiating at my sister's wedding tomorrow, and will be at the rehearsal dinner tonight – he's hosting it, in fact"

Josie: "Nice man. It's good to see some traditions kept up these days."

[Josie may be remarking on the debate leading up to the 2015 decision in the Presbyterian Church USA (PCUSA) to allow same-sex weddings.[32] Like several denominations, this church has searched through and reflected on its traditions and calling, and on its understanding of how to interpret and honor God's will, prompting its decision to offer marriage to same-sex couples.]

Susan: "Say, aren't those pink flowers over there rhododendrons?"

Josie: "Why yes."

Susan: "They're Emma's favorite flowers. Could you squeeze in just a couple in the arrangement for her?"

Josie: "No problem.

[Josie grabs a couple, and begins to re-tie a ribbon around the arrangement, embossed with the Bloomington Blooms logo.]

Josie: "Your sister has a lovely name, don't run into many Emmas."

Susan: "Yes, but that's not my sister, it's the woman she's marrying."

Josie, taken back: "What?!"

Susan: "Yes – she's marrying her partner going on nine years, but now that it's legal, they're finally tying the knot, as respectable people still do."

Josie, alarmed: "Respectable? That's not how I see it. I can't sell you these flowers – I suppose I should say "I'm sorry", but I'm not. It's what I believe in."

Susan, incredulous: "Excuse me? What do you believe in? We all go to the same church and adhere – I'm assuming – to the same religion, believe in the same things, share the faith of our church. What do you mean, you can't sell me the flowers?"

Josie, adamant: "Homosexuality goes against my religious beliefs. Besides, the owners of this shop in Bloomington don't want us to cater to same-sex weddings. I just can't."

---

[32] On March 17, 2015, the PCUSA, the largest Presbyterian body in the United States with 1.7 million members, changed its definition of a Christian marriage to approve performing same-sex weddings in its *Book of Order*, though this won't take effect until June 21. See Bailey (2015). About 71% of PCUSA leaders approved this change, 86 of the 171 Presbyteries which include about 10,959 churches with about 1.8 million members. See Kuruvilla (2015) The PCUSA and other prominent churches such as the Episcopal Church earlier on July 1, 2015, the Evangelical Lutheran Church in America, the Disciples of Christ, Conservative and Reform Judaism, the Society of Friends, and the United Church of Christ all allow same-sex marriages.

[Josie may be channeling the Court's decision in *Thomas*, asserting her right to have her very own religious understanding respected, and she may also have in mind the owners in Bloomington in light of the Court's decision in *Hobby Lobby* which they understand to allow businesses to express their owner's religious beliefs, not to have them infringed even in contradistinction to federal law.]

Susan: "That's ridiculous! I ordered this arrangement weeks ago. You're selling it to *me*, and I'm not gay. And they're not for a wedding, but a rehearsal dinner."

[Susan is trying to convince Josie to sell her the arrangement, perhaps in the hopes of averting what some commentators have feared is likely to happen—that the RFRA exemption with respect to catering to same-sex weddings is not in principle limited just to such occasions, but is likely to expand to all related activities if not to all incidents of same-sex activity, and also across time to any commercial transaction with the same-sex couple.[33] Also, Susan may be trying, in vain as it turned out, to get Joise to sell her the arrangement because she is not gay or in a same-sex relationship.]

Josie: "But that's what the flowers are for – it's all part of the same big ceremony. And, just so you'll know, I do sell flower arrangements to gay people, just not for their weddings."

[Josie may be channeling those commentators who hold the distinction meaningful between refusing to provide services to a gay person and refusing to provide services for an event such as a same-sex wedding, and may also believe that exemptions that allow for the latter are discrete and would not lend themselves to the former. Others may wonder, however, whether this is a distinction without a difference from the perspective of the gay person, just as a Black person would wonder whether refusing to provide services associated with an interracial marriage is a one-time event unconnected to any form of bias couched in race. In both cases, a status-based judgment is at work.]

Susan: "Look, the dinner starts at 6:30pm – I need to get going. Can't you just use some regular ribbon, so no-one sees where the flowers came from?"

Josie: "It's a beautiful arrangement if I do say so myself, so it's bound to come up where it comes from. And that would be dishonest, knowing as I do the real nature of the occasion and knowing what the big boss wants."

[Josie may again be channeling the facts of the case in *Hobby Lobby*, where the Green Family asserted religious proprietorship, so-to-speak, across the entire nationwide chain of over 500 arts and crafts stores in 41 states through the closely held Hobby Lobby Corporation, thinking that if the Greens can do that then surely the much smaller Bloomington Blooms can assert its owners' religious beliefs too.]

Susan, frustrated: "This is absurd. You should have told me."

---

[33] As Taylor Flynn elaborates: "Although framed in terms of marriage and sexual orientation, the exemptions' reach extends far beyond both.... The proposed exemptions touch every aspect of commercial transactions involved in public and private life, as well as any area in which the government offers services, grants, contracts, licenses, or tax-exempt status." See his article "Clarion Call or False Alarm," pp. 238, 244.

Josie, defiant: "I didn't know. We don't ask personal questions, and we're not used to that sort of thing."

Susan, getting infuriated and in a panic over the time: ""That sort of thing"? What's that supposed to mean? You mean, two people who love each other in an actual long-term committed relationship getting married? It's really none of your business – you're not a church, you sell flowers. And we go to the same church – and our Pastor is officiating!"

Josie, feeling her religious oats: "It's what I believe. I don't like it one bit – don't ask me to approve."

Susan: "I'm not asking you to approve. I'm just asking you to sell me the floral arrangement!"

Josie, wanting to be helpful: "There are other flower shops you know."

[Josie may be channeling Douglas Laycock's idea that outside major metropolitan areas "same-sex couples planning a wedding might be forced to pick their merchants carefully, like black families driving across the South half a century ago."[34] Laycock seems to imply that the violation of equality back then was intended to be cured not by a nationwide American principle of equality, but by one subject to local dispensation instead.]

Susan: "Probably closed by the time I'd get there – none nearby anyway. You should have a sign, or post something on your website."

[Susan may again be channeling Douglas Laycock's suggestion that businesses whose proprietors have a religious objection to same-sex weddings and so will not cater to them post a sign in their shop window to alert prospective customers of this, and also to save gay customers the "unfair surprise," the embarrassment of having to be told this in front of others once inside.[35] Of course, the customer need not be one of the two getting married or gay at all, as in this case, and *any* American may be embarrassed that such signs are allowed anywhere in the U.S., marking as they do the inequality of some of their fellow citizens. In addition, Susan and certainly Laycock may not have realized that any legal duty to post a sign in the post-*Hobby Lobby* world would nevertheless implicate Josie in the 'sin' as surely as providing notice that triggers the insurer to provide contraceptives via a different route than the employer insurance provider: "[i]f the merchant has the burden of showing the exemptions, is he not participating in the sin? By providing information on

[34] See Laycock (2008), p. 200. In a more recent essay he affirms his earlier position that "for very small businesses, where the owner is likely to be personally involved in providing any services, we should exempt wedding vendors so long as another vendor is available without hardship to the same-sex couple." See Laycock (2019), p. 29. Ball remarks "how anomalous it is to determine the appropriate outcome of a discrimination claim based on the availability of non-discriminating actors in the same marketplace" in *The First Amendment*, p. 267.

[35] Ibid., pp. 198–199. One religious proprietor's private business practice could well contribute "to a general pattern of stigmatization and exclusion from which people have a reasonable claim to be free", the very aim of public accommodation laws, at least as regards race. See Patten (2017), p. 153.

non-discriminating merchants, he will be facilitating the conduct he refused to be mixed up with."[36]]

Josie, somewhat righteously: "I couldn't do that – it might make us look intolerant, or at least insensitive."

[Josie, oddly enough, may be channeling a large body of literature on religious intolerance in America, a tradition of discrimination by people of faith *for* their religion.[37]]

Susan: "Well, you are!"

Josie: "I'm sorry you feel that way, but I ask you to respect my feelings and honor my religious beliefs and those of the shop owner."

Susan: "You're a bigot, and you're ignorant of your own religion. For the last time, will you please give me the floral arrangement I ordered?"

[Susan is trying to shake Josie loose from the proposition she apparently holds, that the discrimination she is insisting on may not actually be an exercise of religion.]

Josie: "No. I can't, and you can't make me. I think you should leave."

Susan: "You don't have to tell me that. We might see each other again, but before the holidays – in court."

[With that remark Susan left, without her flowers.]

4 Some Considerations for Future Discussion

As the above imagined dialogue makes apparent, any assumption that we may expect any given case to present clear opposing sides is too facile to capture reality as navigated by ordinary citizens, even as their views track theoretical, political, legal, or moral positions available in the literature. Some things stand out and are worthy of further investigation, though we likely will not be able successfully to avoid the significant dignity harm or to navigate away from the question of the legitimate specialness of religion in the law.[38]

[36] See Curtis (2012), p. 200.

[37] See Corrigan and Neal (2010), who put the point rather bluntly: "Religious intolerance is ugly. A story about America without it is a more attractive story, one that more easily pleases and inspires us, one that seems a better fit with what we believe are our ideals, and one that makes us prouder than we might otherwise be.... The Europeans who crossed the Atlantic and colonized the Americas…were not tolerant." See Ibid., pp. 15, 17. Also see Beneke and Grenda (2011), who are equally blunt: "…religion was the United States's first prejudice – and early and inveterate source of bigotry" based in which "humiliating and routinized forms of discriminations were common." See Ibid., pp. 1, 5.

[38] See Bedi (2007) for a spot-on interrogation of the legitimacy of religious exemptions, and how they may perturb religious believers who support them.

4.1 A Parallel to Interracial Marriages

The Good Lord was the original segregationalist.—former Mississippi Governor Ross Barnett[39]

Josie seemed to have an issue with interracial relationships, including marriages, despite indicating her acceptance of the value of bare tolerance with respect to Mrs. Osgood, whose affairs and marriages she says are not her business. Religion was not a reliable ally in the fight against interracial marriage or slavery, and Jeffrey Stout draws a parallel to same-sex marriage, here in the context of an argument promoting greater room for religious discourse in the public space:

> Among the great achievements of American history is the abolition of slavery. How did it come about?... The abolitionists had to persuade American Christians that biblically grounded defenses of slavery were not compelling, despite Saint Paul's advice that slaves should obey their masters and the notion that God had punished blacks as descendants of Ham.... A debate is now raging over the issue of same-sex marriage. Like the debate over slavery, it is full of fear, hatred, and paranoid fantasy.... Some of the biblical passages that mattered greatly in the debate over slavery, such as Galatians 3:28, are receiving extensive attention again.[40]

Religion's role in upholding slavery and subsequent decades-long racial discrimination has been occluded by the history of its more comforting role where it opposed slavery.[41] And, anti-miscegenation laws are an important and relevant aspect of this tradition, religion being the preeminent normative support.[42] One treatment of the religion and race nexus is Forrest Wood's 1990 award-winning history, *The Arrogance of Faith*, which mixes humor with serious historical analysis of the role of sex in the segregation of the South:

> It would not be inappropriate to wonder why the members of a society that not only tolerated but actually exalted an institution as barbaric as human bondage should be squeamish about anyone's private sexual behavior. By the middle of the nineteenth century sexual liaisons between masters and slave women were so widespread that they could no longer be called aberrations.... Southern Christianity was a tribute not so much to the power of slavery as to the fear of a society without slavery...[43]

And religion continued to be the handmaiden of segregation surrounding the *Brown* cases in the 1950s, as historian Jane Dailey relates:

> Certainly both the [Warren] Court and the NAACP recognized that restrictions on sex and marriage lay at the heart of Jim Crow.... State antimiscegenation laws underpinned the

---

[39] See Baume 2015

[40] See Stout (2004), pp. 194, 195.

[41] See Rutherford 1996 which provides extensive documentary evidence of religion as a tool of oppression, including its role in mollifying the African-American slave community and in critiquing the practice of prioritizing religious freedom when it conflicts with what equality arguably would demand.

[42] See Botham 2009, and Washington and Joseph 1970.

[43] See Wood 1990, pp. 200, 334.

> edifice of racial segregation and discrimination in America.... This argument [God's "moral codes" about separation of the races], it is important to note, was not about school segregation per se; it was about its consequences, which segregationists considered to be interracial sex and marriage, leading to race corruption.... More important than the way Christian theology continues to buttress segregationist views within the church has been the effort to use the constitutional protection of religion to expand the social sphere in which segregation could remain.[44]

Anti-miscegenation statutes violated the right to marry considered as "a religious freedom protected by the First and Fourteenth Amendments" and "were in contravention of the Constitution on the day of their inception.... repugnant to the spirit, aims and purposes of the Fourteenth and First Amendments."[45]

The parallels between religious opposition to same-sex marriage and to interracial marriage are clear, and speak to the viability of blithely assuming religion to have only a positive effect on society and to accommodations whenever religious believers claim a law burdens their exercise of religious expression, rather than presents merely an irksome situation of an undesired customer.[46]

Some would argue that allowing businesses to sanction gay people as a class is not akin to "a structural system of oppression, a society-wide conspiracy like Jim Crow."[47] William Eskridge asks the pertinent question, "[a]re Baptists certain that today's antigay readings of the Bible are more reliable than racist readings a generation ago?"[48] His discussion continues:

> Religious doctrine on matters relating to race and sexuality has been relentlessly dynamic: the Word of God has changed constantly.... Because the Bible is a treasure trove of quotable but vague admonitions, the prejudiced reader can find support for many biases and stereotypes.... Hysterical prejudice against African-Americans and gay people have motivated extravagant readings of the Bible to support scandalously bad policies, from slavery to marriage bans, that have harmed America as well as these minorities. In short, religion in American history has often translated – and in effect "laundered" – social prejudice into respectable discourse.[49]

The basis for the parallel is the common religious source, and the name for the 'structural system of oppression' is *heterosexism*, an identity-based discrimination. This common religious source provides respectability to putatively independent secular arguments, but nonetheless the veil was pierced in *Loving* and should be

---

[44] See Dailey (2004), pp. 127, 133, 143.

[45] See Riley (1959), pp. 42–43, 44.

[46] See Oleske Jr (2015) for a very able discussion of these points.

[47] See Douthat 2015 Douthat also believes that "bans on interracial marriage were generally a white supremacist innovation, not an inheritance from Christendom or common law," an opinion that is factually inaccurate if not outright naïve, and that "[j]ettisoning it ["the clear biblical meta-narrative...about male and female"] requires repudiating scripture, history and tradition in a way the end of Jim Crow did not," reflecting further misunderstanding of how traditions are maintained and enforced, and perhaps engaging in a bit of condemnation of some major Christian and Jewish revised understandings. See Ibid.

[48] See Eskridge (2011), p. 708.

[49] Ibid., pp. 713, 714.

pierced now as well to reveal the *shadow establishment* of religion grounding certain of our laws and impermissibly infringing on the equality of a certain class of American citizens.[50] Both structural systems of oppression are undermined by anti-discrimination laws; that is their message:

> [T]he racial caste system, or a similar one based on sexual orientation, is wrong and illegal…. The message sent by allowing religious exemptions is that discrimination is wrong and illegal except when it is right and legal…. General protection against discrimination helps to dismantle the caste system and allow gays to come out, which further dismantles the caste system…. Exemptions undermine that purpose…. It is hard to see why, as a constitutional matter, the Court would allow discrimination against married gays, but not against single gays…. The race analogy may help some see why the harms of discrimination against gays are substantial and why broad exemptions are problematic.[51]

Proponents of religious exemption bills with respect to same-sex weddings such as Governor Pence initially signed into law may attempt to "assure us that this [discrimination] is not what is intended" and that "presumably, the veneer of neutrality in these proposals is necessary to avoid the awkwardness (and likely unconstitutionality) of explicitly singling out a particular, disadvantaged group."[52] But, the "wink-and-nod "textual neutrality" should not occlude from view that basic question: "Why should religiously grounded discrimination be tolerated against gay and lesbian citizens when, regarding racial, religious, gender, national-origin, and other groups, it is not?."[53] Hence, the contemporary shift to freedom of expression, which avoids drawing the obvious parallel to the *Loving* case, where the Court rejected the use of religion to prevent recognition of an interracial marriage.[54]

4.2 An Intra-Religious Dispute

Whereas many commentators posit an opposition between same-sex marriage proponents and religious believers, Josie and Susan, and maybe also Emma, all adhere to the tenets of the same faith, which complicates ascertaining whose exercise of religious expression is being burdened, *if any is*.[55] In the imagined interaction presented above, Susan is the more devout believer, judging from frequency of atten-

---

[50] I developed the notion of a *shadow establishment* of religion in my 2002 manuscript, *Liberal Constitutionalism*.

[51] See Curtis 2012, pp. 203–204, 207, 210.

[52] See Underkuffler 2011 p. 2087.

[53] Ibid., p. 2088.

[54] See Loving v. Virginia, 388 U.S. 1 (1967).

[55] Among churches that perform same-sex marriages are the Presbyterian Church USA, Conservative and Reform Judaism, the Society of Friends, and the Unitarian Universalist Association of Churches. The Disciples of Christ, Evangelical Lutheran Church, the Episcopal Church, and Reconstructionist Judaism each allow individual clergy to decide whether to officiate a same-sex marriage.

dance at religious services, while Josie is more the tries-to-make-it-on-important-holidays religious services attendee.

When Josie says "it's not what I believe in" and "homosexuality goes against my religious beliefs," it's unclear whether this is a statement reflecting her religious beliefs as a member of PCUSA, or her personal beliefs which she may view through the lens of her faith as she personally understands it on her own. In the United States people may hold essentially all manner of idiosyncratic religious views, even those that conflict with the church they claim to be aligned with. While this helps to preserve the freedom to differ and shields persons from a court's prying interrogation, it conceptually devolves down to an individual stating 'this is what I believe my faith demands and that's all the reason there is to it.' Each individual, then, may recourse to faith to launder what to observers might be viewed as raw personal or social prejudice.

By contrast, Susan's exercise of religious belief is consistent with the present understanding of the faith they share, an understanding reflecting PCUSA's active engagement with that faith tradition specifically over the issue of same-sex unions and, we might assume, homosexuality, gay persons as members of the church if not as clergy, and so on. That is to say, though Josie and Susan may offer their views as their conscientiously held beliefs, a court would have difficulty granting Josie and her Bloomington Blooms Flower Shop an exemption *for reason of her exercise of religious expression* being burdened by having to sell a floral arrangement to Susan, without considering that the latter could argue that her exercise is being burdened *as well as* her rightful expectation that a public accommodation conduct business with her. After all, the service Susan is asking for concerns the exercise of a constitutionally protected right, and she may be procuring the floral arrangement entirely on her own and the mention of the same-sex wedding was happenstance.

However, one might opine that Josie is having to violate her religious beliefs or convictions—however conscientiously held or not—by selling the floral arrangement, and so she is the one burdened.[56] Josie complicates this interpretation by asserting that she is also carrying out the religious beliefs of the flower chain's owners, who adhere to a different religion than she does but apparently one with the same opinion as her personal one regarding same-sex marriage. One may speculate that what we have here is more an issue of viewpoint, than one of religion and its exercise. She, of course, may have whatever opinion on anything she wants. It is not her opinion or its source, but her actions that are at issue. And clothing her action in religion—whether her employer's or her personal understanding of her faith tradition that rejected that understanding—may serve to make opaque the actual bias against homosexuality or gay persons really at work, enabling an ambition to discriminate.[57] Not being able to determine which in this context ought to incline the law *not* to grant the exemption.

---

[56] There is no legal criterion for 'conscientiously held', so no legal accountability if not.

[57] Similarly, a gay-friendly racist may cloak his racism by discriminating against a Black gay person under cover of homophobic religious beliefs, thereby engaging in categorically prohibited

4.3 Participating in Sin, the Thin End of the Wedge?

It is not clear whether selling anything constitutes 'participating in sin,' as some would put it in defense of being granted an exemption from public accommodations law even where this imposes a cost on others. In the imagined interaction recounted above, the floral arrangement is not intended for a same-sex wedding, but for a rehearsal dinner hosted by their common pastor, and the buyer is not herself gay. The 'sin' isn't recognized as such by their common faith, nor is sin a legal category but one the law is implicitly recognizing through according recognition to the expression of religious belief, which itself reflects the specialness of religion and its take on various human activities. 'Sin' could not by itself be a legal category except as a manner of speaking about an activity some may wish to dissuade others from participating in, as in 'sin taxes' on consumption of alcoholic beverages or smoking tobacco. To give legal effect to some persons' understanding of 'sin' as a purely religious category is to subject other citizens to their religious dictate, and the error of this is not ameliorated by insulting the subjected parties further by chiding them that "we are *all* in the grip of an unchosen condition, an original problem that our wills alone cannot overcome," as if to make a statement of fact that is in fact merely additional theo-metaphysical belief.[58]

By contrast, one could imagine the relevance of a psychological condition, a social pathology, a practice debilitating to human society or harmful to children. Importantly, neither civil same-sex marriage nor homosexuality, according to the recognized, research-based, scholarly, and informed professional community of experts in the relevant fields, counts in any of those categories.[59] The claimant seeking an exemption because he fears to participate in 'sin' cannot reasonably be understood to refer to an empirically verifiable state of affairs; rather, the claim is theo-metaphysical.[60] The issue is whether such a category of claim warrants the infringement on another person's exercise of his religious freedom or conscientious convictions that same-sex marriage and homosexuality are both blessed, or on his standing as an equal citizen not to be subject to the religious dictate of another as prescribed by law.[61]

---

discrimination. This is a topic for another day, the intersectionality of the injustice religion can facilitate.

[58] See Douthat 2015 (emphasis original).

[59] The American Psychological Association in 2004 advocated for same-sex marriage, as did the American Sociological Association also in 2004, the American Anthropological Association in 2005, and the American Academy of Pediatrics in 2006.

[60] For an argument that any empirical claims or factual propositions made on behalf of religion or religious believers should indeed be subject to the fact-finding power of the courts, see Mason 2010-2011 He argues that religious believers should not be able to masquerade falsifiable propositions to trump civic values. See Ibid, pp. 123, 139.

[61] Kara Loewentheil argues for a "protection, not privilege" principle, because "if religion is to be privileged [when implicating the equality rights of others], then there is no principled way of

Should selling goods from behind the counter be 'participating in sin' on this occasion of an arrangement for a same-sex wedding rehearsal and thus a prompt for a religious exemption from public accommodation law, one wonders what other products or services, or occasions or events they may be intended for that a clerk might be selling as part of her job could be construed as 'participating in sin' and, more importantly, *whether the sinner and not the sin is the real target.*[62] Perhaps in the mind of some traditional religious believers, this is a distinction without a difference, deployed only for public relations purposes so as not to seem intolerant, a concern to which Josie is sensitive.

Then too there is the issue of whether a sales clerk and by association the store in which she is an employee is 'participating' in a deliberate, not incidental sense in anything at all besides the sale, much less 'approving' whatever activity is at issue. Notice how Josie refused to sell the flower arrangement even without the ribbon identifying the store, suggesting that the mere idea of the sale for such an occasion itself is prompting the denial of doing business, rather than a concern for reputation. Is this sufficient to trigger an exemption so as to protect the claimed 'burden' on free exercise or, if it is not, should it be? I believe the answer is no.

May a city trolley driver refuse to let on a passenger whose clothing and comport suggest he is *en route* to a gay pride event? May a sidewalk balloon vendor refuse to sell a bouquet of balloons to a man, learning that they are intended to celebrate a same-sex couple's adoption of a baby daughter? What about the only local men's formal wear store and wedding gown salon? Aren't such transactions a part of daily, ordinary commercial activity that ought to be governed by public accommodation law, regardless of whether there is a state or local anti-discrimination law with respect to sexual orientation?

4.4 The Real Issue: the Specialness of Religion, or Fear of a Society That Doesn't Respect Its Specialness

There has been a long-standing debate in the legal literature as to whether religion is 'special,' which may seem inarguable given its being singled out in the First Amendment.[63] Of course, religion is also mentioned in the un-amended Constitution, in the 'no religious test clause' that some commentators claim conditions the spe-

knowing when to draw the line with regard to infringements on other people's rights." See her article (2014), p. 455.

[62] See Douglas NeJaime and Reva Siegel's excellent discussion of complicity-based conscience claims that, with respect to same-sex marriage, suggest that "[i]n the absence of laws enforcing traditional sexual norms they seek to enforce those norms through a web of religious exemptions" in their article "Conscience Wars," p. 56.

[63] Some of the pertinent literature: Ellis (2006), Gey (1990), Schwartzman (2012), Koppelman (2012), Berg (2012), Smith (1983), Nussbaum (2008), Leiter (2013), and McConnell (2000). McConnell is has been a leading advocate for maximal religious freedom, seeing this norm as

cialness of religion, at least in the eyes of the Founders.[64] Engaging that literature would pull us away from our focus of attention here, where the operating assumption is that religion is indeed special because so many Americans regard it so, but not because of anything inherent to religious doctrine or practice. At any rate, religion was not viewed as so special as to warrant exemptions with respect to race in the 1960s:

> [T]he Civil Rights Act of 1964 passed without an accommodation for those opposed to integration on religious grounds; laws banning interracial marriage fell without measures to accommodate those of faith opposed to interracial relationships; and the courts rejected claims rooted in faith for accommodation to laws banning discrimination in public accommodations and education.[65]

Why be more generous today?

Religious believers have claimed many things to burden their free expression, and particular things when they involve particular people they for religious reasons find trigger a burden. Inter-racial marriage is an obvious example alongside same-sex marriage: in both cases a special relationship is being asserted between religion and either race or sexual orientation such that "it is absolutely essential for individual Christians to be able to restrict the provision of goods and services to homosexuals."[66] Religious believers offer that they "require exceptions from anti-discrimination law relating to sexual orientation because of their need to manifest their religion through expressions about homosexuality…. [as if] curtailing the manifestation of faith-based hostility to homosexuality amounts to a form of discrimination."[67] Such exemptions, however, are "legally anomalous. In no other respects are individuals and for-profit entities excused, on religious grounds, from compliance with non-discrimination laws."[68] That is, prior to *Hobby Lobby*.[69]

---

grounded both in a transcendent reality that has priority to man-made law and in the historical understanding of the Founders' intent with respect to liberty.

[64] Rogers M. Smith suggests that McConnell "overstates" the historical basis for his views in his essay ""Equal" Treatment?" in Monsma and Soper, eds., *Equal Treatment of Religion*, pp. 191–193. For a comprehensive treatment of the views of the Founders, see Stewart (2014), which presents the best treatment of the religiosity and philosophical outlook of the Founders I have recently encountered.

[65] See Melling (2015) p. 183.

[66] See Johnson and Vanderbeck (2014), p. 116.

[67] Ibid., p. 114.

[68] See Lupu and Tuttle (2010), p. 288.

[69] In that case the Court may have opened the door to "corporate theocracy" wherein religious business owners may "profess that a central tenet of their religion bars them from associating with certain other kinds of people." See Luchenitser (2015), pp. 88, 86.

5 Concluding Remarks

At the end of the day, the provision of legal exemptions to public accommodations law on the basis of freedom of religious expression enhanced by a RFRA obscures the discrimination thereby protected, to the detriment of the equal citizenship of American citizens who happen to be in a sexual minority, an infringement on the latter in a way that would not, could not be tolerated were the same infringement directed at persons individually, in pairs, or as a group because of their race.[70] State-authorized departures from equal treatment always risk being constituted as departures from the equal status before the law that is the hallmark of the American political regime, and American citizens who happen to be in a sexual minority rightly perceive themselves inferior in the eyes of the law in a way no one would tolerate for persons of color, who cannot be inferiorized in public accommodation law for reason of someone else's freedom of religious expression. Douglas Laycock's *via media* between religious believers and their gay opponents—in his view, a false dichotomy—misses the mark widely with his recommendations, even if they are stop-gap, because the harms caused by public indicia of different treatment—e.g., legal signage—are dignity harms, among others, against citizens who seek equal participation in American life, and not a "mere inconvenience" in a marketplace "sprinkled with public notices of discriminatory intent," and these harms do not have a parallel for the religious believer who purports to be exercising her religious freedom through, say, the commercial activity of selling flowers, as in the imagined dialogue recounted earlier.[71]

References

Bailey SP (2015) Presbyterian Church (USA) changes its constitution to include gay marriage. The Washington Post (March 17, 2015), online at http://www.washingtonpost.com/news/acts-of-faith/wp/2015/03/17

Ball CA (2017) The first amendment and LGBT equality: a contentious history. Harvard University Press, Cambridge

Baume M (2015) Blast from the past: states using 'Religious Freedom' to Justify Segregation. The Huffington Post (March 26, 2015), online at http://www.huffingtopost.com/matt-baume/states-using-religious-freedom...

[70] Louise Melling reminds us that "[t]he court in *Piggie Park* [a chain of barbeque restaurants in the South that wished not to serve Black people] did not ask whether the customers could have been accommodated elsewhere.... African Americans could not achieve equality if we continued to sanction discrimination in businesses that otherwise opened their doors to the public." See her article (2013), p. 253.

[71] See Laycock (2008), pp. 198, 200. The important notion of 'dignity harm' to same-sex couples or, rather, to the individual gay individuals, is explored in Flynn (2010) pp. 237, 246, 254, and Melling (2015), p. 189.

Bedi S (2007) What is so special about religion? The dilemma of the religious exemption. J Polit Philos 15(2):235–249
Beneke C, Grenda CS (eds) (2011) The first prejudice: religious tolerance and intolerance in early America. University of Pennsylvania Press, Philadelphia
Berg TC (2012) Secular purpose, accommodations, and why religion is special (Enough). Univ Chicago Law Rev 79
Botham F (2009) Almighty god created the races: Christianity, interracial marriage, & American law. The University of North Carolina Press, Chapel Hill
Chandler K (2015) Couples Wed in Alabama County. The Orange County Register (February 13, 2015): News page 10
Cook T (2015) Gov. Mike Pence signs 'religious freedom' bill in private. Indy Star (April 2, 2015), online at http://www.indystar.com/story/news/politics/2015/03/25
Corrigan J, Neal LS (eds) (2010) Religious intolerance in America. A documentary history. The University of North Carolina Press, Chapel Hill
Curtis MK (2012) A unique religious exemption from antidiscrimination laws in the case of gays? Putting the call for exemptions for those who discriminate against married of marrying gays in context. Wake Forest Law Rev (Spring 2012). 47
Dailey J (2004) Sex, segregation, and the sacred after brown. J Am Hist 91:1
David T, DeMillo A. (2015) Indiana unveils changes to religion bill; Arkansas in flux. (April 2, 2015), online at http://www.aol.com/article/2015/04/02/indiana-unveils-changes-to-religion-bill
Douthat R (2015) Interview with a Christian. Sunday Review (April 4, 2015), online at http://www.nytimes.com/2015/04/05/opinion/sunday/rosss-douthat-interview
Ellis A (2006) What is special about religion? Law and Philosophy 25:2(March, 2006)
Eskridge WN Jr (2011) Noah's curse: how religion often conflates status, belief, and conduct to resist antidiscrimination norms. Georgia Law Rev 45
Flynn T (2010, Fall) Clarion call or false alarm: why proposed exemptions to equal marriage statutes return us to a religious understanding of the public marketplace. Northwest J Law Soc Policy 5:2
Ford Z (2015) The true intent of Indiana's 'Religious Freedom' Bill, According To The People Who Helped Write It. (March 31, 2015), online at http://www.thinkprogress.org/lgbt/2015/03/31/3640801/conservatives-indiana
Gey SG (Fall 1990) Why is religion special?: Reconsidering the accommodation of religion under the religion clauses of the first amendment. Univ Pittsburgh Law Rev 52
Gill ER (2019) Free exercise in the liberal polity: conflicting interpretations. PalgraveMacmillan/Springer, Cham
Hamilton MA (1998) The religious freedom restoration act is unconstitutional, period. J Const Law 1:1
Holland S (2015) Most Americans side with gays in religious freedom disputes: Reuters/Ipsos poll. (April 9, 2015) at http://www.reuters.com/article/2015/04/09/us-usa-religion-poll-id
Johnson P, VanderbeckRobert RM (2014) Law, religion and homosexuality. Routledge, Oxford
Karst KL (1989) Belonging to America: equal citizenship and the constitution. Yale University Press, New Haven
Koppelman A (2012) Religion's specialized specialness. Univ Chicago Law Rev 79
Kuruvilla C (2015) Presbyterian Church (USA) embraces LGBT-inclusive definition of marriage. The Huffington Post (March 17, 2015), online at http://www.huffingtonpost.com/2015/03/17/pcusa-lgbt-book-of-order_n_
Laycock D (2008) Afterword. In: Laycock D, Picarello AR Jr, Wilson RF (eds) Same-sex marriage and religious liberty: emerging conflicts. Rowman & Littlefield, Lanham
Laycock D (2014) Religious liberty and the culture wars. Univ Ill Law Rev No. 3
Laycock D (2019) Liberty and justice for all. In: Eskridge WN Jr, Wilson RF (eds) Religious freedom, LGBT rights, and prospects for common ground. Cambridge University Press, Cambridge
Leiter B (2013) Why tolerate religion? Princeton University Press, Princeton

Loewentheil K (Winter 2014) When free exercise is a burden: protecting third parties. In: Religious Accommodation Law. Drake Law Review 62
Luchenitser AJ (2015) A new era of inequality? Hobby Lobby and religious exemptions from anti-discrimination laws. Harv Law Policy Rev 9
Lupu IC, Tuttle RW (Fall 2010) Same-sex equality and religious freedom. Northwest J Law Soc Policy 5:2
Mason CE (2010-2011) What is truth? Setting the bounds of justiciability in religiously-inflected fact disputes. J Law Relig 26:1
McConnell MW (Fall 2000) The problem of singling out religion. DePaul Law Rev 50
Melling L (2013) Will we sanction discrimination?: can "Heterosexuals Only" be among the signs of today? UCLA Law Rev Disc 60
Melling L (Winter 2015) Religious refusals to public accommodations laws: four reasons to say No. 38. Harv J Law Gender
Monsma SV, Christopher Soper J (eds) (1998) Equal treatment of religion in a pluralistic society. William B. Eerdmans, Grand Rapids
NeJaime D, Siegel R (2015 Forthcoming) Conscience wars: complicity-based conscience claims in religion and politics. Yale Law J 124
Nussbaum MC (2008) Liberty of conscience: in defense of america's tradition of religious equality. Basic Books, New York
Oleske JM Jr (2015) The evolution of accommodation: comparing the unequal treatment of religious objections to interracial and same-sex marriages. Harv Civil Rights-Civil Libert Law Rev 50
Patten A (2017) The normative logic of religious liberty J Polit Philosophy 25(2)
Pyke A (2014) Texas Lawmaker Wants Constitutional 'License to Discriminate' Against LGBT Workers And Customers. (November 11, 2014), online at http://thinkprogress.org/lgnt/2014/11/11/3591183/texas-license-to-discriminate
Ravitch FS (2016) Freedom's edge: religious freedom, sexual freedom, and the future of America. Cambridge University Press, Cambridge
Riley LH (1959) Miscegenation statutes – a re-evaluation of their constitutionality in light of changing social and political conditions. South Calif Law Rev 32 (1958–1959)
Robertson C, Dewa S (2015) In defiance, Alabama sets itself far apart. The Orange County Register (February 12, 2015): News page 3
Rutherford J (1996) Equality as the primary constitutional value: the case for applying employment discrimination laws to religion. Cornell Law Rev 81:5
Savage DG (2015) Backlash against religious freedom laws helps gay rights in Indiana, Arkansas. Los Angeles Times (April 4, 2015) at http://www.latimes.com/nation/la-na-religious-rights-analysis
Schwartzman M (Fall 2012) What if religion is not special? Univ Chicago Law Rev 79:4
Smith ME (1983) The special place of religion in the Constitution. The Supreme Court Review
Smith PJ (2014) Who decides conscience? RFRA's Catch-22. J Law Policy 22:727
Somashekhar S (2015) Christian activists: Indiana law tried to shield companies against gay marriage. The Washington Post (April 3, 2015), online at http://www.washingtonpost.com/politics/christian-activists-indiana
Stewart M (2014) Nature's god: the heretical origins of the American republic. W. W. Norton, New York
Stout J (2004) Thoughts on religion and politics. In: Dionne EJ Jr, Elshtain JB, Drogosz KM (eds) One electorate under god? A dialogue on religion & American politics. Brookings Institution Press, Washington, DC
Terkel A (2015a) Indiana governor signs anti-gay 'Religious Freedom' bill at private ceremony. The Huffington Post (March 26, 2015), online at http://www.huffingtonpost.com/2015/03/26/indiana-governor-mike-pence
Terkel A (2015b) LGBT protections included in fix for Indiana's 'Religious Freedom' law. The Huffington Post (April 2, 2015), online at http://huffingtonpost.com/2015/04/02/indiana-lgbt-protections

The Kansas City Star. Kansas Kills Protection of LGBT State Workers. In The Orange County Register (February 13, 2015): News page 10
Underkuffler LS (2011) Odious discrimination and the religious exemption question. Cardozo Law Rev 32
Washington J, Joseph R (1970) Marriage in Black and White. University Press of America, Lanham
Wood FG (1990) The arrogance of faith: christianity & race in America from the colonial era to the twentieth century. Northeastern University Press, Boston

Ethical Vigilantism and Natural Justice: Outline for a Theory of International Criminal Law

Win-chiat Lee

Abstract In this paper, I offer a general defense of what I call "ethical vigilantism" and argue that it provides the basis for universal jurisdiction and the legitimacy of international criminal law. Following David Luban, I argue that any entity exercising "vigilante jurisdiction" would have to bootstrap itself into legitimacy by delivering high-quality natural justice. International criminal law will have to be vigilantism, in my view, as long as we find it undesirable to enter the world-state to achieve the requisite political authorization for its enforcement.

1 Introduction

It may be objected that international criminal law is a misnomer and that it is not really law. This kind of objection can be the result of a general skepticism about international law. But there can also be reasons specific to international criminal law (ICL). In this paper I consider the objection that international criminal law is antithetical to the rule of law because its enforcement is nothing more than glorified vigilantism.

I should note at the outset that what I mean by ICL is broader than what it commonly refers to, i.e., what is enforced under the jurisdiction established for the International Criminal Court (ICC) by the Rome Statute. Parts of ICL enforced by the ICC is not subject to the vigilantism objection for the obvious reason that the ICC is established by a treaty of the signatory states who, as a result of the treaty, have consented to give up some of their authority over certain crimes to the ICC to exercise.

If one thinks that the exercise of legitimate political authority is essential to the rule of law, then clearly the vigilantism objection would make sense only for the kind of law the enforcement of which involves the exercise of jurisdiction by an

W.-c. Lee (✉)
Department of Philosophy, Wake Forest University, Winston-Salem, NC, USA
e-mail: leew@wfu.edu

G. A. Babst, W.-c. Lee (eds.), *Contemporary Facets of Injustice*, AMINTAPHIL: The Philosophical Foundations of Law and Justice 13,
https://doi.org/10.1007/978-3-031-93783-5_9

entity not authorized to do so.[1] We standardly think that the exercise of legitimate political authority is associated with the state, but only *vis-à-vis* its citizens (as well as others who happen upon its territory) and over its territory. Since we do not have a world-state encompassing every state or all of humanity and having political authority over them, any agent outside a particular state imposing, enforcing, or adjudicating legal norms against that state's citizens for crimes committed on its territory, without authorization, is, by definition, not exercising legitimate political authority and therefore contravening the rule of law, even if the agent is another state. We may call such agents "vigilantes." By that, we mean that they are self-appointed, *unauthorized* agents taking the law (what this refers to needs specification in each case) into their own hands, regardless of whether they are individuals, states, or other kinds of entities. The enforcement and adjudication of ICL committed in one state often involves an agent outside that state—either another state or an international entity—who lacks political authority over that state.

Thus, the International Military Tribunal convened by the Allied governments in 1945 was acting as a vigilante when it prosecuted and tried former high Nazi officials for crimes committed outside of Allied territories or against non-Allied citizens. Similarly, Israel was acting as a vigilante in 1961 when its secret service agents captured Adolf Eichmann from Argentina and sent him to Israel for trial for crimes including crimes against humanity. Similarly, Spain was acting as a vigilante in 1998 when it exercised universal jurisdiction and attempted to extradite General Augusto Pinochet, the former dictator of Chile, from Britain to Spain to answer charges of human rights violation committed against Chilean Citizens on Chilean soil. More recently (2022), but similarly, Germany was also acting as a vigilante in prosecuting and convicting in two cases involving Syrian officers committing international crimes against other Syrians on Syrian soil.

The above cases involve the exercise of universal jurisdiction—a jurisdiction that may be claimed by a state solely because of the nature of the crime, regardless of where it is committed or what the nationality of the alleged perpetrators or victims of the crime is. That is what makes them examples of vigilantism. Cases involving the International Criminal Court (ICC) are more complicated and generally do not involve vigilantism since they do not involve the exercise of universal jurisdiction. Generally, the ICC only exercises jurisdiction over states that are signatories to the Rome Statute. One can therefore claim that the ICC is *authorized* by the signatory states to prosecute crimes committed on their territories, over which the signatory states have jurisdiction originally.

Things are more complicated when it involves non-signatory states. In an ongoing case, the ICC was also acting as a vigilante in indicting and issuing warrant for the arrest of President Omar el-Bashir of Sudan for crimes that include crimes against humanity he allegedly committed against other Sudanese Citizens on

[1] This sentence might appear to be paradoxical because it seems to refer to ICl as both law and not law. But the problem can be overcome in drawing a distinction between law in the strict sense and law that is sufficiently similar and still falls short in some regards to be law in the strict sense (in ways that need to be specified in the specific case).

Sudanese soil when Sudan is not a signatory state to the Rome Statute. Such cases require referral by the UN Security Council. Since the UN Security Council is not a political state and does not have political authority over states including Sudan, it cannot confer to the ICC authority it does not have either.

However, to say that something is vigilantism is not necessarily to condemn it, even if we may think it *generally* a bad thing. Similarly, to say that something is extra-legal (strictly speaking) or a contravention of the rule of law is not necessarily to condemn it either, even if we may think the rule of law is *generally* a good thing. There may be circumstances under which vigilantism is morally justified and legitimate, or even required, and may be the only option available for forestalling impunity for serious harms. For example, in what political philosophers call "the state of nature," i.e., the state of affairs where there is not a state, vigilantism may be the only way in which justice can be delivered in situations where harm is perpetrated.[2] However, as will be made clear later, only some accounts of "the state of nature", such as the one provided by John Locke, will be able to connect the exercise of vigilantism to justice.

Even where vigilantism is justified, however, it does not mean anything goes or there are no ethical constraints for its exercise. If we think that there is such a thing as vigilante justice, i.e., that it is not an oxymoron, we need to specify the conditions under which it can be brought about. However, even more important, just because vigilantism may be justified under some circumstances, it does not follow that we do not have an even greater responsibility to bring about conditions under which such justified vigilantism is no longer needed.

In this chapter, I shall take up the question of vigilantism in international criminal law in three stages, each corresponding to one of the three sections respectively. In Section I, I argue that there is a certain kind of philosophical account of the legitimacy of international criminal law—an account to which I subscribe in Lee (2010)—that lends itself to the charge of legitimizing vigilantism. In fact, the problem goes deeper. In this kind of account, the legitimacy of international criminal law is itself grounded in the legitimacy of vigilantism. In Section II, I argue that in the absence of relevant legitimate political authority in cases involving core international crimes, each one of us may have the right to exercise vigilantism in relation to certain harms committed against individuals. The exercise of vigilantism in such a situation is not necessarily a horrible thing and need not lead to chaos if we consider the ethical principles that constrain how and by whom it is to be exercised. Such ethical constraints, I argue, are what may indeed give us some order and priority for the claiming of jurisdiction over international crimes.

Ethical constraints, being what they are, do not provide clear and indisputable norms or assurances that respecting such norms will be reciprocated, without which there will always be some fundamental problems of injustice associated with the

[2]An interesting and controversial recent case is Haiti which has been ravaged by gang violence. In the absence of effective law enforcement, the exercise of vigilantism has provided people with some protection from crimes. Nevertheless, it is also clear that the exercise of vigilantism in Haiti is brutal and, for that reason, unjust. See New York Times 2023.

exercise of vigilantism. These problems may require us, in the first place, as a matter of duty of justice, to abandon vigilantism, establish political authority, and enter a political state to be governed by the rule of law. In Section III, I argue that we are again confronted with the same problems in international criminal law, now at the global scale. However, we no longer have the option of establishing international criminal law as the rule of law in the strict sense because establishing political authority in relation to the application and adjudication of international criminal law would require us to enter a world state, which we may also have good reasons—some related to justice—to resist. More important, international criminal law will also be applicable to the world-state if it exists. Vigilantism, I argue, will again be involved when international criminal law is applied to the world state under the same conditions that make it applicable to states.

We are stuck, as a result, with an international criminal law that is vigilantism but, hopefully, one exercised within ethical limits. We may perhaps achieve a relatively systematic or orderly and even uniform approach to international criminal justice in this way. But it is still not the rule of law in the strict sense without disengaging the rule of law from the exercise of political authority.

2 Default Jurisdiction and Vigilantism

There is a certain kind of philosophical account of the legitimacy of international criminal law that lends itself to the charge that it is nothing more than a glorified form of vigilantism. I shall call it the Default Jurisdiction Account (DJA). I have argued for this kind of account of international criminal law in Lee (2010). Altman and Wellman (2004) have also put forward a similar view in their defense of international criminal law. I take Luban (2004) to be an account of a more specific crime in international criminal law, namely, crimes against humanity, along the same vein. The detail of what I shall present here, however, is mainly my version of this argument.

DJA is the kind of account of international criminal law that does not appeal to harm to the international community as a fundamental notion on which to ground the idea of international crimes.[3] It does not argue for the universal or international jurisdiction over international crimes by claiming that they harm the international community as a whole while other such crimes do not. This part of DJA is motivated by the skepticism that the international community can be harmed in relevant ways or that there is such a thing as the international community at all in the relevant sense. For DJA, the more fundamental issue, rather, concerns jurisdiction more directly. To account for the legitimacy of international criminal law, according to DJA, one has to justify more fundamentally the universal or other international

[3] Larry May proposes, for example, what he calls "the international harm principle" in May (2004). See especially Ch. 5.

jurisdiction exercised by states or international bodies, such as the International Criminal Court (ICC), over an international crime as the consequence of the loss of the exclusive jurisdiction over them by the territorial state, i.e., the state on whose territory the crime is committed.

DJA takes what is known as the Westphalian model, i.e., the model of the world of equal sovereign states, and the attendant principle of non-interference with each other's affairs, to be the way things ought to be in the normal course of events.[4] According to the Westphalian model, all crimes that happen on a state's territory should be exclusively subject to that state's jurisdiction and are essentially domestic in that sense. Some allowances, however, must be made for extra-territorial jurisdictions even in the Westphalian model because crimes perpetrated on one state's territory might involve another state's nationals (either as perpetrators or as victims) or affect another state's interests. There may be other grounds for extra-territorial jurisdiction, but they will have to do with some *connections* a state has to the crime over which it is claiming extra-territorial jurisdiction.

According to DJA, however, there are certain conditions that cannot be violated for the Westphalian model to hold among states. This is because part of the justification of the existence of a state is, among other things, to protect its citizens against harms, especially serious ones.[5] The further claim is that a state may not be able to do so effectively without monopolizing the use of force and excluding others from imposing or enforcing law or adjudicating violations committed on its territory. Given this function of the state, if the state itself, through its agents, perpetrates serious harms against its citizens, or condones such harms, or fails on a regular basis to protect its citizens against such harms, it will lose the legitimacy of the full extent of the monopoly of the use of force or the exclusion of others from adjudicating crimes committed on its territory it otherwise enjoys, especially in relation to the crimes or the serious harms it itself (through its agents) has committed or condoned.[6] This is, according to DJA, what constitutes the core part of international criminal law[7] and how another state or an international body, without having any

---

[4] The reference to this conception of sovereign states as Westphalian is more Altman and Wellman's than my own.

[5] The kind of harm would have to be *mala in se*. Altman and Wellman put their point in terms of violation of basic human rights. I am fine with that. That might leave things less (or more) vague, but that also give us more to account for. For a discussion of the relation between *mala in se* and basic human rights and their role in ICL. See Lee (2022).

[6] The loss of the monopoly of the use of force allows for humanitarian intervention as well. On this account, then, the justification of humanitarian military intervention and international criminal law are two sides of the same coin.

[7] Interestingly, core international crimes on this account would be crimes committed within a state's territory—either perpetrated by the state (or its agents) against its citizens or condoned by the state or failed to be prevented as a result of a more general failure of the state. Thus, in the case of war crimes, it would be war crimes committed in the context of a civil war or of a failed state that constitute the core case of war crimes as an international crime. This makes sense. In the case of war crimes committed by one state against another state or its citizens on the latter's territory, the latter has not lost its exclusive jurisdiction over such war crimes as a result.

connection to these crimes, may exercise extra-territorial jurisdiction to prosecute and adjudicate the crimes over which the territorial state has now lost its exclusive jurisdiction. When a state or an international body may claim jurisdiction over a crime without any connection to the crime at all but solely because of the nature of the crime, we call that kind of jurisdiction "universal jurisdiction."[8]

However, it does not follow from the fact that the territorial state has lost exclusive jurisdiction over a certain crime that others may now come in, also claiming jurisdiction over it. If others have never had jurisdiction over such crimes, then they will still not have jurisdiction over such crimes even if the territorial state has lost its exclusive jurisdiction over them. Thus, for DJA to work, it must begin with the assumption of a *default* such that in the absence of a political authority that can legitimately exclude others from exercising jurisdiction over certain crimes on a certain territory, those others without political authority have the right to prosecute and adjudicate such crimes. If by "vigilantes" we mean people taking the law into their own hands, i.e., enforcing the law, adjudicating violation, and punishing the guilty without political authority, then the default condition is that vigilantism of some sort is legitimate. If the universal jurisdiction exercised by states or international organizations over the core international crimes is the result of this default, i.e., if states and international organizations may exercise universal jurisdiction over such crimes because *anyone* may exercise jurisdiction over them in the absence of a relevant legitimate political authority, then the legitimacy of international criminal law is grounded in the legitimacy of vigilantism of some sort.

How do we understand or justify this idea that the default in the absence of a relevant legitimate political authority is that each and every one may exercise jurisdiction over certain harms done to individuals. I think John Locke's discussion of jurisdiction in the state of nature, which I shall refer to as "natural jurisdiction," is helpful here. For our purposes, we do not need to subscribe more to the notion of the state of nature in Locke's theory than to think of it as a heuristic device to help us understand the norms that should govern our affairs in relation to one another in the absence of political authority. Nor do we need to buy, for our purposes, more into the notion of the natural law than that there is a set of laws—*enforceable* moral norms presumably—that is not positive law. With these qualifications, I suggest that we take natural jurisdiction in Locke to be the default jurisdiction in the absence of a relevant legitimate political authority.

In the *Second Treatise*, Locke writes,

---

[8]The jurisdiction exercised by international tribunals is fundamentally universal jurisdiction, the same as what is sometimes exercised by national courts, unless it is like the jurisdiction that ICC exercises over signatory states, which, as previously discussed, is nothing more than the jurisdiction over their territory and nationals signed over to the ICC by these states. In cases involving non-signatory states, as I have argued, the jurisdiction exercised by ICC is also universal. Thus, in my account, there is no separate argument for something called "international jurisdiction" exercised by international tribunals than the one given for universal jurisdiction in general. This is perhaps what fundamentally sets my account apart Altman and Wellman (2004) and May (2004), for which *international* jurisdiction plays a special role that needs to be accounted for.

> "...the law of nature would, as all other laws that concern men in this world, be in vain if there were nobody that, in the state of nature, had a power to execute that law, and thereby preserve the innocent and restrain offenders. And if any one in the state of nature may punish another for any evil he has done, every one may do so. For in that state of perfect equality, where there is no superiority or jurisdiction of one over another, what any may do in prosecution of the law, every one must needs have a right to do."[9]

The argument, basically, is this:

1. If anyone has jurisdiction in the state of nature over another for the violation of the law of nature, then everybody has jurisdiction over the violation.
2. Someone has jurisdiction over the violation of the law of nature in the state of nature.

Therefore,

3. Everyone in the state of nature has jurisdiction over the violation of the law of nature.

This is a rather straightforward *modus ponens* argument.

Locke's reason for the conditional claim in premise 1 is that it follows from the principle of equality, i.e., the principle that no one is superior or subordinate to another in power in the state of nature.[10] That principle seems reasonable.

Do we have reason to confirm the antecedent in the conditional in premise 1, as Locke does in premise 2, and allow the *modus ponens* to go through? Locke's reason for accepting premise 2, as stated in the passage quoted in the above, is that the law of nature would be "in vain" without any one to execute it. I suppose what Locke has in mind that no law, natural or positive, would make sense as *law* if it is not enforceable. Perhaps the idea is that law is not really *law* if it can be violated with impunity, regardless of whether there exists a legitimate political authority to enforce it. This might also suggest that what Locke has in mind as *law* in the state of nature is not just any moral norm, but the kind of moral norm that is enforceable because there is an interest in not having ~~it~~ violated with impunity. Regardless, Locke seems to think that for the law to be enforced or enforceable, *someone* must have the power or the right to enforce it. This seems to be Locke's reason for premise 2 in the argument.

So here we have a way of understanding and justifying individual universal jurisdiction as natural jurisdiction and as the default in the absence of a legitimate political authority. In this we need not follow Locke all the way to his account of the state—how it comes into existence, how it is legitimate and what the limits of its legitimate authority are. The relevant point is that the state, when legitimate, preempts the default and legitimately monopolizes the use of force and excludes others internally as well as externally from enforcing and adjudicating the law on its

[9] Locke (1980), II. 7.

[10] One may also argue for the reciprocity of jurisdiction as a consequence of equality. The idea, presumably, is that if I have jurisdiction over you in the state of nature and we are equal to each other, then you would also have jurisdiction over me.

territory.[11] When the state fails to meet the basic conditions of its legitimacy as political authority, a reversion to the default takes place whereby natural universal jurisdiction reigns (so to speak).

With the return of the natural jurisdiction of vigilantes, we might as well say that we have reverted at least in part back to anarchy. There is some truth to this claim of anarchy, but only in the sense of the lack of a relevant political authority and not necessarily in the sense of chaos. More important, in the absence of legitimate relevant political authority, it is not just any vigilantism that is morally legitimate and acceptable. Rather, as explained in the following section, vigilantism, where legitimate, is subject to a set of ethical constraints. Compliance with these constraints, I shall argue, gives rise to a certain orderliness we would like to find in the exercise of jurisdiction in international criminal law. Furthermore, if the exercise of jurisdiction in international criminal law amounts to a partial reversion back to the state of nature, it is not the state of nature as described by Locke where only *individual* vigilantes are available to carry out the execution of the law of nature. Since the partial reversion back to the state of nature on this kind of account involves some states turning predatory towards their citizens or simply failing as states, it presupposes a state of affairs that has *states*. What are available as vigilantes in such a "state of nature" are not only individuals and a variety of groups, but also states, state institutions, such as national courts, and possibly international institutions, such as regional and international courts, which are generally stronger candidates than individuals for delivering justice as enforcers and adjudicators.

3 Universal Jurisdiction and the Ethics of Vigilantism

David Luban, in his account of crimes against humanity, is explicit about the connection of such crimes to what he calls "vigilante jurisdiction" as the jurisdiction implicit in such crimes.[12] By "vigilante jurisdiction," Luban means the jurisdiction "in which the criminal becomes anyone and everyone's legitimate enemy."[13] Luban realizes that the notion of vigilante jurisdiction is, in his words, "monstrous," but only because the "vigilante cannot be trusted to determine who is guilty and who is not, nor to moderate their punishments to fit the crime."[14] Here Luban is clearly referring to our popular conception of vigilantes, individuals or in groups, using their rather idiosyncratic and random approaches to justice if that is what they are at

---

[11] It is important to note that in Locke's theory, the contract to enter civil society is only among members of that civil society. Nonmembers never give up their natural jurisdiction to that civil society *vis-à-vis* its members. In this regard, the exclusion of nonmembers by a civil society from exercising their jurisdiction cannot be justified on Locke's theory. I am grateful to Clark Thompson for pointing this out.

[12] Luban (2004), p. 140.

[13] Luban (2004), p.140.

[14] Luban (2004), p.141.

all interested in delivering. But more important, in my view, we find vigilantism appalling because of its association with individuals or groups executing the law themselves where there *is* relevant and functional *legitimate* political authority operating in the area.

None of this implies that when national or regional or international courts and tribunals are used to prosecute or adjudicate crimes against humanity, they are exercising jurisdiction fundamentally different in kind than vigilante jurisdiction. In fact, Luban thinks that the universal jurisdiction exercised by national courts and international tribunals over crimes against humanity is "derived from the vigilante jurisdiction," and is legitimate only insofar as such courts and tribunals satisfy conditions of natural justice.[15]

This last requirement of satisfying conditions of natural justice is what makes all the difference.[16] It shows that if ordinary vigilantes are as interested in and as capable of implementing due process, fair trials, fair use of evidence, protection of the rights of the accused, and doling out fair punishments for the convicted as some of national courts and international tribunals, they will be just as legitimate as the prosecutors and adjudicators for crimes against humanity. By the same token, if the courts and the tribunals are as disinterested or inapt in satisfying conditions of natural justice as those "monstrous" individual vigilantes, they will be as illegitimate as prosecutors and adjudicators of crimes against humanity. Courts, tribunals, and individuals alike all act without political authority in this kind of situation and their legitimacy equally relies on satisfying the conditions of natural justice. The superiority of national courts or international tribunals as legitimate prosecutors and adjudicators of crimes against humanity thus consists solely in their ability and their reliability in satisfying the conditions of natural justice.[17] This is the reason why Luban argues that international tribunals such as the International Military Tribunal at Nuremberg in the aftermath of WWII "bootstrap themselves into legitimacy by the quality of justice they deliver."[18] The bootstrap approach is precisely to achieve legitimacy without political authority. That will have to do as the approach for all the other international tribunals, as well as the national courts involved in the prosecution and adjudication of crimes against humanity committed outside their territory.

What interests me, however, is also a broader set of ethical concerns the bootstrap approach entails. It is important to remind ourselves that we are talking about

---

[15] Luban (2004), p. 143.

[16] The point is that only enforcing and delivering natural justice and not any positive law or private interests can justify the exercise of vigilantism in lieu of a *legitimate* political authority. Dumsday (2006) similarly argues that vigilantes are to be motived by the concern for justice, although he also adds "the good of the community" as a possible legitimate motive for vigilantism (p.58)."

[17] One can understand this kind of "superiority" of jurisdiction as not by nature in the relevant sense. If one subscribes to Locke's idea of the natural equality of all persons in the state of nature, any kind of "superiority" of one jurisdiction over another in the absence of legitimate political authority would have to be reconciled with the idea of natural equality.

[18] Luban (2010), p. 579. Dumsday (2006) would lead to the same result.

not just any kind of vigilantism, but ethical and legitimate vigilantism. On the bootstrap approach, self-appointed vigilantes bootstrap themselves into legitimacy by delivering justice in the absence of relevant legitimate political authority. Since justice is the aim of and the justification for practicing this kind of vigilantism, it should also provide guidance to how such vigilantism is to be practiced. I am interested more specifically in the kind of *deference* that natural justice might require in the exercise of vigilante jurisdiction, as subjecting one alleged crime to multiple jurisdictions simultaneously is itself a form of natural injustice.

Let us return to the Lockean heuristic for a moment. In the Lockean state of nature, there are presumably ethical principles governing the exercise of vigilante jurisdiction insofar doing justice is the aim of such practice. The point of the universal executive power in the state of nature is to thwart impunity. But not just any exercise of the executive power in the state of nature would result in holding perpetrators of harm to account and bring about justice. Process is supremely important. Arguably, a fair and just process is generally more reliable in determining guilt accurately. We may also have a natural duty to determine an alleged violator's guilt in a fair and just way. Thus, in exercising our executive power of the law of nature in the state of nature, the previously mentioned requirements of natural justice, such as due process, can be presumed to apply although some of them may be difficult to implement without institutions and by individual efforts alone. An arbitrary or random process of determining guilt, or no process at all, is not the determination of guilt and therefore not a proper exercise of executive power.

Generally, if a person does not have reasonable expectation that she would be able to deliver justice in a case or if there is someone else willing to adjudicate who would be able to obtain more readily the proper evidence and determine guilt or innocence more accurately than she does in a case, then she should refrain from and not insist on exercising jurisdiction over it. In fact, it may even be wrong for her to do so. For example, if, for one reason or another, such as language, cultural, or physical barriers, one will be unable to obtain the proper evidence and therefore has no confidence for arriving at a correct judgment in a certain case, one should not exercise one's right to adjudicate in that case. If there is a known person or group of persons willing to adjudicate, but without the aforementioned barriers and therefore more capable of delivering justice in that case, then one should defer to them.

Furthermore, suppose there is a violation of natural rights in the state of nature and someone is already there to adjudicate the violation. If I also want to exercise jurisdiction over the same case, it does not seem to be a violation of my right to prevent me from doing so, especially if I am no more likely to deliver justice in this case.[19] There is, however, clearly a problem of injustice if more than one person asserts and exercises jurisdiction over it. It is clearly unjust to subject the same violation to multiple jurisdictions simultaneously or otherwise expose it to double or even multiple jeopardy, but the injustice is even more severe if the multiple jurisdic-

[19] This would make the executive power exercised by individuals in the Lockean state of nature more like a liberty right than a claim right (in the Hohfeldian sense) in that one is free to exercise such an executive power, but cannot make a claim against others to make such exercise possible.

tions also use different procedures and standards for proving guilt. Thus, it would be highly desirable and even a matter of duty of justice to reach a consensus or common understanding among the vigilantes regarding the ordering of claims of jurisdiction and, where there is a consensus or common understanding, for them to abide by it. Without it, there would be significant obstacles for vigilantes to bootstrap themselves to legitimacy.

It is not difficult to see how these ethical constraints on vigilante jurisdiction apply to the arena of international criminal law, especially in matters concerning deference in exercising jurisdiction. Even though individuals (or bands of them) exercising jurisdiction over international crimes is not a realistic worry, theoretically (by DJA) they may be justified in doing so. But individuals should defer to national courts or international tribunals where they are available, even though they are all *equally* self-appointed in the sense that they act without political authority, for the obvious reason that national courts and international tribunals have the means, such as institutional practices, and are more likely to satisfy the conditions for natural justice.[20] Also, among national courts and international tribunals there should also be priority ordering of the available forums in terms of their ability to deliver justice to certain cases so that one court or tribunal should defer to another if the latter is available and willing to prosecute and adjudicate these cases. Some of the reasons for deference to a particular forum may be quite specific to a case—involving considerations such as language, culture and the availability of evidence and witnesses. Other reasons may be more general. The reason for preferring an international tribunal over a national court exercising universal jurisdiction, for example, may have to do with the former being less likely to be fraught with political interests and biases. A regional court or a hybrid court (i.e., a court that combines a national court and an international tribunal) may be preferable to an international tribunal in general also for closer ties to the victims and the perpetrators of a certain international crime. Although there are ethical considerations that govern whether one forum should defer to another for the prosecution or adjudication of a certain case of international criminal law violation, it is also clear that these considerations often yield conflicting results and can lead to disagreements and challenges about which forum is the best to proceed with the case. If the disagreements are serious and the challenges are reasonable, it will compromise the bootstrapping approach to legitimacy for these forums for it will be disputable whether justice is best served by having a case prosecuted or tried in a certain forum.

[20] That means that if there are no national courts or international tribunals available for this purpose, then individual vigilantes might gain more claim to the right to adjudicate these international crimes by being the next best forums available. Thus, national courts or international tribunals might have a duty to assert universal jurisdiction in these cases just to prevent these cases from going to the "next best" forums which are not unlikely to be much good at all. Altman and Wellman (2004) make a similar point but more as a "practical matter" and not as a moral concern. They write, "...as a practical matter, one of the foremost virtues of instituting an effective system of international criminal law is precisely that it will undercut the motivation of miscellaneous individuals to resort to vigilante justice." (P. 64)

The establishment of the ICC is no doubt a significant improvement over the use of *ad hoc* international criminal tribunals, such as ICTY[21] and ICTR.[22] It has given clarity and definition to the crimes that can be prosecuted as international crimes. Just as important if not more, it regularizes and standardizes the process by which these crimes are prosecuted and adjudicated. However, I would like to note two points about the ICC here. First, as previously discussed (Section 1), what the ICC exercises may also be universal jurisdiction in some cases, no different than what Spain exercised when it tried to extradite Pinochet to Spain for prosecution. These are cases involving non-signatory states, but with UN Security Council referrals. Second, where the ICC is also exercising universal jurisdiction, the ethics of vigilantism including the principles of deference also applies. Interestingly, the ICC subscribes to the Principle of Complementarity which defers the prosecution and adjudication of international crimes to national courts that are able and willing to carry it out.[23] However, this still leaves open many issues concerning when a national court and which national court the ICC should defer to and what standards the ICC should use to make judgments concerning these issues. Regardless, the deference to national courts may also perpetuate the problem of a multiplicity of norms involved in international criminal law prosecution and adjudication.

Treaties and conventions regarding several international crimes, as well as the Rome Statute, can be seen as steps in the right direction, i.e., towards a consensus or common understanding and developing common norms regarding the execution of international criminal law. The more things move in that direction, the more justice is embodied in the exercise of universal jurisdiction by national courts and international tribunals in prosecuting and adjudicating international crimes, and thus the more Lubanian bootstrapping into legitimacy there is in the international criminal law regime. But there is still no *guarantee* that international criminal law and its execution will develop into a more centralized and unified set of norms. Furthermore, compliance with that set of norms will still be voluntary. This is the reason that international criminal law will always fall short of the ideal of the rule of law.

[21] International Criminal Tribunal for the Former Yugoslavia.

[22] International Criminal Tribunal for Rwanda.

[23] It is not clear from the point of view of delivering justice in these cases, whether the national courts are always the superior forums. In the case of the national court of the territorial state, a case can be made. But since these are international crime cases, the territorial state is often the state that is implicated in the crimes itself. The national courts outside of the territorial state may be even more questionable in terms of their superiority as forums compared to the ICC. See Philippe (2006) for an interesting discussion of the relation of complementarity to universal jurisdiction in the context of the ICC.

4 World-State and the Rule of Law

One of the notions central to the appeal of the bootstrapping approach is that of delivering natural justice. But that is also its main problem. For Immanuel Kant, most important as a source of insecurity in the state of nature is the subjectivity of each person's judgment about justice. In *The Metaphysical Elements of Justice*, Kant writes,

> "The necessity of public lawful coercion does not rest on a fact, but on an a prior Idea of reason, for, even if we imagine men to be ever so good-natured and righteous before a public lawful state of society is established, individual men, nations, and states may never be certain that they are secure against violence from one another, because each will have his own right to do what *seems just and good to him*, entirely independently of the opinion of others."[24]

Couple Kant's claim here with Locke's claim that we are the executors of the law of nature, we will find a rather unappealing picture of the state of nature as a place for justice to be done. This does not bode well for the bootstrapping approach under consideration in the application of international criminal law because of its reliance on judgments concerning natural justice. Although one can make a case that having conflicting norms applied (in the sense of enforcing rights and adjudicating conflicts) to a person because others have well-motivated, but conflicted judgments about what justice requires is itself a form of injustice, Kant does not seem to go that far. Instead, he draws a distinction between injustice (*Ungerechtigkeit*) and the absence of justice (*Rechtlosigkeit*) and claims that a controversy concerning justice in the state of nature where no competent judge is present to render an authoritative decision that has the force of law only amounts to the latter.[25] The authority and the rule of law Kant is referring to has to with *political* authority associated with the state. Regardless of whether the problem is injustice or the absence of justice in the state of nature, Kant's solution is to enter political society, i.e., the state, and establish the rule of law. Kant's view is that we have a duty of justice to enter contract with others to form a political society subject to the rule of law. In Kant's view, individual rights can be protected and guaranteed only when norms are dictated and enforced coercively with authority, i.e., the political authority of the state.

That is precisely what we do not have in the bootstrapping approach to legitimacy in international criminal law. In the best-case scenario, despite attempts by national courts and international tribunals to implement what they judge to be a just process of determining guilt, it may still amount to justice not being done or being absent in Kant's sense. We have relied on the ethics of vigilantism in the previous section to argue for a normative demand for arriving at some common norms. But as long as compliance is voluntary and not enforced with the coercive authority of law, no rights of the victims or the accused are *guaranteed*.

---

[24] Kant (1965), p.76. The emphasis is mine.

[25] Kant (1965), p. 76.

But this may be the best we can do in international criminal law. We may generally have a duty of justice to resolve the problem of the absence of justice by establishing and entering a state. But presumably a world-state of which we, including the individual nation-states, are all members, i.e., organizing all of humanity into a political state, is the scale of the state solution that is needed to address the problems of absence of justice in matters related to what I have called core international crimes, namely, crimes involving a state's violation of its conditions of legitimacy. We have international criminal law as law in the strict sense only if it is stipulated as positive law, enforced by coercive force and adjudicated authoritatively against states and their citizens by a world-state wielding political authority.

The problem is clear. We do not have a world-state and are unlikely to have one in the foreseeable future. We may not want a world-state in any case and may even have, as our duty of justice, reason to resist having one.[26] This may be sufficient explanation of why we have to live with the fact that international criminal law is less than law in the strict sense and, instead, aim at the kind of ethical vigilante enforcement of international criminal law that bootstraps itself into legitimacy. More important, even the world-state, if we had one, could turn abusive or predatory in perpetrating harm against its citizens or simply fail to perform its protective function, in which case international criminal law would then be also applicable to it. As a result of the state—the world-state in this case—losing its exclusive jurisdiction to prosecute and adjudicate these crimes, we would now revert to the default, i.e., vigilante jurisdiction. Any person or entity asserting this vigilante jurisdiction would presumably also have to bootstrap itself into legitimacy by doing the right thing, namely, satisfying conditions of natural justice, in prosecuting and adjudicating international crimes implicating the world-state.

5 Conclusion

I begin this chapter with the objection to international criminal law as not really the rule of law in the strict sense because its enforcement lacks the backing of legitimate political authority and is therefore no more than vigilantism. My defense of

[26] Kant himself famously rejects the idea of world-state. On this he is followed by many of the contemporary writers on global justice such as John Rawls and Charles Beitz. In *Perpetual Peace,* Kant writes,

"The idea of international right [i.e., law] presupposes the existence of many *separate*, independent, adjoining nations; and although such a situation is itself a state of war…, yet this situation is rationally preferable to their being overrun by a superior power that melds them into a universal monarchy. For laws invariably lose their impact with the expansion of their domain of governance, and after it has uprooted the soul of good a soulless despotism finally degenerates into anarchy." Kant (1983), pp. 124–125. However, Louis-Philippe Hodgson questions the consistency of Kant's rejection of the world-state and argues that Kant in fact should require bringing about the world-state based on the same kind of justice considerations that requires bringing about states to begin with. See Hodgson (2012).

international criminal law is, ironically, to bear out this objection, but to argue that it is nonetheless legitimate—morally legitimate, that is—if it is vigilantism practiced within ethical constraints and delivering justice. International criminal law has no choice but be vigilantism because it takes its place outside the exercise of legitimate political authority and the rule of law in the strict sense, i.e., where political authority, due to abuse, becomes illegitimate. Impunity for certain crimes may be the price we have to pay if we refuse to leave room for international criminal law because of its vigilantism and dubious status as the rule of law.

References

Altman A, Wellman CH (2004) A defense of international criminal law. Ethics 115(1):35–67

Dumsday T (2006) On cheering Charles Bronson: the ethics of vigilantism. South J Philos XLVII:49–67

Hodgson L-P (2012) Realizing external freedom: the Kantian argument for a world-state. In: Ellis E (ed) Kant's political theory: interpretations and applications. Pennsylvania State University Press, College Park PA, pp 101–134

Kant I (1965) The metaphysical elements of justice. Ladd J transl. Bobbs-Merrill, Indianapolis

Kant I (1983) Perpetual peace and other essays. Humphrey T transl. Hackett, Indianapolis

Lee W-C (2010) International crimes and universal jurisdiction. In May L, Hoskins Z (eds) International criminal law and philosophy. Cambridge University Press, New York, pp 15–38 References

Lee W-C (2022) International crimes and human rights. In: Khan BU, Bhuiyan MJH (eds) Human rights and international criminal law. Brill, Leiden, pp 3–22

Locke J (1980) The second treatise of government. In: Macpherson CB (ed) Hackett, Indianapolis

Luban D (2004) A theory of crimes against humanity. Yale J Int Law 29:85–167

Luban D (2010) Fairness to rightness: jurisdiction, legality and the legitimacy of international criminal law. In: Besson S, Tasioulas J (eds) The philosophy of international law. Oxford University Press, New York, pp 569–588

May L (2004) Crimes against humanity, a normative account. Cambridge University Press, Cambridge

New York Times (2023) Vigilante justice rises in Haiti and crime plummets. https://www.nytimes.com/2023/06/03/world/americas/haiti-crime-gangs-vigilantes.html

Philippe X (2006) The principles of universal jurisdiction and complementarity: how do the two principles intermesh? Int Rev Red Cross 86(862):375–398

No Right to Be Forgiven

Rodney C. Roberts

Abstract This paper suggests a theory of rectificatory justice, the essential elements of which include restoration, compensation, and the idea of a just apology. The aim is to show that, given an argument from this conception of rectificatory justice, there is no right to be forgiven. No right to be forgiven should be ascribed to the perpetrators of injustice. Two arguments that are not grounded in any particular theory of rectificatory justice, the Agency Argument and the Expressive Argument, have been offered in support of a right to be forgiven; however, neither of these arguments succeeds.

1 Introduction

The correct answer to the question "Is There a Right to Be Forgiven?" (Maring 2020), is "no." No right to be forgiven should be ascribed to the perpetrators of injustice. Although he thinks that a right to be forgiven "seems unfair to victims," Luke Maring nevertheless finds two arguments he offers in support of a right to be forgiven, the Agency Argument and the Expressive Argument, "compelling" (Maring 2020, p. 1114). My aim in this paper is to suggest a theory of rectificatory justice and show that, given an argument from this conception, there is no right to be forgiven. Moreover, neither of the arguments offered by Maring in support of a right to be forgiven succeeds.

R. C. Roberts (✉)
East Carolina University, Greenville, NC, USA
e-mail: robertsr@ecu.edu

G. A. Babst, W.-c. Lee (eds.), *Contemporary Facets of Injustice*, AMINTAPHIL: The Philosophical Foundations of Law and Justice 13,
https://doi.org/10.1007/978-3-031-93783-5_10

2 Justice

The idea of "justice," or of a thing being "just," always includes some consonance with principles of moral right. When we are concerned with a person's nature, "we speak in terms of excellence… of character;" however, when we are concerned with the way a person's "actions affect other people, we speak in terms of justice" (Urmson 1988, pp. 71–72). Like "[t]he concept of Right, insofar as it is related to an obligation corresponding to it … [justice] has to do, *first*, only with the external and indeed practical relation of one person to another" (Kant 1991, p. 56). So, while being frugal in one's spending might be said to be consonant with principles of moral right, and being fair in one's dealings with others might also be said to be consonant with principles of moral right, only the latter is a matter of justice. Justice "is a distinct segment of morality;" it is a subset of the principles of moral right (Hart 1994, p. 157). "There is no such thing as justice *within* an individual. When the concept of justice relates to an individual, it concerns relationships *between* [that individual] and other individuals or between [that individual] and a group (including the large group that constitutes the organized society of the State)" (Raphael 1990, p. 117). The concept of justice may also relate to groups and their relationships between each other (Buchanan 1991).

Since justice is not the whole of morality, and since the issues with which it must concern itself are of considerable breadth, we can think of justice as a genus of morality. Implicit in the classification of justice as a genus, is that there are particular species of justice which come under it. I suggest that there are only two species of justice: *distributive justice* and *rectificatory justice*. Distributive justice is concerned with establishing a just distribution. Since liberal democracies like the United States of America are very much concerned with civil and political rights, it makes sense to think that rights (or perhaps more specifically, rights and duties) constitute that which liberal democracies are concerned with distributing justly. The ultimate standard of distributive justice is "the principle of consideration;" the state, insofar as it embodies the notion of distributive justice, "distributes rights (on a basis of proportionate equality or equity) to the pursuit of those interests," i.e., those ends, which individuals and groups in a community take to be good, "prescribing, at the same time, the duties and obligations implied in the distribution of rights" (Lamont 1941, p. 12). When rights circumscribe the sphere of just behavior and those rights are transgressed, the prescribed system of distributive justice has broken down; an injustice has occurred.

3 Rectificatory Justice

To rectify something is to set it right. Hence, rectificatory justice is the species of justice concerned with righting injustice; the aim of rectificatory justice is to set unjust situations right. When a right to property has been violated by way of theft, e.g., justice requires, first and foremost, that the exact same item of property be returned to the owner whenever possible. Consequently, the first essential element of rectificatory justice is *restoration*. In cases where immediate restoration is not possible and the owner suffers some additional loss or harm as a result of the injustice, justice requires that the owner be compensated for that loss or harm. Likewise, when restoration of property is not at issue (a violation of one's right to bodily integrity, e.g.) individuals ought to be compensated for any unjust loss or harm. *Compensation* is the second essential element of rectificatory justice.

To compensate for something is to counterbalance it, to provide something equivalent in value to the thing. "The root of 'compensate' is to 'weigh,' that is, to weigh different things together in order to establish a balance between them… 'compensation' carries the connotation of providing something *equivalent* in value to that which has been lost" (Lomasky 1987, p. 142). Since currency is thought to make things commensurate, this compensatory value may often come in the form of currency. In the context of distributive justice, compensation may be provided in order to alleviate some disadvantage or natural loss that is thought to unduly hinder members of society, helping to ensure that they have an equal opportunity to compete for positions and resources. Distributive compensation may be due when, e.g., individuals are disadvantaged by accidents or "acts of God." When members of society suffer a loss or harm as a result of injustice, rectificatory compensation is required as a means of providing something equivalent in value to that unjust loss or harm (this is what is often meant by "reparation(s)").

The third essential element of rectificatory justice is *apology*.[1] Since restoration and compensation can only address unjust losses or harms, rectificatory justice requires an apology in order to address the wrong of an injustice. What makes an injustice a *wrong* is the lack of respect shown to individuals when their rights are violated. Therefore, the righting of a wrong is accomplished by way of an apology—an acknowledgement of wrongdoing that includes the reaffirmation that those who suffered an injustice have moral standing and are worthy of respect. It is typically thought that legitimate apologies must necessarily be sincere and that sincerity requires emotions like sorrow, regret, or remorse. Some even think that a sincere, legitimate, apology justifies the belief that, by apologizing, the apologizer has committed to behavioral reform; that the apologizer promises not to repeat a particular wrongful act. I think this popular view of apology is mistaken.

Thinking of apology in this way may be the result of forming a conception of apology within the context of the whole of morality. However, as we have already observed, justice is not the whole of morality, it is only a distinct segment of morality. Consequently, the content of apologies in response to injustice is prescribed by justice, not by the whole of morality. When an apology is given following an injustice, it is not an apology all things considered that justice requires, that is, not what

[1] Punishment is the fourth essential element of rectificatory justice. This is so because, unlike restoration, compensation and apology, all of which address what the victims of injustice are due, punishment addresses what may be due to the perpetrators of injustice (Roberts 2002).

we might call a *moral apology*. What is required following an injustice is a *just apology* (Roberts 2017).

Contrary to those who think that when rendering a legitimate apology one must *really* be sorry for that which they are apologizing, the just apology does not include as a necessary condition that those who apologize have certain feelings. Just apologies need only be sincere in the sense that the person uttering the words is making a true statement about the unjust act, and is making a commitment to providing, or at least earnestly attempting to provide, compensation. Would it be better if the person apologizing was racked with guilt, shame, sorrow, and regret when uttering the words? Of course it would. Would this being the case make the apology a more substantive acknowledgment of the victim's moral worth than just making a statement? Perhaps. In any event, justice is not in the business of prescribing which feelings people ought to have and when they ought to have them. Rather, it is in the business of prescribing the way we ought to act toward one another. Justice is that sphere of morality which functions as the primary arbiter of social behavior. It may be that morality in a general sense calls for feeling sorrow, regret or remorse when we have committed an injustice, but there is no ground for this requirement in justice.

The just apology includes a statement that expresses an acknowledgement by the actor, or the actor's representative, that the action was wrong. It is in this way that an apology addresses the wrong of an injustice. Consequently, an apology is due after an injustice whether or not the victim has sustained any unjust loss or harm. However, this is not to deny the essential relationship between apology and compensation where the latter legitimizes the former. Since rectificatory justice requires that unjust losses be restored or compensated for, apologies purported to be given in cases where compensation is due but not provided (or at least earnestly attempted) are illegitimate. This is so because, in such cases one's actions are (at best) inconsistent if one acknowledges the injustice perpetrated, but fails to provide an equivalent in value for the losses or harms sustained by the victim as a result of that injustice. Moreover, in cases where there is an unjust loss, it is in large part by way of fulfilling (or earnestly attempting to fulfill) the restorative or compensatory requirements of rectificatory justice that a perpetrator's apology is rendered sincere.

Since face-to-face speech is the most effective and the most personal way in which we communicate complex ideas to each other, just apologies ought to be given verbally and face-to-face by the perpetrator of the injustice whenever possible, or by the perpetrator's representative when it is not. Beyond one-on-one apologies where groups are involved, all members of the groups concerned should have a reasonable chance of hearing the apology. In state-rendered apologies for major injustice, e.g., the number of relevant parties may run into the millions. In such cases the apology ought to be broadcast widely. The apology should also be widely published, both for the record and so that any relevant parties who did not hear the apology have a reasonable chance of experiencing it subsequently, such as through viewing recordings or reading the text of the apology.

The conception of a just apology makes better sense of the idea of demanding an apology than do apologies in which particular feelings are required. If we think that the person apologizing must be "really sorry" for the injustice in order to render a legitimate apology, then it seems odd that we should ask, much less demand, that one be given. In such cases we would be demanding that people possess certain feelings. What justice requires from the perpetrator is to act justly in the wake of injustice, to endeavor to make things right; not to have particular feelings. To demand a just apology is to demand an acknowledgement of the perpetration of an injustice and the taking of responsibility by the perpetrator (or the perpetrator's representative) for ensuring that compensation is provided for any unjust loss or harm. A demand is sometimes necessary because in our non-ideal world people may need to be reminded that justice requires an apology following injustice. Like a mother who brings her child face-to-face with someone the child has wronged and commands, "Tell Mr. Jones you're sorry," adults may need to be reminded when an apology is due. This is part of developing what John Stuart Mill describes as the external sanction of "the hope of favor and the fear of displeasure from our fellow creatures" (Mill 2001, p. 28). Our moral faculty, while "susceptible of being brought by cultivation to a high degree of development," is sometimes too weak to prompt us to act justly on our own (Mill 2001, p. 31). As Aristotle reminds us, we are not born with prudence and wisdom, they arise in us and grow "mostly from teaching," that is why the possession of these virtues only comes with "experience and time" (Aristotle 1999, p. 18 (1103a 15)). It therefore makes sense to think that when an acknowledgment of wrongdoing is "expressed" in an apology it will sometimes include more than having put the acknowledgement into words. It may also include a sense in which (pursuant to the Latin origin of 'express') the acknowledgment is obtained in part by way of pressure; that the apology was pressed or squeezed out of a reluctant apologizer.

The conception of a just apology also makes better sense of the idea of a national or state-to-state apology than do apologies in which particular feelings are required. Here the concern has been that national or state-to-state apologies require entire groups to feel sorrow, remorse or regret in order for the apology to be legitimate. Since it seems likely that there will be many cases in which everyone in the apologizing group will not have the requisite feelings, an apology where one or more of those feelings is necessary for a legitimate apology means that national and state-to-state apologies will often be impossible; not so with the just apology.

Finally, the just apology does not have as a necessary condition that it be sincere in the sense that by apologizing one commits oneself to not repeating a particular wrongful act. Kant suggests this point when he observes that "[a]nyone can be free, as long as I do not impair his freedom by my *external actions*, even though I am quite indifferent to his freedom or would like in my heart to infringe upon it" and thereby perpetrate an injustice (Kant 1991, p. 56). Wronging a person and then wanting to wrong them again in the very same way may speak ill of my character, but it is not unjust. Although I acted unjustly toward you in the past, my present desire to do so again is not itself an injustice. It is therefore difficult to see how a commitment to refrain from the performance of a particular wrongdoing can follow from an acknowledgement of having perpetrated that wrongdoing.

There is no obvious reason why we should infer a commitment to refrain from repeating an act from the mere fact of having denounced the past performance of that act. Of course, even when we have not apologized, if X is an injustice for which an apology is due, then X is a rights violation that we already had a duty not to do in the first place. Hence, *a fortiori*, we ought not to do X again.

4 The Argument from Rectificatory Justice

According to the argument from rectificatory justice, there is no right to be forgiven for the perpetration of an injustice:

(1) The sphere of justice is circumscribed by rights.
(2) Justice has that which is external in actions as its object.
(3) Justice does not have that which is internal in feelings as its object.
(4) Justice cannot require the possession of any particular feelings.
(5) "Forgiveness is primarily a matter of how I *feel* about you (not how I treat you) (Murphy, Hampton 1988, p. 21).
(6) Therefore, perpetrators of injustice have no right to be forgiven by their victims.

Since justice is only a distinct segment of morality, and since it seems possible that victims of injustice can forgive their perpetrators on moral grounds, some may think this presents a difficulty for my argument; it does not. Nothing I have said forecloses the possibility that victims can have moral reasons for forgiving their perpetrators—only the possibility that perpetrators have a *right* to be forgiven by their victims. If we consider forgiveness a virtue, e.g.,

> then it must be that sometimes it is not merely permissible that I forgive but that I *ought* to forgive and can be properly criticized if I do not. Perhaps nobody has a *right* to be forgiven (imposing on others a perfect duty to forgive him), but surely forgiveness—if a virtue—must be like charity in at least this way: Just as charity requires that I sometimes ought to assist those having no right to my assistance, so does forgiveness require that I sometimes ought to forgive those having no right to my forgiveness (Murphy, Hampton 1988, p. 29).

Forgiveness "is conceptually connected with supererogatory acts of generosity and charity. It is something we ask or hope, rather than demand, for ourselves, and grant, rather than owe, to others." (Calhoun 1992, p. 81).

Contrary to my conclusion (6), both the Agency Argument and the Expressive Argument claim that there is a right to be forgiven. However, as I will now endeavor to show, since both arguments contain at least one false premise, and since analysis of each argument prompts a rectificatory justice-based rationale for finding their conclusion false, neither argument succeeds.

5 The Agency Argument

According to the Agency Argument:

(1) "[P]eople have a right that we respect their agency" (Maring 2020, p. 1112).
(2) "[R]espect for agency requires us to judge [an amends-making offenders'] actions fairly (i.e., not discounting amends made while emphasizing lowlights)" (Maring 2020, p. 1112).
(3) "[I]f we judge amends-making offenders fairly, we will forgive them" (Maring 2020, p. 1112).
(4) Therefore, wrongdoers who have done everything necessary for moral repair of the perpetrated injustice (i.e. they have rectified the injustice), have a right to be forgiven by their victims.

As stated, premise (3) asserts that fair judgement of amends-making offenders is a sufficient condition for their victims to actually forgive them (*will* forgive). Since this would render moot any need for a right of amends-making offenders to be forgiven grounded in a victim's judgment (we will all do it when such offenders are judged fairly), premise (3) is perhaps better understood as the normative claim: "If we judge amends-making offenders fairly, we have a duty to forgive them." In order for the Agency Argument to succeed, it must be the case that fair judgement of amends-making offenders is a sufficient condition for a duty on the part of their victims to forgive them; however, it is not a sufficient condition. "How can my hurting you and then trying to undo the harm, actions all of my choice and not yours, put you under an obligation to do something which did not exist before?" (Swinburne 1989, p. 82). Surely there is no way that it can. Fulfilling the requirements of justice in the wake of injustice is the sole responsibility of the wrongdoer and is only a matter of what the perpetrator must do to make things right; and this is as it should be. Fair judgement of a wrongdoer's rectificatory efforts only counts insofar as an assessment of the injustice's rectification is concerned, it in no way counts as ground for some action on the part of their victim. Hence, fair judgement of amends-making offenders is not a sufficient condition for a duty on the part of their victims to forgive them; premise (3) is false.

Moreover, fair judgement of amends-making offenders cannot be a sufficient condition for a duty on the part of their victims to forgive them, because a necessary condition for forgiveness is that victims feel a certain way about their offenders. Since offenders can be forgiven only if their victims possess certain feelings toward them, and since justice cannot require us to possess any particular feelings, victims of injustice do not have a duty to forgive their perpetrators. There being no duty on the part of victims to forgive their perpetrators, perpetrators have no right to be forgiven by their victims. Hence, the conclusion (4) of the Agency Argument is also false.

6 The Expressive Argument

According to the Expressive Argument:

(1) "[W]ithholding forgiveness" or "[r]efusing to forgive" a wrongdoer "who has done everything necessary for moral repair" of the perpetrated injustice, "expresses that the wrongdoer is unfit" for "a community of equals;" it marks the wrongdoer "as Other, as unequal, as a degraded or broken moral agent" (Maring 2020, p. 1109).
(2) "[M]oral agents have a right against being the target of degrading or Othering messages that are inapt" (Maring 2020, pp. 1109–1110).
(3) "[T]elling people who do not deserve to be shunned that they are unfit for the moral community" is wrong (Maring 2020, p. 1110).
(4) Therefore, wrongdoers who have done everything necessary for moral repair of the perpetrated injustice (i.e. they have rectified the injustice), have a right to be forgiven by their victims.

Those who endorse premise (1) think that an utterance like "I forgive you" expresses moral equality between victim and perpetrator, and that withholding forgiveness or refusing to forgive with an utterance like "I will not forgive you" or "I refuse to forgive you," expresses moral inequality between victim and perpetrator. However, neither withholding forgiveness nor refusing to forgive constitutes an expression of moral inequality. As Maring rightly notes, "[i]t is a commonplace that wrongdoing is expressive," and that it "communicate[s] something about the victim's worth" (2020, p. 1109). This is because "when we are treated with contempt by others it attacks us in profound and deeply threatening ways" (Murphy, Hampton 1988, p. 25). Injustices perpetrated against us do not only "hurt us in some tangible or sensible way," they "are also *messages*—symbolic communications" (Murphy, Hampton 1988, p. 25). Like wrongdoing, the expression "nigger" clearly communicates something about a person's worth (Roberts 2010). It has been described as "a chief symbol of white racism that "reinforce[s] the stereotype of the lazy, stupid, dirty, worthless parasite" (Pilgrim, Middleton 2012). White folk calling Black folk "nigger" can have an immediate and injurious impact on the hearer(s) and on Black folk out of earshot as they learn about more repeated instances of this derogatory term being used. It does so by "remind[ing] the world that you are fair game for physical attack," by "evok[ing] in you all of the millions of cultural lessons regarding your inferiority that you have so painstakingly repressed," and by "imprint[ing] upon you a badge of servitude and subservience for all the world to see" (Lawrence III 1993, p. 74). Relying on "the unalterable fact of the victim's race and on the history of slavery and race discrimination in this country," it is "always a dignitary affront, a direct violation of the victim's right to be treated respectfully." As Richard Delgado reminds us, "[o]ur moral and legal systems recognize the principle that individuals are entitled to treatment that does not denigrate their humanity through disrespect for their privacy or moral worth." "Nigger" expresses a judgement that the victim "is entitled to less than that to which all other citizens are entitled" (Delgado 1993, p. 94).

In sharp contrast to "nigger," expressions like "I will not forgive you" and "I refuse to forgive you" do nothing to communicate disrespect, inferiority, or moral inequality. Withholding forgiveness or refusing to forgive may communicate that the victim does not possess the feelings necessary for forgiveness, but they say nothing about the perpetrator. This being the case, premise (1) of the Expressive Argument is false. Moreover, since perpetrators of injustice who have done everything necessary to rectify their injustice do not have a right to the expression of moral equality from the victim that forgiveness is thought to entail, the conclusion (4) is also false.

Prescription and justification are two essential elements of a right. "[A]lmost all theorists regard rights as, in some sense, justified," and "any genuine right must involve some normative direction of the behavior of persons other than the holder" (Martin, Nickel 1980, p. 165 n.2, 167). Rights are prescriptive relations that we ascribe to persons; they are relations in which at least one of the members is justified in having some other member(s) act, or refrain from acting, in a certain way. The justification for the behavior required by a given right is often expressed by terms like 'natural,' 'moral,' 'legal,' and 'civil.' Saying that a right is a moral right tells us that the right has its justification in sound moral argument, whether or not such reasoning is grounded in a formal normative theory. "[T]o assert the existence of a moral right is merely to assert the existence of a set of moral reasons bearing upon human conduct in that very special way in which rights have practical relevance" (Wellman 1985, p. 170). In other words, having a moral right entails "having a moral justification for limiting the freedom of another" and for "determin[ing] how another shall act" (Hart 1955, p. 178, 177 n. 6). We do not go about our day-to-day lives expressing moral equality toward each other. Rather, we demonstrate our understanding that all individuals are equally worthy of respect by respecting everyone's rights. Only in the wake of an injustice perpetrated against us, and then only by way of an apology, do any of us have a right to something like an expression of moral equality. Grounded in the injustice perpetrated against them, victims of injustice have a right to the acknowledgement of wrongdoing that includes the reaffirmation that they have suffered an injustice and that they have moral standing. By apologizing the perpetrator reaffirms that the victim is a person and is therefore worthy of respect. Since perpetrators of injustice who have done everything necessary to rectify their injustice do not have a right to the expression of moral equality from their victims that forgiveness is thought to entail, they have no right to be forgiven by their victims.

7 Conclusion

If my analysis holds, given an argument from rectificatory justice, there is no right to be forgiven. Moreover, neither the Agency Argument nor the Expressive Argument, both of which have been offered in support of a right to be forgiven, succeeds.

References

Aristotle (1999) Nicomachean ethics, 2nd edn (trans: Irwin T). Hackett, Indianapolis
Buchanan A (1991) Secession: the morality of political divorce from Fort Sumter to Lithuania and Quebec. Westview Press, Boulder
Calhoun C (1992) Changing one's heart. Ethics 103:76–96
Delgado R (1993) Words that wound: a tort action for racial insults, epithets, and name calling. In: Matsuda MJ, Lawrence CR III, Delgado R, Williams Crenshaw K (eds) Words that wound: critical race theory, assaultive speech, and the first amendment. Westview Press, Boulder, pp 89–110
Hart HLA (1955) Are there any natural rights? Philosoph Rev 64:175–191
Hart HLA (1994) The concept of law, 2nd edn. Oxford University Press, New York
Kant I (1991) The metaphysics of morals (trans: Gregor M). Cambridge University Press, Cambridge
Lamont WD (1941) Justice: distributive and corrective. Philosophy 16:3–18
Lawrence III CR (1993) If he hollers let him go: regulating racist speech on campus. In: Matsuda MJ, Lawrence III CR, Delgado R, Williams Crenshaw K (eds) Words that wound: critical race theory, assaultive speech, and the first amendment. Westview Press, Boulder pp. 53–88
Lomasky LE (1987) Persons, rights and the moral community. Oxford University Press, New York
Maring L (2020) Is there a right to be forgiven? Philosophia 48:1101–1115
Martin R, Nickel JW (1980) Recent work on the concept of rights. Am Philosophical Quart 17:165–180
Mill JS (2001) In: Sher G (ed) Utilitarianism, 2nd edn. Hackett, Indianapolis
Murphy JG, Hampton J (1988) Forgiveness and mercy. Cambridge University Press, New York
Pilgrim D, Middleton P (2012) Nigger and caricature. https://www.ferris.edu/HTMLS/news/jimcrow/caricature. Accessed 6 Jan 2021
Raphael DD (1990) Problems of political philosophy, 2nd edn. Humanities Press, Atlantic Highlands
Roberts RC (2002) Justice and rectification: a taxonomy of justice. In: Roberts RC (ed) Injustice and rectification. Peter Lang, New York, pp 7–28
Roberts RC (2010) The morality of using 'nigger.'. In: Golash D (ed) Freedom of expression in a diverse world. Springer, Dordrecht, pp 87–100
Roberts RC (2017) Race, rectification, and apology. In: Zack N (ed) The oxford handbook of philosophy and race. Oxford University Press, New York, pp 516–525
Swinburne S (1989) Responsibility and atonement. Oxford University Press, Oxford
Urmson JO (1988) Aristotle's ethics. Blackwell, Oxford
Wellman C (1985) A theory of rights: persons under laws, institutions, and morals. Rowman & Allanheld, Totawa

Generative AI and Deepfakes: Challenges to Epistemic Justice and Comprehensive Regulations

Yi Deng

Abstract In response to epistemic challenges posted to the public by hyper-realistic characters in AI-generated synthetic media, this chapter aims to answer the question: to what extent is generative AI responsible for its generated texts, images, audio, or videos, especially in situations involving deepfakes? I argue that generative AI models such as an artificially intelligent speech generator or a Generative Adversarial Network (GAN) should be accountable for the transparency and truthfulness of its generated output due to its practical impacts on the public, particularly considering the injustice and potential epistemic threats posed by political deepfakes. The latest trend in AI regulations, as presented by the 2024-implemented EU Artificial Intelligence Act (AIA) and the 2024-signed California AI Transparency Act, shows the move toward a more comprehensive regulatory framework for AI, which aligns with my argument on AI accountability.

The paper's earliest version "Digital Being and Fake Voice" was presented at XXVIII World Congress of the International Association for the Philosophy of Law and Social Philosophy (IVR), a special workshop: New Technology and (Non-) Human Agency: Risks, Responsibilities, and Regulation in July 2017. Special thanks to the workshop organizers Vesco Paskalev and Peter Cserne, fellow workshop participants, and the conference attendees. The paper's later version was presented at Georgia Philosophical Society 2022 Annual Meeting, UGA, and the latest version was presented at AMINTAPHIL 2023 conference and UNG HAP Works in Progress group. I appreciate all the feedback and comments from the conference participants, attendees, and fellow colleagues. Special thanks to Russell Waltz for writing comments on my paper at the 2023 AMINTAPHIL meeting. I also greatly appreciate comments from editors Gordon Babst and Win-chiat Lee.

Y. Deng (✉)
University of North Georgia, Dahlonega, GA, USA
e-mail: yi.deng@ung.edu

G. A. Babst, W.-c. Lee (eds.), *Contemporary Facets of Injustice*, AMINTAPHIL: The Philosophical Foundations of Law and Justice 13,
https://doi.org/10.1007/978-3-031-93783-5_11

1 Introduction

I was initially intrigued by the development of an artificially intelligent speech generator. In 2017, a Canadian startup Lyrebird announced a software that can imitate almost any human voice, and released a series of public demos on fake voices of politicians.[1] In my initial investigation, inquiring about such a type of AI generator's accountability and responsibility for the voice they deliver, I asked a question: to what extent is an AI generator responsible for its generated content, such as audio, video, images, or prose? During the recent years, hyper-realistic characters generated by AI, say, voice or photographic images, have been in the direction of being hardly distinguishable from the ones by humans. The technology milestone was signified by the development of the generator in Generative Adversarial Networks (GANs) (Goodfellow et al. 2014; Goodfellow et al. 2020). With machine learning advancement, the availability of high-quality realism generated by generative AI has emerged in public life with a wide range of implications, such as in the movie industry and the education sector. Along with those benefits of AI-generated hyper-realistic media (Pataranutaporn et al. 2021), some notorious instances of deepfake videos during recent years drew public and professional attention and concerns over the moral limit and legal restrictions of AI-generated media. The compound phrase "deepfake," a combination of "deep learning" and "fake," refers to a generation of false or modified media through a technique of machine learning (Abdulreda and Obaid 2022). Known to the public as AI-based "face-swapping," instances of swapping celebrity face into pornography in 2017 initially brought "deepfake" from reddit users in r/CeleFakes to the mainstream's attention (Nguyen et al. 2022). Later in 2018, major platforms including Reddit banned pornographic deepfakes. With the rising availability of face-swapping tools, illustrated in instances like BuzzFeed's deepfake ObamaPeele video created through FakeApp in 2018,[2] showed the instant influences of non-pornographic use of the deepfake techniques on a massive scale (Goggin 2019). In 2019, the popularity and easy accessibility of the Zao face-swapping app went viral for public debates but also revealed the potential of deepfake techniques into commercial markets (Agence France-Presse in Shanghai 2019; Doffman 2019; de Seta 2021).

---

[1] A brief history of Lyrebird AI, which was acquired by Descript in 2019, can be found on Descript's website. https://www.descript.com/lyrebird. A Lyrebird's 2017 demo of a fake discussion about Lyrebird among fake Barack Obama, fake Donald Trump, and fake Hillary Clinton can be found on SoundCloud: https://soundcloud.com/user-535691776/dialog.

NPR listed the demo's transcript. See NPR, "New Software Can Mimic Anyone's Voice" (2017). https://www.npr.org/2017/05/05/527013820/new-software-can-mimic-anyones-voice.

A series of Lyrebird public demos on fake Obama and fake Trump can still be found on SoundCloud: https://soundcloud.com/user-535691776.

[2] The ObamaPeele video can be viewed on the BuzzFeed website. See Silverman C (2018) How To Spot A Deepfake Like The Barack Obama–Jordan Peele Video. https://www.buzzfeed.com/craig-silverman/obama-jordan-peele-deepfake-video-debunk-buzzfeed.

In this chapter, I inquire into the moral accountability of generative AI for generating hyper realistic characters in media like video data, audio, images, or even text or prose.[3] To begin with, I would point out that AI generated hyper-realistic characters involved in deepfakes, particularly in political deepfakes, may deprive the public's right to determine the veracity of information and disrupt the public's ability to vote. Such epistemic perplexities with the potential to develop into a type of epistemic injustice call for theoretical considerations and regulatory frameworks on AI. The latest regulations on AI, represented by the EU AIA and the California Transparency Act, show the regulatory directions on AI towards a more comprehensive regulations, and Governor Newsom's veto on S.B. 1047 on September 29, 2024 signaled the need for a more unified framework bringing together science communities, the tech industries, government agencies, consumers, and the public. My argument for AI's moral accountability, inferring the requirement for transparency at a threshold and further for trustworthy, starts with metaphysical considerations of AI's nature rather than thick moral presumptions, and it aims to support a more unified framework for AI regulations by reevaluating and reinforcing AI's relation to the public.

2 Epistemic Threats and Deepfakes

A 2023 study (Mai et al. 2023) found that human capacities in detecting deepfake speeches are limited, with an accuracy of 73% in an experiment with 529 participants, regardless of language impact in English and Mandarin. Another study involving 280 participants found limited human capacities of detecting static deepfake images generated by StyleGAN2, with detection accuracy of only 60 to 64% of the time, "only just above chance" (Bray et al. 2023). An earlier study shared the similar results and concerns that "synthetically generated faces…are nearly indistinguishable from real faces and are judged more trustworthy" (Nightingale and Farid 2022). These studies have revealed a type of epistemic threats in human capacity to distinguish deepfakes from real images or speeches, and repeatedly remind us of human overconfidence in detection abilities, given that AI is continually advancing in generating more realistic outputs as algorithms develop. Regrettably, human performance improvement remains disproportionately slow in an era flooded with synthetic deepfake medias. It is observed that increasing listeners' awareness of deepfake speeches only slightly improves the accuracy rate (Mai et al. 2023), and neither of the human interventions, including familiarization exercise or explicit advice, significantly improved human performance (Bray et al. 2023). Worse still, humans' tendency to believe what they see, as in

[3] In the last two years, the most widely discussed text prose AI generator is ChatGPT. A brief history of ChatGPT can be found on the OpenAI website (2022): https://openai.com/index/chatgpt/.

"seeing-is-believing," makes them more vulnerable to influences from deepfakes (Köbis et al. 2021).

Admittedly, the mere existence of hyper-realistic characters in generated deepfake media poses epistemic threats to human detection capacities, and furthermore, such perplexities in discerning truth, coupled with decreasing reliability of human detection, may lead to actual negative impacts, for example, in cases of political deepfakes. Scholars have expressed their concerns about the urgent threats from deepfakes, especially when used maliciously in politics or international affairs, potentially distorting democratic discourse (Chesney and Citron 2019). An earlier example of political deepfakes included a synthetic fake video of the Ukrainian President Volodymyr Zelenskiy telling the solider to surrender their fight against Russians, whose falsity was not hard to detect (Allyn 2022). However, along with AI's rapid development in the last two years, the quality and quantity of deepfakes have reached a level where humans must admit their detection limitations. As the Guardian reported, "more than 100 deepfake video advertisements impersonating Rishi Sunak were paid to be promoted on Facebook in the last month alone," showing manipulation risks in elections arising from the advanced quality and a large quantity of AI-generated deepfake medias due to the low cost and ease of use of these tools (Quinn 2024). Not to speculate about the epistemic mistrust of and vulnerability to a flood of deepfakes—one instance of political deepfake, for example, an AI-generated robocall of U.S. President Joe Biden in Jan 2024 urging New Hampshire voters not to vote in the state's primary election, was able to demonstrate potential harms, or at the very least, directly disrupt the electoral process. Another instance of political deepfake involved a viral audio recording of Michal Šimečka, leader of the liberal Progressive Slovakia party discussing election fraud, posted to Facebook in two days before Slovakia's October 2023 election. The instance of Slovakia's election deepfakes, which showed how timely AI-generated misinformation can unsettle voters and bring challenges for fact-checkers to respond during elections, may have indeed influenced the election result (Weiner and Norden 2023). One relevant aspect of the background on Slovakia's election deepfakes is Meta's manipulated media policy then, the version implemented in November 2020. [4] While the policy covered the removal of synthetic videos at the time, it had a loophole that left fabricated audio outside its scope (Weiner and Norden 2023). Meta's manipulated media policy has been criticized for this loophole by an oversight board, which was addressed and updated this year.[5] Still, Slovakia's instance with the irreversible election result occurred in the context of Meta's policy loophole during a precisely calculated election timeline. Admittedly, those instances of political deepfakes reveal the public's vulnerabilities to election manipulation and disruption considering the recognized human limitations in detecting AI generated

---

[4] See versions of Meta's Manipulated Media Policy: https://transparency.meta.com/nl-nl/policies/community-standards/manipulated-media/#policy-details.

[5] See the oversight board's notes on Meta's changes in response to criticisms: https://www.oversightboard.com/news/meta-makes-significant-changes-to-manipulated-media-policy/.

falsehood and call for a reevaluation of generative AI's nature and the new direction of its regulations.

3 Deepfakes and Regulatory Trends

Given the detection limits, responses to deepfakes have been promoted by industries' development of deepfake detection technologies. Alongside, the latest trend in AI regulation, as presented by the EU Artificial Intelligence Act (AI Act), the world's first comprehensive regulation on AI, newly implemented on August 1, 2024, and the California AI Transparency Act signed by California Governor Gavin Newsom on September 17, 2024, shows the move toward a more comprehensive regulatory framework for AI. Further, Governor Newsom's veto on S.B. 1047 (the AI safety act) on September 29, 2024, combined with the industries' resistance and leading scientists' open rejection of S.B. 1047, may signal that the future AI regulatory framework needs to unite the tech industry, scientific communities, consumers, government agencies, and the public.

The phrase "AI's Media Integrity" mentioned in the 2020 Kaggle's Deepfake Detection Challenge (DFDC) with an objective to seek techniques in detecting deepfakes (Benpflaum et al. 2019) may vision the ethical demand for AI media or AI (Dolhansky et al. 2020). Other challenges like DeeperForensics Challenge 2020 @ ECCV SenseHuman Workshop (Jiang et al. 2021; Jiang et al. 2022),[6] 2020 Open Media Forensics Challenge organized by the National Institute of Standards and Technology (NIST) (Guan et al. 2021) and Multi-Forgery Detection Challenge 2022 (Li et al. 2022) also showed the development of deepfake detection as a direction to address deepfakes' epistemic challenges.

Along with the development of deepfake detection, the latest industry recommendations and the evolving legal regulations may indicate certain moral imperative for AI models or AI systems, particularly the transparency requirement, perhaps as a response to the epistemic injustice described above. In section 2 of *PAI's Responsible Practices for Synthetic Media* (2023), "Practices for Builders of Technology and Infrastructure," suggestion #4 "be transparent to users about tools and technologies' capabilities, functionality, limitations, and the potential risks of synthetic media," suggestion #5 "Take steps to provide disclosure mechanisms for those creating and distributing synthetic media," and suggestion #6 "When developing code and datasets, training models, and applying software for the production of synthetic media, make best efforts to apply indirect disclosure elements (steganographic, media provenance, or otherwise) within respective assets and stages of synthetic media production," advocate for the inclusion of a disclosure mechanism for the production of synthetic media (Partnership on AI 2023). In October 2022,

---

[6] The overview of DeeperForensics Challenge 2020 @ ECCV SenseHuman Workshop can be found on the following website: https://competitions.codalab.org/competitions/25228.

the White House Office of Science and Technology Policy issued *The Blueprint for an AI bill for Rights: Making Automated Systems Work for the American People*, identifying five principles as guidelines for automated system and AI usage and development.[7] The third principle that "you should know that an automated system is being used and understand how and why it contributes to outcomes that impact you," reinforces the public's right to know in response to the above epistemic injustice, in which deepfakes deprive our right to determine the veracity of AI generated content and threaten our capacity to know the truth.

Though the White House's *Blueprint* has no-binding force so far, the European Parliament adopted its negotiating position on the Artificial Intelligence (AI) Act: first regulation on artificial intelligence in June 2023 (European Parliament press releases 2023). The European Union's AI Act (AIA) imposes regulations on generative AI (GAI) that "designing the model to prevent it from generating illegal content; designing the model to prevent it from generating illegal content; publishing summaries of copyrighted data used for training" (European Parliament, "EU AI Act: first regulation on artificial intelligence", 2023). In March 2024, the Artificial Intelligence Act was approved by the European Parliament and established the legal framework on transparency requirements for labeling artificial or manipulated content (European Parliament Press Releases 2024),[8] and it was newly implemented on August 1, 2024, as the world's first comprehensive regulation on AI. Article 2 of the AIA specifies the scope of the regulations, as applied to providers, deployers, importers, and distributors of AI systems.[9] For transparency obligations for specific AI systems, Article 50(2) mandates providers of AI systems "ensure that the outputs of the AI system are marked in a machine-readable format and detectable as artificially generated or manipulated," and article 50(4) requires deployers of AI systems "disclose that the content has been artificially generated or manipulated."[10] Regarding personal data, General Data Protection Regulation (GDPR) applies in addition to AIA. In general, AIA adopts a risk-based approach and a horizonal regulatory framework, assigning obligations variably among systems that carry different

[7] Those five principles include:

"You should be protected from unsafe or ineffective systems.

You should not face discrimination by algorithms and systems should be used and designed in an equitable way.

You should be protected from abusive data practices via built-in protections and you should have agency over how data about you is used.

You should know that an automated system is being used and understand how and why it contributes to outcomes that impact you.

You should be able to opt out, where appropriate, and have access to a person who can quickly consider and remedy problems you encounter." (The White House 2022)

[8] Up-to-date analyses of the EU AI Act can be found on the website: https://artificialintelligenceact.eu/.

[9] Article 2 of the EU AI Act (AIA) can be found on the website: https://artificialintelligenceact.eu/article/2/.

[10] Article 50 of the EU AI Act (AIA) can be found on the website: https://artificialintelligenceact.eu/article/50/.

levels of risk, mainly applicable for high-risk AI systems, and Article 95 introduces the voluntary application of requirements for non-high-risk AI systems,[11] exempt from the mandate obligations for high-risk systems as listed in AIA chapter III.

At this moment, September 5, 2024, the U.S. regulatory focus is on the California Gov. Gavin Newsom's decisions on AI bills with the deadline of September 30, 2024, to sign or veto bills passed by the legislature.[12] Those AI-related California bills include S.B. 1047 (the AI safety Bill) on tech companies liability for harm from their AI models, S.B. 942 (the AI Transparency Act) on tech companies' obligations to provide AI detect tool, and A.B. 2355, on the disclosure of usage of generative AI in political advertisements. On September 17, 2024, Newsom has signed A.B. 2655 (Defending Democracy from Deepfake Deception Act of 2024), A.B.2355 (Political Reform Act of 1974: political advertisements: artificial intelligence), and A.B.2839 (Elections: deceptive media in advertisements) as responses to concerns about political deepfakes and their growing impact on the elections. As Newsom addressed in his statement, "safeguarding the integrity of elections is essential to democracy, and it's critical that we ensure AI is not deployed to undermine the public's trust through disinformation – especially in today's fraught political climate. These measures will help to combat the harmful use of deepfakes in political ads and other content, one of several areas in which the state is being proactive to foster transparent and trustworthy AI."[13] Specifically, A.B. 2655 will require large online platforms remove or label deceptive election-related content during a specified period.[14] A.B.2355 will mandate a disclaimer for the use of AI in political advertisements with the following disclosure "Ad generated or substantially altered using artificial intelligence."[15] A.B. 2839, effective immediately, prohibits the distribution of "materially deceptive" media of a candidate during a specified period, with exemptions, such as those for "satire or parody" that includes a disclosure statement: "This __ has been manipulated for purposes of satire or parody."[16] In

---

[11] Article 95 of the EU AI Act (AIA) can be found on the website: https://artificialintelligenceact.eu/article/95/.

[12] The details of the California bills can be tracked on the California Legislative Information website: https://leginfo.legislature.ca.gov/faces/home.xhtml.

[13] A.B. 2355 (Cal. Sep 17., 2024) https://leginfo.legislature.ca.gov/faces/billNavClient.xhtml?bill_id=202320240AB2355.

[14] According to A.B. 2655's definition, "'deepfake' means audio or visual media that is digitally created or modified such that it would falsely appear to a reasonable person to be an authentic record of the actual speech or conduct of the individual depicted in the media."

A.B. 2655 (Cal. Sep 17., 2024) https://leginfo.legislature.ca.gov/faces/billNavClient.xhtml?bill_id=202320240AB2655.

[15] Artificial intelligence is defined in A.B. 2355 as "an engineered or machine-based system that varies in its level of autonomy and that can, for explicit or implicit objectives, infer from the input it receives how to generate outputs that can influence physical or virtual environments."

A.B. 2355 (Cal. Sep 17., 2024) https://leginfo.legislature.ca.gov/faces/billNavClient.xhtml?bill_id=202320240AB2355.

[16] "Materially deceptive content" as defined in A.B. 2839 means "audio or visual media that is intentionally digitally created or modified, which includes, but is not limited to, deepfakes, such

addition to bills on political deepfakes, Newsom have signed S.B. 926 and S.B. 981 on September 19, 2024, addressing sexually explicit deepfakes.

On September 19, 2024, Newsom has approved S.B. 942 the California AI Transparency Act, which will require a provider "make available an AI detection tool" and "offer the user the option to include a manifest disclosure in image, video, or audio content, or content that is any combination thereof, created or altered by the covered provider's GenAI system."[17] As S.B.942 defines, "'covered provider' means a person that creates, codes, or otherwise produces a generative artificial intelligence system that has over 1,000,000 monthly visitors or users and is publicly accessible within the geographic boundaries of the state."[18] S.B. 942 goes into effect January 1, 2026.

In the spotlight of the current regulation debate, the controversial S.B. 1047 AI safety bill has faced resistance from the tech industry (Vynck and Oremus 2024). On September 29, 2024, Newsom has vetoed S.B.1047. In his veto message, Newsom pointed out that S.B.1047 doesn't concern "smaller, specialized models" but only focus on "the most expensive and large-scale models," nor "take into account whether an Al system is deployed in high-risk environments."[19] The veto on S.B. 1047 sent a signal that the future AI regulatory framework needs to unite the tech industries, scientific communities, consumers, government agencies, and the public. Newsom's specific concerns about different levels of risk requiring distinct regulations echo the EU AIA's risk management approach, which categorizes AI systems into unacceptable, high, minimal, and no risk, with specific obligations for high-risk systems. AIA's risk management has been criticized for its limited regulations, far-reaching exceptions due to lobbying, enforcement limitations, and loopholes like self-assessment (Wachter 2024), but Wachter notes that in a positive way the AIA breaks through the traditional regulatory framework—such as "a product-safety framework"—by offering remedies for infringements of individual right. Still, a normative threshold and corresponding responsibilities are particularly necessary for an effective AI regulatory framework (Wachter 2024). A moral vision for trustworthy and responsible AI can also be revealed from the National Institute for Standards and Technology (NIST)'s *NIST-AI-600-1, Artificial Intelligence Risk*

that the content would falsely appear to a reasonable person to be an authentic record of the content depicted in the media."

A.B. 2839 (Cal. Sep 17., 2024) https://leginfo.legislature.ca.gov/faces/billNavClient.xhtml?bill_id=202320240AB2839.

[17] S.B. 942 (Cal. Sep. 19., 2024) https://leginfo.legislature.ca.gov/faces/billNavClient.xhtml?bill_id=202320240SB942.

[18] Ibid.

[19] "By focusing only on the most expensive and large-scale models, SB 1047 establishes a regulatory framework that could give the public a false sense of security about controlling this fast-moving technology. Smaller, specialized models may emerge as equally or even more dangerous than the models targeted by SB 1047 - at the potential expense of curtailing the very innovation that fuels advancement in favor of the public good."

California Governor Gavin Newsom's full veto message is available on the California government website: https://www.gov.ca.gov/wp-content/uploads/2024/09/SB-1047-Veto-Message.pdf.

Management Framework: Generative Artificial Intelligence Profile (GenAI Profile) and NIST's *AI Risk Management Framework* (AI RMF 1.0) (Autio et al. 2024). Following President Biden's Executive Order on *Safe, Secure, and Trustworthy Development and Use of Artificial Intelligence* (Executive Order No. 14110, 2023), NISTs GenAI Profile released on July 26, 2024, serves as a companion source for AI RMF, NIST AI 100-1, released in January 2023. Implementing a comprehensive approach to risk management, the AI RMF depicts trustworthy AI systems with moral characters like "valid and reliable, safe, secure and resilient, accountable and transparent, explainable and interpretable, privacy-enhanced, and fair with harmful bias managed," and calls for "balancing tradeoffs among the trustworthiness characteristics" (Tabassi 2023). Among the list of trustworthiness characteristics for AI systems, "valid & reliable is a necessary condition of trustworthiness" and "accountable & transparent ... is related to all other characteristics" (Tabassi 2023). Together, these newly implemented or signed regulations, and the latest guidelines show a normative framework for responsible AI systems or AI models from a comprehensive approach. However, the veto on S.B. 1047 reminds us of the challenges and divisions, perhaps indicating the need for a more unified framework that brings together scientific communities, the tech industry, government agencies, consumers, and the public.

4 A Metaphysical Argument for AI's Accountability

A future direction for AI regulations, especially considering the epistemic challenges posted by deepfakes, I believe, calls for comprehensive consideration and a fine balance between technological innovation and risk management. A holistic consideration of stakeholders and relevant agents including AI providers, deployers, and users, may also involve a reevaluation of the nature of AI systems or AI models. Zoom-in reflections on AI's nature may offer new perspectives on our relations with AI to address the epistemic injustices discussed earlier. That's why my argument for AI's moral accountability, inferring the requirement for transparency at a threshold and further for trustworthy, starts with metaphysical considerations of AI's nature rather than thick moral presumptions, and such a reevaluation and reinforcement of AI's relation to the public aims to support a more unified framework for AI regulations.

Questions related to the nature of generative AI could include the following: How real is generative AI, such as an Artificially Intelligent Speech Generator (AISG), Generative Adversarial Networks (GANs), or ChatGPT? Is generative AI mere representation of human beings' mental states, without which its existence has no ground? Can generative AI exist out of the human mind, or does generative AI exist in us? First, I argue that generative AI like AISG, GAN or ChatGPT is real in terms of its relation to us by appealing to Lucy Allais's concept of "manifest reality" (Allais 2015) within the context of Kant's distinctions between *things in themselves* and *things as appearance*. Later, I would declare generative AI model's accountability to be transparent and truthful about the generated output due its manifest reality to us.

How real is generative AI like an Artificially Intelligent Speech Generator (AISG), Generative Adversarial Networks (GANs), or ChatGPT? Within Kant's distinctions between *things in themselves* and *things as appearance*,[20] I first concentrate on a claim that generative AI appears to us. One way to explain a claim that generative AI's appearance is to assert that the reality of generative AI is mere representation of our experience, and that generative AI does not exist without its connection with perceivers or its imitated objects. Alternatively, according to an extreme idealist interpretation, generative AI merely exists in the mind or some mental states, either of a perceiver's or of a developer's mind. A possible **objection** against AI's moral accountability could be that generative AI exists as constructions out of what exists merely in our mind. If it is so, neither AI model nor AI system is accountable for the falsity of those generated deepfakes.

Instead of the interpretations on AI's appearance mentioned above, I appeal to Lucy Allais's concept of "manifest reality" (Allais 2015) and argue that generative AI is real in terms of its relation to us. Allais labels her approach as a moderate metaphysics within debates between extreme metaphysical interpretation and deflationary views (non-metaphysical views). She offers an interpretation of Kant's transcendental idealism with accommodation of realism by highlighting both metaphysical and epistemological components to the distinctions between *things in themselves* and *things as appearance*. Take color as an example to Allais' relational account. Allais describes colour as "a directly presented, external, but mind-dependent features of mind-independent things" (2015, p.103). Similarly, generative AI has some mind-dependent features including those generated hyper-realistic characters but as mind-independent things it does not exist merely in the perceiver's mind. Those mind-dependent features[21] are not just perceivable by us, but also (essentially) manifest generative AI themselves to us. Particularly for its computational qualities, those are essential manifest qualities, which are "relational, mind-dependent qualities of things which can be present in perceptual experience, and

[20] There have been two traditional interpretations of Kant's distinctions between the above two types of things: extreme metaphysical interpretation and deflationary views (non-metaphysical views). Extreme metaphysical interpretations classify Kant as either a noumenalist or a phenomenalist due to the ontological distinctions between "non-sensible things'" and "appearance." On the other side, deflationary views deny the metaphysical distinctions between two worlds, but address those epistemological and methodological distinctions about one world, such as the "conditions of cognition" (Allison 2015), Kant's rejection of the "given" (Abela 2002), or distinctions between intrinsic and external properties (Langton 1998). In general, deflationary views do not see Kant's commitments to things in themselves.

[21] Interestingly, some unique features of generative AI do not belong to traditional categories of qualities, but lie in its non-spatio-temporal features, such as its computational natures from Bit. With those considerations, we can no longer limit the scope of our cognition to spatio-temporal things but call for an account of non-spatio-temporal reality, such as Informational Structural realism (ISR). However, in this paper, even not relying on an account of non-spatio-temporal reality, I argue for AI's relational realism.

which do not present us with qualities things have as they are in themselves, independent of their perceptually appearing to us" (Allais 2015, p.124). That is to assert that generative AI is real in the sense that it possesses manifest qualities. Even as perceptual appearance, voices and images generated by generative AI are not mere representations of our experience, in the case of physical voices, but, further, through its generated voices, generative AI is communicating to us. Through its communication, it reveals its capacity to affect our actions and choices, illustrated by those political deepfake cases.

A recurring **objection** to my argument could be that appearances of those hyper-realistic generated characters can be merely reduced to properties of generative AI. If so, generative AI's essential features are still mere constructions out of what exists merely in our mind, exempt from its moral responsibilities. **A common way** to elaborate the objection would be that AI as a human creation is not responsible for the epistemic injustice posted by deepfakes, but it is only humans, either the AI developer, or those who initiate, upload, or distribute a fabricated video, especially those holding malicious purposes be countable for the epistemic threats upon the public.

As for the common objection, one point to clarify is that a metaphysical argument for AI's accountability does not exclude the liability of the specific agent involved in deepfakes. However, considering the easy accessibility of open source deepfake software, it seems somewhat overreaching to place a direct moral responsibility on those earlier developers. For example, for Generative Adversarial Networks (GANs), a type of generative AI, Ian Goodfellow was considered as GANfather. By 2018, four years after Goodfellow et al. published the article on GAN in 2014, hundreds of related papers had been published (Giles 2018). It seems perplexing to blame those scientists who initially shared their codes for the harms caused by later synthetic images. Still again, this claim does not dismiss the liabilities of current stakeholders in deepfake creation and distribution, especially those involved defamation.

I will then respond to **the metaphysical objection**. It is true that those hyper-realistic characters generated by generative AI as appearances may involve mind-dependent nature to some extent, but those appearances of generated characters can't be merely reduced into essential properties of generative AI. The special essence of generative AI as things in themselves may still be unknowable to us, but *grounds* those appearances to us, independently of our cognition as perceivers, given our inability sometimes in distinguishing generated representations from real appearances. I am not confident to declare that generative AI as things in themselves cause those appearances at this point, and such a claim needs more sophisticated justification about causality, but at least I could safely claim that generative AI affects us through those appearances, admittedly mind-dependent appearance and sometimes incognizable to us.

I will use Generative Adversarial Networks (GANs) as an example to show that appearances of generated characters can't be merely reduced to properties of GANs. GANs consist of two neural networks, including the generator and the discriminator. "A generative model G that captures the data distribution, and a discriminative model D that estimates the probability that a sample came from the training data rather than G" (Goodfellow et al. 2014). Its adversarial training includes the generator's learning to increase the probability of generating synthesized samples that fool the discriminator and the discriminator's increasingly perfect classifications of the fake samples generated by the generator from real samples. If the discriminator (D) successfully differentiates fake samples from real samples, the generator (G) updates its model to catch up to the generator's classification. Till the generator updates its model to the level when the discriminator fails to distinguish fake instances from real samples, the generator can be considered as good and could successfully produce newly high-quality outputs, say, pseudo-real, hyper-realistic images, voices, or synthesized videos, sometimes hardly distinguished by a human observer. In Goodfellow's 2014 paper, the optimization for the generator and the discriminator is a type of a minimax game to train both models. Compared to some traditional generative models, say, energy-based models (EBMs) whose objective is to optimize a single model to generate new data that represents the similar distribution given the training data, GANs aim to optimize two modelsets simultaneously. In rapidly developed computer vision among its various applications, GANs can generate realistic images and manipulated videos (Dubey and Singh 2023), all of which cannot be reduced to properties of GANs in the same sense that red color is an external property of a red apple.

Additionally, I shall go through various types of generative AI, including the VAEs, GANs, and Large Language Models (LLMs) to illustrate that appearances of generated characters can't be merely reduced as essential properties of generative AI. Machine learning models are generally divided into supervised learning (including classification and regression) and unsupervised learning, say, clustering, depending on the use of labeled datasets. Generative AI is typically considered as unsupervised or self-supervised machine learning. A comparison with a variety of generative models, including (variational autoencoders) VAEs, GANs, Normalizing Flows, Energy-Based to Autoregressive Models, or other hybrid approaches within these types, may involve features like "training and test speed, parameter efficiency, sample quality, sample diversity, and ability to scale to high resolution data" (Bond-Taylor et al. 2022). None of the above features, however, can exactly mirror those generated hyper-realistic characters, say, the color red. Both as latent variable models (LV), variational autoencoders (VAEs) in the above comparison are marked with "exact densities," in density estimation, having tractable density function to describe underlying probability distributions of training data, while GANs have intractable density starting from random noise as input. With both encoding and decoding components, traditional autoencoders involve mapping the raw data into latent variable vectors as compressed representations of training data and reconstructing the original input data by learning latent variables, while its training is to optimize the divergence between the reconstructed data and the original input data. Like traditional autoencoders, VAEs can generate new images, similar but not strict reconstructions of original data by allowing randomness to each latent variable and computing its probabilistic distribution. Since VAEs aim to minimize the reconstruction loss and the VAE loss, some properties of the latent space taken into consideration are its continuity and completeness, which are not perceivable characters of its generated output.

Moreover, a claim that AI's generated output can't be reduced to mere properties of generative AI can be supported by the fact that similar models might generate different types of representations, say, textual generation, image synthesis, or video synthesis. For example, Large Language Models (LLMs) as a subfield of generative AI and natural language processing with a large amount of trained multimodal dataset primarily in textual data can generate "human-like languages" (Bariah et al. 2023). Besides, other types of generated outcome could include general inferences, predications, or simulations.

Next objection could be that our ignorance of things in themselves reveals our limited abilities to know the truth, and exempt generative AI's accountability to speak the truth. My response is that our limitation to distinguish those fake hyper-realistic characters from authentic ones does not entail the global skepticism of knowledge, nor deny our perceptual functions nor cognitive capacities in general. To demonstrate, I will explore again a specific architecture of generative AI and deepfakes. For example, a type of generative AI model behind deepfakes, Cycle-Consistent Adversarial Networks (CycleGAN) could learn to translate an image or audio source from a source domain to a target domain (Zhu et al. 2017) and generate face-swapping or fake videos in which celebrities were voicing fabricated information. The condition to generate deepfakes by CycleGAN still relies on our perception and understanding of the original image in the source domain. Additionally, acknowledging that our ignorance of things in themselves is insufficient to assert the non-existence of things in themselves. As Langton suggested for Kant's claim about our ignorance of things in themselves, "although we cannot know *how* a thing is in itself (*wie es an sich beschaffen sei*), we must none the less acknowledge the *existence* of things in themselves" (Langton 1998, p.22). According to it, our ignorance of things in themselves would simply reveal our limits to know the essential nature of things and does not release individuals nor AI from being accountable in general.

In sum, I argue generative AI is real in the sense that through generated hyper-realistic characters AI has the capacity to affect the public's choices and actions, such as negatively impacting us through epistemic challenges posed by political deepfakes. Those epistemic challenges including humans' detection limits do not entail global skepticism of knowledge nor exempt AI from its responsibilities involved. On the contrary, due to its manifest reality in relation to us, generative AI should be accountable for those epistemic injustices posted by deepfakes, entailing its obligation to be transparent and truthful at a minimum standard, ideally being trustworthy.

5 Conclusion

In this chapter, I present a moderate metaphysical argument for AI's moral responsibilities to be transparent and truthful by appealing to Lucy Allais's concept of "manifest reality" as a response to the epistemic threats posted by deepfakes, especially cases involved political deepfakes. The latest trends of AI regulations and recommendations show the move toward a more comprehensive regulatory framework for AI, which aligns with my argument.

My moderate metaphysical argument aims, first, to avoid starting with a thick value assumption, as it may be a common source of division in conflicts. Secondly, reevaluation of AI as real in its relation to us is not to spark fear, a common motive behind risk control, but to reinforce our relations with AI, possibly toward a reciprocal alliance. This shift in outlook may help reconcile the regulatory divisions between the scientific communities, the tech industries, government agencies, and the public, with a holistic goal of unifying technological innovation and the protection of private and public rights. Third, a comprehensive approach on AI regulations ideally calls for all stakeholders and relevant agents accountable, while with AI's far-reaching impacts some instances of deepfakes may involve too numerous stakeholders or agents, making either ineffective or too ambiguous to identify liabilities among many. On the one side, if we want to identify all relevant stakeholders, leaving out AI from the list does seem incomplete. On the other side, when cases involve the deprivation of individual rights, remedies need to be offered under the principle of justice. Singling out AI's moral responsibilities may help execute some internal activities, in cases of deepfakes, either mandating detection tools, offering watermark, labeling synthetic content, or assessing the veracity of content. To clarify, I am not arguing for AI as an autonomous agent, which is beyond the scope of this paper. However, reinforcing AI's manifest reality while perceiving AI not merely as constructions in our mind may be a collaborative mindset in bringing communities together and working on AI-human reciprocal alliance, regardless of whether artificial general intelligence (AGI) is achieved or not.

References

A.B. 2355 (Cal. Sep 17., 2024). https://leginfo.legislature.ca.gov/faces/billNavClient.xhtml?bill_id=202320240AB2355

A.B. 2655 (Cal. Sep 17., 2024). https://leginfo.legislature.ca.gov/faces/billNavClient.xhtml?bill_id=202320240AB2655

A.B. 2839 (Cal. Sep 17., 2024). https://leginfo.legislature.ca.gov/faces/billNavClient.xhtml?bill_id=202320240AB2839

Abdulreda A, Obaid A (2022) A landscape view of deepfake techniques and detection methods. Int J Nonlinear Anal Appl 13(1):745–755. https://doi.org/10.22075/ijnaa.2022.5580

Abela P (2002) Kant's empirical realism. Oxford University Press, New York

Agence France-Presse in Shanghai (2019) Chinese deepfake app Zao sparks privacy row after going viral. The Guardian. https://www.theguardian.com/technology/2019/sep/02/chinese-face-swap-app-zao-triggers-privacy-fears-viral

Allais L (2015) Manifest reality: Kant's idealism and his realism. Oxford University Press UK, Oxford

Allison H (2015) Kant's transcendental deduction. An analytical-historical commentary. Oxford University Press, Oxford

Allyn B (2022) Deepfake video of Zelenskyy could be 'tip of the iceberg' in info war, experts warn. NPR. March 16. https://www.npr.org/2022/03/16/1087062648/deepfake-video-zelenskyy-experts-war-manipulation-ukraine-russia

Autio C, Schwartz R, Dunietz J, Jain S, Stanley M, Tabassi E, Hall P, Roberts K (2024) Artificial intelligence risk management framework: generative artificial intelligence profile, NIST Trustworthy and Responsible AI. National Institute of Standards and Technology, Gaithersburg, MD. https://doi.org/10.6028/NIST.AI.600-1

Bariah L, Zhao Q, Zou H, Tian Y, Bader F, Debbah M (2023) Large generative AI models for telecom: the next big thing? https://doi.org/10.48550/arXiv.2306.10249. arXiv:2306.10249 [cs.CL]

Benpflaum BG, Djdj KI, Tester JE, Elliott JL, Metherd J, Elliott J, Mozaic, Culliton P, Dane S, Kim W (2019) Deepfake Detection Challenge. Kaggle. https://kaggle.com/competitions/deepfake-detection-challenge

Bond-Taylor S, Leach A, Long Y, Willcocks C (2022) Deep generative modelling: a comparative review of VAEs, GANs, normalizing flows, energy-based and autoregressive models. IEEE Trans Pattern Anal Mach Intell 44(11):7327–7347. https://doi.org/10.1109/TPAMI.2021.3116668. arXiv:2103.04922 [cs.LG]

Bray SD, Johnson SD, Kleinberg B (2023) Testing human ability to detect deepfake images of human faces. J Cybersecur 9(1):tyad011. https://doi.org/10.1093/cybsec/tyad011. arXiv:2212.05056 [cs.HC]

Chesney R, Citron D K. (2019). Deep Fakes: A Looming Challenge for Privacy, Democracy, and National Security (July 14, 2018). 107 *California Law Review* 1753, U of Texas Law, Public Law Research Paper No. 692, U of Maryland Legal Studies Research Paper No. 2018-21. SSRN: https://ssrn.com/abstract=3213954. https://doi.org/10.2139/ssrn.3213954

de Seta G (2021) Huanlian, or changing faces: Deepfakes on Chinese digital media platforms. Convergence 27(4):935–953. https://doi.org/10.1177/13548565211030185

Doffman Z (2019) Chinese Deepfake App ZAO Goes Viral, Privacy of Millions 'At Risk'. Forbes. https://www.forbes.com/sites/zakdoffman/2019/09/02/chinese-best-ever-deepfake-app-zao-sparks-huge-faceapp-like-privacy-storm

Dolhansky B, Bitton J, Pflaum B, Lu J, Howes R, Wang M, Ferrer C (2020) The DeepFake detection challenge (DFDC) Dataset. https://doi.org/10.48550/arXiv.2006.07397. arXiv:2006.07397v4 [cs.CV]

Dubey S, Singh S (2023) Transformer-based generative adversarial networks in computer vision: a comprehensive survey. https://doi.org/10.48550/arXiv.2302.08641., arXiv:2302.08641 [cs.CV]

European Parliament (2023) EU AI Act: first regulation on artificial intelligence. https://www.europarl.europa.eu/topics/en/article/20230601STO93804/eu-ai-act-first-regulation-on-artificial-intelligence

European Parliament Press Releases (2023) MEPs ready to negotiate first-ever rules for safe and transparent AI. https://www.europarl.europa.eu/news/en/press-room/20230609IPR96212/meps-ready-to-negotiate-first-ever-rules-for-safe-and-transparent-ai

European Parliament Press Releases (2024) Artificial Intelligence Act: MEPs adopt landmark law. https://www.europarl.europa.eu/news/en/press-room/20240308IPR19015/artificial-intelligence-act-meps-adopt-landmark-law

Exec. Order No. 14,110, 3 C.F.R. 657-699 (2023). https://www.govinfo.gov/content/pkg/CFR-2024-title3-vol1/pdf/CFR-2024-title3-vol1-eo14110.pdf

Giles M (2018) The GANfather: the man who's given machines the gift of imagination. February 21. https://www.technologyreview.com/2018/02/21/145289/the-ganfather-the-man-whos-given-machines-the-gift-of-imagination/

Goggin B (2019) From porn to 'Game of Thrones': how deepfakes and realistic-looking fake videos hit it big. Business Insider. https://www.businessinsider.com/deepfakes-explained-the-rise-of-fake-realistic-videos-online-2019-6

Goodfellow I, Pouget-Abadie J, Mirza M, Xu B, Warde-Farley D, Ozair S, Courville A, Bengio Y (2014) Generative adversarial networks. arXiv:1406.2661

Goodfellow I, Pouget-Abadie J, Mirza M, Xu B, Warde-Farley D, Ozair S, Courville A, Bengio Y (2020) Generative adversarial networks. Commun ACM 63(11):139–144. https://doi.org/10.1145/3422622

Guan H, Lee Y, Diduch L, Zhang J, Ghorbanian Bajgiran I, Kheyrkhah T, Fontana P, Fiscus J (2021) Open media forensics challenge (OpenMFC) 2020–2021: Past, Present, and Future, NIST Interagency/Internal Report (NISTIR), National Institute of Standards and Technology, Gaithersburg, MD, [online], https://doi.org/10.6028/NIST.IR.8396, https://tsapps.nist.gov/publication/get_pdf.cfm?pub_id=933191

Jiang L, Guo Z, Wu W, Liu Z, Liu Z, Change CL, Yang S, Xiong Y, Xia W, Chen B, Zhuang P, Li S, Chen S, Yao T, Ding S, Li J, Huang F, Cao L, Ji R, Lu C, Tan G (2021) DeeperForensics challenge 2020 on real-world face forgery detection: methods and results. https://doi.org/10.48550/arXiv.2102.09471. arXiv:2102.09471v1 [cs.CV]

Jiang L, Wu W, Qian C, Loy C.C. (2022) DeepFakes detection: the DeeperForensics dataset and challenge. In: Rathgeb, C., Tolosana, R., Vera-Rodriguez, R., Busch, C. (eds) Handbook of Digital Face Manipulation And Detection. Advances in computer vision and pattern recognition. Springer, Cham. doi:https://doi.org/10.1007/978-3-030-87664-7_14

Köbis NC, Doležalová B, Soraperra I (2021) Fooled twice: people cannot detect deepfakes but think they can. iScience 24(11):103364. https://doi.org/10.1016/j.isci.2021.103364

Langton R (1998) Kantian humility: our ignorance of things in themselves. Oxford University Press, Oxford

Li J, Luo M, Liu J, Chen T, Wang C, Liu Z, Liu S, Yang K, Shao X, Chen K, Liu B, Guo M, Guo Y, Ao Y, Gao P (2022) Multi-forgery detection challenge 2022: push the frontier of unconstrained and diverse forgery detection. https://doi.org/10.48550/arXiv.2207.13505. arXiv:2207.13505 [cs.CV]

Mai KT, Bray S, Davies T, Griffin LD (2023) Warning: Humans cannot reliably detect speech deepfakes. PLoS ONE 18(8):e0285333. https://doi.org/10.1371/journal.pone.0285333. arXiv:2301.07829 [cs.HC]

Nguyen T, Nguyen Q, Nguyen D et al (2022) Deep learning for deepfakes creation and detection: a survey. Comput Vision Image Understand 223:103525. https://doi.org/10.1016/j.cviu.2022.103525

Nightingale SJ, Farid H (2022) AI-synthesized faces are indistinguishable from real faces and more trustworthy. Proc Natl Acad Sci USA 119(8):e2120481119. https://doi.org/10.1073/pnas.2120481119

Partnership on AI (2023) PAI's Responsible Practices for Synthetic Media: A framework for Collective Action. https://syntheticmedia.partnershiponai.org/

Pataranutaporn P, Danry V, Leong J et al (2021) AI-generated characters for supporting personalized learning and well-being. Nat Mach Intell 3:1013–1022. https://doi.org/10.1038/s42256-021-00417-9

Quinn B (2024) Slew of deepfake video adverts of Sunak on Facebook raises alarm over AI risk to election. The Guardian. January 12. https://www.theguardian.com/technology/2024/jan/12/deepfake-video-adverts-sunak-facebook-alarm-ai-risk-election

Regulation (EU) 2024/1689 of the European Parliament and of the Council of 13 June 2024 laying down harmonised rules on artificial intelligence and amending Regulations (EC) No 300/2008, (EU) No 167/2013, (EU) No 168/2013, (EU) 2018/858, (EU) 2018/1139 and (EU) 2019/2144 and Directives 2014/90/EU, (EU) 2016/797 and (EU) 2020/1828 (Artificial Intelligence Act) (Text with EEA relevance) http://data.europa.eu/eli/reg/2024/1689/oj

S.B. 926 (Cal. Sep 19, 2024). https://leginfo.legislature.ca.gov/faces/billNavClient.xhtml?bill_id=202320240SB926

S.B. 942 (Cal. Sep. 19., 2024). https://leginfo.legislature.ca.gov/faces/billNavClient.xhtml?bill_id=202320240SB942

S.B. 981 (Cal. Sep 19., 2024). https://leginfo.legislature.ca.gov/faces/billNavClient.xhtml?bill_id=202320240SB981

Tabassi S (2023) Artificial Intelligence Risk Management Framework (AI RMF 1.0). NIST Trustworthy and Responsible AI, National Institute of Standards and Technology, Gaithersburg, MD. https://doi.org/10.6028/NIST.AI.100-1

The White House (2022) Blueprint for an AI Bill of Rights: Making Automated Systems Work for the American People. https://www.whitehouse.gov/ostp/ai-bill-of-rights/

Vynck GD, Oremus W (2024) California Gov. Gavin Newsom's desk is overflowing with AI bills. The Washington Post. September 5. https://www.washingtonpost.com/politics/2024/09/05/california-gov-gavin-newsoms-desk-is-overflowing-with-ai-bills/

Wachter S (2024) Limitations and Loopholes in the EU AI Act and AI liability directives: what this means for the European Union, the United States, and beyond. Yale J Law Technol 26(3):671–718

Weiner DI, Norden L (2023) Regulating AI and synthetic media in the political Arena. The Brennan Center, December 5. https://www.brennancenter.org/our-work/research-reports/regulating-ai-deepfakes-and-synthetic-media-political-arena/

Zhu JY, Park T, Isola P, Efros A (2017) Unpaired Image-to-image translation using cycle-consistent adversarial networks. https://doi.org/10.48550/arXiv.1703.10593. arXiv:1703.10593 [cs.CV]

GPSR Compliance
The European Union's (EU) General Product Safety Regulation (GPSR) is a set of rules that requires consumer products to be safe and our obligations to ensure this.

If you have any concerns about our products, you can contact us on

ProductSafety@springernature.com

In case Publisher is established outside the EU, the EU authorized representative is:

Springer Nature Customer Service Center GmbH
Europaplatz 3
69115 Heidelberg, Germany

www.ingramcontent.com/pod-product-compliance
Lightning Source LLC
Chambersburg PA
CBHW061458051025
33560CB00033B/12
9783031937828